9

THE UNITED STATES IN PRAGUE, 1945–1948

WALTER ULLMANN

EAST EUROPEAN QUARTERLY, BOULDER
DISTRIBUTED BY COLUMBIA UNIVERSITY PRESS
NEW YORK

1978

EAST EUROPEAN MONOGRAPHS, NO. XXXVI

Walter Ullmann is Associate Professor of History at
Syracuse University

EAST EUROPEAN MONOGRAPHS

The *East European Monographs* comprise scholarly books on the history and civilization of Eastern Europe. They are published by the *East European Quarterly* in the belief that these studies contribute substantially to the knowledge of the area and serve to stimulate scholarship and research.

1. *Political Ideas and the Enlightenment in the Romanian Principalities, 1750-1831.* By Vlad Georgescu. 1971.

2. *America, Italy and the Birth of Yugoslavia, 1917-1919.* By Dragan R. Zivojinovic. 1972.

3. *Jewish Nobles and Geniuses in Modern Hungary.* By William O. McCagg, Jr. 1972.

4. *Mixail Soloxov in Yugoslavia: Reception and Literary Impact.* By Robert F. Price. 1973.

5. *The Historical and National Thought of Nicolae Iorga.* By William O. Oldson. 1973.

6. *Guide to Polish Libraries and Archives.* By Richard C. Lewanski. 1974.

7. *Vienna Broadcasts to Slovakia, 1938-1939: A Case Study in Subversion.* By Henry Delfiner. 1974.

8. *The 1917 Revolution in Latvia.* By Andrew Ezergailis. 1974.

9. *The Ukraine in the United Nations Organization: A Study in Soviet Foreign Policy. 1944-1950.* By Konstantin Sawczuk. 1975.

10. *The Bosnian Church: A New Interpretation.* By John V. A. Fine, Jr. 1975.

11. *Intellectual and Social Developments in the Habsburg Empire from Maria Theresa to World War I.* Edited by Stanley B. Winters and Joseph Held. 1975.

12. *Ljudevit Gaj and the Illyrian Movement.* By Elinor Murray Despalatovic. 1975.

13. *Tolerance and Movements of Religious Dissent in Eastern Europe.* Edited by Bela K. Kiraly. 1975.

14. *The Parish Republic: Hlinka's Slovak People's Party, 1939-1945.* By Yeshayahu Jelinek. 1976.

15. *The Russian Annexation of Bessarabia, 1774-1828.* By George F. Jewsbury. 1976.

16. *Modern Hungarian Historiography.* By Steven Bela Vardy. 1976.

17. *Values and Community in Multi-National Yugoslavia.* By Gary K. Bertsch. 1976.

To my mother
and
to the memory of my father

Contents

Contents

Preface

Only in a limited sense may the present book be called an account of American-Czechoslovak relations. In order to lay claim to such a title, source materials from both partners ought to be available for examination. Since Czechoslovak sources pertaining to this study were not available and are not likely to become available in the near future, it was necessary to rely heavily and, at times exclusively, on American materials. To be sure, some important Czechoslovak documentation could be secured from secondary works and, on occasion, even in original form, but this was the exception rather than the rule. This being so, the book's title more accurately reflects its contents than a general account of relations between the two countries.

Since it is reasonable to assume that in any partnership each of the parties wishes to appear in a favorable light, the absence of Czechoslovak documentation is even more deplorable. On the other hand, it prompted a doubly careful scrutiny of American materials, if only to compensate for it to the degree that this was possible. So, for example, Embassy versions of Czechoslovak press reports were checked against the originals to see whether innuendo or out-of-context quotations had been used. As far as possible, similar techniques were applied to ascertain the reliability and the overall calibre of the communications. As long as Czechoslovak sources remain inaccessible, this seemed the only viable alternative.

In view of all this, it must be anticipated that once researchers will have access to the Prague archives, some conclusions arrived at in this study may have to be altered. But, such is the nature of scholarship, its beauty, its fascination.

I gratefully acknowledge the assistance given me by my colleagues and friends. Professor Radomír Luža of Tulane University and my colleague William Stinchcombe and former colleague Dietrich Orlow read the manuscript at its various stages and made many a helpful suggestion which put some issues into different focus and forced me to rethink others. Mr. James Hastings of the National Archives in Washington went well beyond the call of duty in making the various research materials available to me. I have benefited from an exchange of views with Mr. Mark Steinitz of the University of Maryland, himself a student of the subject. Constance Rajala typed and proofread the manuscript and assisted me with the index; she also took care of some of the more obvious Slavicisms in my English.

I should also like to thank the American Philosophical Society and Syracuse University for their financial assistance which greatly facilitated my going to Washington on research leave.

While all these individuals and institutions had a hand in my work, I alone remain responsible.

Syracuse, New York   W.U.
March 1977

Introduction

American-Czechoslovak relations go back to 1918, the year of the founding of the Czechoslovak Republic. Even prior to the Czechoslovaks' official declaration of their independence on October 28, 1918, the United States government had given both *de facto* and *de jure* recognition to the Czechoslovak National Council which, in the absence of a formally constituted government, administered the affairs of the future state. Although it was France which took the lead at the Paris Peace Conference by championing the Czechoslovak cause and looking after the interests of its fledgling protégé, the United States usually followed the French lead; in so doing, America gave the infant republic the necessary prestige and support which are indispensable on such historic occasions.

The early link between Czechoslovaks and Americans was of a twofold nature. On the one hand, there was the liberal and democratic orientation of the Czech and Slovak leaders who championed the creation of the new Czechoslovak state. In this respect, Masaryk, Beneš and Štefánik had all established creditable records among the leaders of the Entente. On the other hand, antedating World War I and the struggle of Czechs and Slovaks for independence, there were President Masaryk's personal connections and family ties in the United States. Not only was Masaryk married to an American, Charlotte Garrigue, but his subsequent encounter with the wealthy and influential American industrialist Charles R. Crane opened both doors and pursestrings to Masaryk and his movement. Crane, from whose longtime interest in the cause of the Western Slavs the Czechs derived particular benefit, introduced Masaryk to Secretary of State Lansing and, subsequently, President Wilson. In talks with Wilson in the spring of 1918, the future President of Czechoslovakia convinced Wilson that his Point Ten of the famous Fourteen Points, the one dealing with federalization of Austria-Hungary and the free development of its subject nationalities, could well be interpreted by Vienna as simply a restructuring of the Empire in a different form. Such an interpretation, in turn, might frustrate the ambitions for complete independence of Czechs and Slovaks and other nationalities. In order to forestall this, he asked Wilson to clarify his views on the matter and, in response to this request, the Department of State on June 28th issued a statement which made it unequivocally clear that the United States championed complete freedom for all the Slavs then living under Hapsburg or Hohenzollern domination. The statement further superseded a previous declaration by Lansing on May 29th, in which the Secretary of State demanded much the same, but in more general terms.

There were yet other connections between Americans and Czecho- slovaks. There was Antonín Dvořák, the famous Czech composer, who for a number of years took up residence in the United States and rose to the prestigious post of director of the National Conservatory of Music (1892–1894). The American scene left a lasting imprint on the Czech musician, of which the *New World Symphony* is most likely the best known testimonial. Bohuslav Martinů, another Czech composer, and, on the lighter side, the well-known and immensely popular Rudolf Friml found the American milieu conducive to their creative efforts. The former, best known for his symphonic music, spent many of his most productive years in the United States; the latter, a long-time resident of Hollywood, left his lasting imprint on the country with such operettas as *Rose Marie* and *The Vagabond King*.

In view of this auspicious beginning, the course of United States– Czechoslovak relations during the inter-war years is bound to appear anticlimactic. But then, so was the diplomacy of the victorious powers in general. The United States' withdrawal from the European scene, the Czechoslovaks' preoccupation with the building and securing of their new state, as well as the general "return to normalcy," all played their part in portraying the period as one which lacked further ties and initiative. This, however, does not mean that U.S.-Czechoslovak re- lations had cooled; they merely took on a normal, run-of-the-mill appearance. Legations rather than embassies, staffed with the then customary number of personnel and as yet devoid of the scores of special attachés and offices so common in today's diplomatic world, carried on the business between Washington and Prague.[1] Again, it was the times which had much to do with this seemingly routine treat- ment of each other. Not even the rise to power in Germany of Adolf Hitler and its subsequent threat to the continued existence of the Czechoslovak state did much to change this apparently tranquil state of affairs. During the years before and immediately after Munich, the sympathies of millions of Americans were undoubtedly with the

Czechs; the United States government, although equally critical of Hitler's actions, continued to adhere to a line of strict neutrality. With the final destruction of Czechoslovakia in March, 1939, the American Legation in Prague closed its doors, although a consulate-general remained open until America's entry into World War II.[2] Contrariwise, the Czechoslovak Legation in Washington continued to function and all during the war provided a most important rallying point for the cause of a Czechoslovakia to be resurrected after the war.

Like his predecessor in World War I, President Eduard Beneš, who left his country days after Munich and began a voluntary exile of six years, almost immediately went to work on behalf of Czechoslovakia's restoration. After a brief stint as a guest lecturer at the University of Chicago, Beneš settled in London; with a handful of associates, he began the painful process of putting the pieces together. He was aided in his task by a score of former Czechoslovak diplomats in Allied and pro-Allied countries, who managed to keep open Czechoslovak legations and consulates. The United States' decision to allow the Czechoslovak Legation in Washington to remain open gave important moral and political support to the Czechoslovak cause. The Legation played an important part in the struggle for Czechoslovak liberation and when, in 1943, President Roosevelt accredited his diplomatic representative to President Beneš' London government, both missions were elevated to the rank of embassies.

As routine as U.S.-Czechoslovak relations might have been up to the outbreak of the Second World War, they took on a different appearance during the war and after the conclusion of hostilities in the European theatre, in May, 1945. This was partly due to the changing nature of post-war international relations, but even more so due to the heightened interest of the United States in Central and Eastern Europe, and Czechoslovakia in particular.

The researcher, whose findings on pre-war United States-Czechoslovakia relations in American archival collections were modest at best, is now confronted with ample materials ranging over a wide variety of subjects. Much greater American involvement in European affairs, the vast expansion of diplomatic relations, and the emergence of the United States and the Soviet Union as superpowers all contributed to this new concern. For the American Embassy in Prague, the new tasks were formidable. The situation had changed similarly in terms of the political importance of the Prague post. From its past role as an average-size legation without any special political significance, the new embassy had become one of the most sensitive American diplomatic missions.

Things were not made easier for the new ambassador by his having to start from scratch. Contrary to his Czechoslovak counterpart, who did not have to relinquish his base of operations during the war and who now merely had to expand facilities in order to resume full-scale relations between the two countries, the American Ambassador, Laurence A. Steinhardt, literally had to reopen shop. Although Prague, unlike some other East European capitals, had experienced relatively little physical damage during the war, facilities and services were at a premium in 1945. While some of the officials in the State Department's political division might well have come to see the new importance of Prague, the administrative and personnel branches responsible for staffing, supplies and allowances still treated Prague in a miserly and routine way. Some of Ambassador Steinhardt's first messages from his new post, addressed to the administrative and personnel divisions, vividly bespeak his urgent needs. Thus, in a lengthy and bitter communication to his friend and fellow foreign service officer, George V. Allen, then Assistant Director of the State Department's North African and Mid-Eastern Division, Steinhardt angrily complained about the incompetence and inefficiency of the Department's administrative and personnel branches, expressing his conviction that "until the political divisions are given almost complete control over personnel and a considerable degree of control over administration . . . the present ills will not be cured. In other words, the chief of a political division should have the say as to how many officers there should be at a given post and who they should be, and not as appears to have been the case for some time, not even be consulted as to personnel."[3] Some weeks later, and in a more relaxed mood, Steinhardt wrote to Walton C. Ferris, Assistant Chief of the State Department's personnel division, and told him that the Embassy was "still required to fetch 'visiting firemen' as well as Government officials and business men from Ruzyne airfield."[4]

Steinhardt's problems in Prague were further augmented by the enormous and frequently entirely novel tasks which his infant embassy was expected to perform. The changing and constantly expanding nature of diplomatic relations, the inclusion into legitimate diplomatic activity of an ever increasing number of cultural and propaganda matters, the expansion into often purely technical fields and the concomitant creation of attaché positions were only part of his new responsibilities. The war and its attendant problems and tragedies, with thousands of persons searching for relatives and displaced persons and others requesting entry visas in ever increasing numbers, added to the Embassy's already formidable workload.

Last, but by no means least, there was the Czechoslovak government, which "has been bombarding us with notes — several every day — about missing property and their relations with the U.S. Third Army, while at the same time the 22nd Corps in Plzen must of necessity refer innumerable matters to us."[5]

To attend properly to all these tasks would have been difficult enough, even if the Embassy had been properly staffed with the prerequisite number of trained foreign service personnel. But neither they, nor sufficient clerical and technical help, was available. Except for John Bruins, the Counselor of Embassy and after Steinhardt the ranking U.S. diplomat in Prague, the Embassy lacked both senior and junior foreign service officers and literally operated on a skeleton clerical staff. While hundreds of trained radio operators were being sent back to the United States after completion of their military service, the Prague Embassy, as well as other American diplomatic establishments in liberated European countries, urgently needed their services. The Ambassador deplored the needlessly complicated and costly procedure of sending back to the United States trained men, many of whom had expressed a desire for continued service overseas, and then recruiting and training others in the U.S. for shipment to American missions abroad. Sarcastically, he commented to Francis Williamson, his long-time friend at the Department's Division of Central European affairs: "I realize that this argument [to keep trained radio operators in Europe and to transfer them from the Army directly to the State Department for service in American diplomatic missions] is too business-like to fit into the kind of mentality that prevailed at Pearl Harbor on or before December 7, 1941, and it still exists in quite a few army circles."[6]

The situation was equally unsatisfactory when it came to the securing of local labor. The highly inflated Czechoslovak currency was a meager incentive for work in the immediate post-war times; a population accustomed to shirking work during the past years, when many jobs were directly related to Germany's war efforts, had not quite overcome this state of mind. "They [the Czechs] are enjoying a sort of lethargical holiday for which I do not blame them after six years of German occupation followed by some months of Russian occupation."[7]

Ambassador Steinhardt's complaints to his friends and associates concerned the question of representation allowances. It is a well known fact that successful diplomacy, like business, is frequently carried out at social functions. This approach to the affairs of state assumed even greater proportions after World War II, and Steinhardt, whose Embassy in Prague was rightly considered by him a pivotal point in East-West relations, found the State Department's annual allowance of three thousand dollars pitifully inadequate. To be sure, ambassadors are expected to be men of means, and rare are the occasions when a representation allowance covers a man's actual expenditures. Still, in comparison to other American missions abroad — and Steinhardt went to great lengths to mention more than a dozen of them whose allowances were superior to his post — the sum allocated to Czechoslovakia seemed grossly inadequate to him. Blaming once again an ill-informed and incompetent administrative and personnel division for this state of affairs, he was nonetheless aggravated by the fact that Washington had as yet failed to perceive the new and immense importance of Prague in the post-war years.[8]

It was against this inauspicious background that the United States reopened its Embassy in Prague, a city which for the next almost three years became a critical testing ground for the competing interests of the World War II allies. Defeat of Germany had been the primary, if not the only, aim, but with success, the long-standing problem of the exact relationship that Czechoslovakia was to play in Europe came to the fore. In the three years after victory, few Americans and not enough Czechoslovaks foresaw the full dimensions of the dilemma of Czechoslovakia, pressed between Soviet and American aspirations.

I

The Liberation of Prague

Although more than three decades have elapsed since the conquest of Czechoslovakia by the Allied forces, the liberation of Prague has remained a much disputed and bitter chapter in Czechoslovak-American relations. Wartime diplomacy, considerations as to which of the Great Powers should have a dominant influence in the liberated country, Slav brotherhood, but, above all, sheer and naked power politics, all played their parts in this particularly traumatic episode of Czechoslovak history.

Two points of view, the military and the political, were squarely pitted against each other from the very beginning. From a purely military point of view, the U.S. forces, then stationed less than 100 miles from the beleaguered Czechoslovak capital, should have advanced to its rescue. Such a decision would seem to be further supported by the fact that by late April and early May of 1945, German troops had virtually ceased to resist on the Western front, while desperately fighting on in the East. The once-proud *Wehrmacht* was more willing to surrender to the Anglo-Americans; the "Bolshevik menace," on the other hand, had to be resisted to the end.

The political angle brought forth entirely different considerations. The whole course of wartime diplomacy of the Big Three, and the Teheran and Yalta conferences in particular, had made it clear that a restored Czechoslovakia, while independent, was definitely to be in the Soviet sphere of influence. Just exactly what this meant was never clearly spelled out and, in tradition with Big Power diplomacy, perhaps even purposely left vague. As interpreted by the United States and Great Britain, independence denoted exactly what it said, although even they were willing to concede that an eventual anti-Soviet orientation of a future Czechoslovakia was both unacceptable and undesirable. To the U.S.S.R., on the other hand, Czechoslovakia could remain independent only as long as it faithfully followed and supported the political goals of the Soviet Union. Only on one issue did East and West see eye-to-eye, unintentional as such a meeting of minds may have been: the very presence of one's military forces in the liberated Czechoslovak capital was likely to give that power a tremendous political advantage and was bound to influence significantly the state of affairs in Czechoslovakia.

It is little wonder, then, that during the final weeks of the war in Europe the question of the liberation of Czechoslovakia and its capital city of Prague came to be a frequent subject of inter-Allied communications. At first it seemed that, contrary to Poland, Czechoslovakia was not likely to become a similar bone of contention between East and West. In January of 1945, at a meeting of the Czechoslovak Council of State in London, Foreign Minister Jan Masaryk could report that at Yalta the Allies had nothing but praise for his country and that the Czechoslovaks had shown "great skill [and gave] the Big Three [the] least trouble."[1] Soon after, however, these kind words seemed to be little more than the proverbial calm before the storm. Both Russian and Anglo-American diplomacy quite clearly foresaw the political value of an eventual military occupation of the three capitals in the heart of Europe: Berlin, Vienna and Prague. Thus, in assessing Russian chances for success in Central Europe, it was thought by the Soviet General Staff that an "attack on Berlin could be carried out only with a guarantee of success, since otherwise the political and military consequences of failure would be severe and irreparable for the Soviet Union."[2] High-ranking Western military officers and diplomats similarly weighed their own prospects. Field Marshal Montgomery speculated that in order to achieve a proper equilibrium of forces in Europe, American and British armies had to occupy the capitals of the three countries in that continent's heartland: Berlin, Prague and Vienna. In line with this thinking, he tried to convince General Eisenhower to consider the situation from a political, as well as from a purely military, point of view. "If the higher direction of the War had been handled properly by all political leaders of the West, and suitable instructions given to Supreme Commanders, we could have grabbed all three before the Russians," Montgomery reminisces in his memoirs. And, as far as Prague was concerned, the British Field Marshal is equally outspoken. Quoting Bradley's reminiscences, he wholeheartedly agrees with the American general's opinion that "[General] Patton could probably have been in Prague within 24 hours."[3]

There was much substance to Bradley's comment, since on May 5th, the day when Czech resistance against the Germans erupted in the capital, Soviet forces, in spite of their spectacular advance during the past weeks, were still well over 100 miles northeast of Prague. General

Patton's Third Army, on the other hand, was in Pilsen, some seventy miles west of the city. Prague radio, in the hands of the Czech insurgents, was broadcasting desperate appeals for help, in view of the determination of the Germans to crush resistance at any cost, no matter how pressed their own situation in the various other theaters of war.

The Czechoslovak exile government, while still in London, kept close watch over the military operations and was eager to have its own forces join the Allies in the liberation and occupation of Czechoslovak territory. Since Czechoslovak units, fighting in the ranks of the Soviet Army, had joined in its advance into Slovakia, it was considered only right by the Czechoslovak government that Czech military formations attached to the Western armies should do likewise. A report from the Office of Strategic Services, dated April 11, conveyed the suggestion of "prominent Czechs in London" that the Czech Brigade "was to be transferred to the American Third Army, so that it might enter Czechoslovakia supported by American troops, and if it were to bring with it extra arms and ammunition so that it could raise and equip troops in the country, it could then serve under American guidance as a balance to the Russian influence."[4] A week later, General Bosý, Chief of the Czechoslovak Military Mission in Great Britain, wrote to Sir Charles Portal, the Chief of the British Air Staff, and requested that three Czechoslovak Fighter Squadrons should "be employed in operations on the Western Front in the battle for Czechoslovakia." If these three squadrons would be included "in the Tactical Air Force operating over Czechoslovak territory, [then] they would be among the first to use [Czechoslovak] airfields."[5]

The London Czechs knew that these and similar requests which they had addressed to the British and American authorities previously were not likely to bring instant and favorable responses. While details were not as yet fully known to them, "they [were] said to fear that the strategy decided upon at Yalta [would] prevent such a move."[6] Yet another report, this time American in origin, boded ill for the cause of the West in the future Czechoslovakia. A U.S. request for the establishment and equipping, by American forces, of a number of Czechoslovak Light Infantry battalions had been presented to the Czechoslovak government in London; unable to accept the offer for fear of offending the Russians, the Czechs first stalled and then referred the request to their Ministry of National Defense. The Ministry had since been moved to the liberated areas of Czechoslovakia which were under Soviet control and where the U.S. demand would certainly fall on deaf ears. Colonel Anthony Biddle informed Major-General H. R. Bull, Eisenhower's aide-de-camp, of these developments and added a number of his own observations on the Czechoslovak situation. His message, dated May 4, is of particular interest in view of its author's familiarity with both the Czechoslovak and the Polish exile governments in London. Having reported on the resignation of General Ingr, the pro-Western Czechoslovak Minister of National Defense, and three other senior officers, Biddle quoted "an unusually reliable Czechoslovak source" that these resignations were requested by the newly-formed and leftist-oriented Košice government. Weighing these and other developments, the Colonel observed that "the picture, as it is presently taking form, bears all the earmarks of a house-cleaning by the new political forces which are now in the saddle" and "that in light of what would appear the political orientation of these new forces, considerations of questions such as light infantry battalions may necessarily not be confined to Košice (the provisional seat of the Czechoslovak government); indeed, may have to be referred elsewhere for decision."[7] In a supportive note, Hubert Ripka, Acting Czechoslovak Foreign Minister, approached both Philip Nichols, the British Ambassador to Beneš' exile government, and Rudolf Schoenfeld, the U.S. chargé d'Affaires who was later to represent his country in Prague, and asked them to impress upon the British government the urgency of the various Czechoslovak requests for the transfer of Western-based Czechoslovak Army units to the liberated territory.[8] Ripka told Nichols that all the Czechoslovak ministers who were still in London welcomed the arrival of United States forces in Czechoslovakia. On the other hand, Nichols quotes Ripka as saying that the Communists were depressed about it, and for obvious reasons. The presence of both Soviet and American forces in Czechoslovakia would ultimately be of advantage to the new Czechoslovak government, inasmuch as the withdrawal of the Americans would provide Prague with an important lever in bringing about the withdrawal of the Russians.[9] Simultaneously with this explanation of the overall political situation, Ripka and Ingr approached the British General Staff with the request for transfer of the Czechoslovak Armored Brigade to Czechoslovakia.

Beneš himself did not conceal his joy when he learned that Patton's armies had indeed entered Czechoslovakia from the west. Informed about it by his political secretary, he is reported to have greeted the event with exclamations of uncontrolled joy and emotion, a rare phenomenon with the otherwise reserved President. After he had shared the news with his wife Hana, he immediately issued directives for a congratulatory telegram to be sent to Patton.[10]

In an attempt to strengthen the position of those who favored the occupation of substantial parts of Czechoslovakia by American armies as a counterweight to the Soviet Army's occupation of the remainder, Ripka now tried to conclude a civil affairs agreement between Czechoslovakia and the United States. Quite obviously, he reasoned, such an agreement would be visible proof of Western interest in his country. With this in mind, Ripka approached Schoenfeld and suggested to him the conclusion of a temporary agreement which would cover civil affairs between the two governments. Schoenfeld forwarded Ripka's request to Washington, but was told that such an agreement could be concluded only in Washington.[11] It would appear, then, that at the time the United States did not seriously consider military occupation of major parts of Czechoslovakia, since it is not to be assumed that Washington would not have prepared for it if its intentions were different.

While the London Czechs were thus clearly rebuffed by the Americans, and now could do little more than sit back and hope for the best, the British were not about to give up on their attempts to convince Washington of the political wisdom of having Western armies in Czechoslovakia. On April 27th, the British Chiefs of Staff decided to send a special message to Eisenhower, once again pointing out the enormous importance of Prague. They suggested his capturing the city, if at all this was possible.[12] Three days later, Prime Minister Churchill sent a personal message to President Truman, asking that Eisenhower be made aware of the political significance of the Czechoslovak capital; he further requested Truman to issue to the appropriate United States military commanders the appropriate instructions for further advance into Czechoslovakia, as Churchill himself had already done in his instructions to the British staff.[13]

Repeatedly, the British attempted to convince their American allies of the high stakes involved in the Czechoslovak question. Thus, Secretary of State Edward R. Stettinius, then in San Francisco for the opening conference of the United Nations, found himself the recipient of a top secret communication which he had just received from his British counterpart, Anthony Eden. He immediately informed the Acting Secretary of State of this renewed British attempt to bring about the liberation of Prague by American forces: "In our view the liberation of Prague and as much as possible of the territory of Western Czechoslovakia by the United States troops might make the whole difference to the post-war situation in Czechoslovakia and might well influence that in nearby countries. On the other hand, if the Western Allies play no significant part in Czechoslovakia's liberation, that country may go the way of Yugoslavia."[14] General Eisenhower had told Churchill about his strategic plans and had made it clear that his main efforts were directed against the Southern redoubts, one of the last strongholds of German resistance. Churchill was "however, unaware whether General Eisenhower has been apprized [sic] of the significance of Prague" and the "British Chiefs of Staff have been asked to draw attention to the United States Chiefs of Staff to this matter."[15]

In retrospect, it would appear that the British position more accurately reflected the actual political chances of the Allies, regarding post-war Czechoslovakia. Quite obviously, and in spite of adherence to zones of influence negotiated by the Big Three during the war, the case of Czechoslovakia was not necessarily a closed one. As late as 1975, thirty years after the actual events, Czechoslovak historians themselves readily admit to the potential situation which might have developed in their country, had it been liberated by American rather than Russian troops. Recounting the events of those days, one of them states rather explicitly that "from what had been said so far, it is clear that the entry of American troops into Prague could have significantly altered political conditions in Czechoslovakia."[16]

In Prague, meanwhile, fighting was in full swing. Although aware of their imminent defeat, German Army and SS units, stationed in Bohemia, were to fight it out until the bitter end. Under the command of Field Marshal Schoerner and the SS General, Count Pückler, the Germans were now attempting safe passage to American lines, since it was to Patton's Third Army rather than to the Soviets that they wished to surrender. On May 4th, Eisenhower commanded United States troops to advance all the way to the Moldau, but subsequently rescinded his order. Why he did so has ever since remained a subject of much scholarly dispute. Czechoslovak sources see in Eisenhower's decision an act of deference to the Soviet Chief of Staff, General Antonov, and, furthermore, an unwillingness on the part of the Americans to aid a genuine "people's revolt."[17] On the other hand, American explanations, most of which came directly from President Truman and his military commanders, are based on two arguments: the military, according to which the capture of Prague was of limited strategic value, and the political, which stresses the desirability of continuing former President Roosevelt's policy towards Russia and avoiding any offensive action.[18]

These decisions from the highest quarters notwithstanding, there were U.S. diplomats and ranking civil servants who obviously disagreed with such a policy and pointed to the relative ease with which the Czechoslovak capital could have been occupied by American troops. Thus, for example, on May 6th, Acting Secretary of State Joseph Grew suggested to Robert Murphy, Truman's newly-appointed political representative for occupied Germany, an American advance all the way to the Moldau, a step which would "make the Russians negotiate on equal terms."[19] Grew was upset over "unilateral" decisions by the Russians made only weeks before. He was angered over Russian recognition of the new Austrian government without prior consultation with the Western allies. He similarly resented the stubborn refusal of the Soviets to grant the Americans use of an airfield in their zone of occupation and, most recently, the Soviet refusal to permit Western diplomats, Americans in particular, to proceed to their posts in liberated Czechoslovakia, as Soviet Ambassador Valerian Zorin had done weeks before. Grew had a simple solution to bringing Russian high-handedness to an end: namely, to "get tough" with them. While he was aware that his considerations were purely political rather than military, he was determined to present them, even though he admitted that eventual decisions would have to be made "primarily on military grounds."[20]

The generals themselves considered such a move perfectly feasible, as can be seen from the following message from Murphy to Stettinius. Though still without direct lines of communication and using the good offices of Jefferson Caffery, the American Ambassador to France, Murphy cabled as follows: "Chief of Staff informed me that it would have been a comparatively simple matter for the U.S. Third Army to have penetrated deeply into Czechoslovakia and to have taken Prague . . . In the absence of a directive, however, Eisenhower pushed south."[21]

The two ranking experts of the State Department's Central European desk, James W. Riddleberger and Francis T. Williamson, "literally crawled to the White House on [their] hands and knees to try to persuade the powers to send American armies to Prague."[22]

Ironically, twenty years after the event, even the Prague press admitted — by accident or by design — that even after Eisenhower's decision to respect Antonov's request and to halt his advance, "the Americans continued to look for ways and means by which they could disregard the agreement with Soviet headquarters, and negotiated with representatives of the Czech National Council in Prague, on the evening of May 7th, expecting to be asked by them to continue their advance."[23] Josef Smrkovský, vice-chairman and ranking Communist member of the Czech National Council, reminiscing on the events of those days, speaks of a message by General Patton according to which, on May 8th, at 4 a.m., Patton would enter Prague with his tank formations and crush the German resistance, should the Czech National Council ask him to do so. Smrkovský goes on to say:

> It was clear to us, however, how politically dangerous an offer this was. We were aware that letting the Americans into Prague would mean to make liberators out of them. We were not that much interested in the fighting . . . the awareness of the political consequences of an American occupation of Prague gave us a clear answer: we did not send a delegation from the Czech National Council to General Patton.[24]

The decision of the United States, based primarily, although not exclusively, on military considerations was thus countered by a purely political stand on the part of the U.S.S.R. and the Czechs themselves. But so, for that matter, was much of the whole diplomacy of World War II, with the Americans still largely interested in winning the war while the sights of the Soviets were already pitted on a victorious peace.

From New York, Ambassador Steinhardt, who had not as yet proceeded to his post in Czechoslovakia, expressed his keen disappointment over the U.S. decision not to advance to Prague. Writing to chargé Schoenfeld, then still in London, Steinhardt voiced his and the State Department's original hope "that the Third Army would be instructed to enter Prague — which it could readily enough have done, but for some reason which we still do not quite understand the American Chiefs of Staff could not see their way clear to giving the necessary instructions." The best thing that now could be hoped for was to prevent an early withdrawal of U.S. troops from Pilsen and to "at least stay there until the Embassy has been established in Prague and until the general picture in Czechoslovakia has cleared up."[25]

Steinhardt's communication best illustrates the rather delicate situation that had developed during the preceding weeks and the continuing interdependence of political and military action. The fact that Soviet troops had advanced into Czechoslovakia from the east had established the necessary prerequisites for Ambassador Zorin's ability to take up his post on liberated Czechoslovak soil, an opportunity so far denied the Americans.

By late 1945, the political implications of the American decision not to enter Prague in early May had become abundantly clear. In conversation with H. Freeman Matthews and James Riddleberger, chief of the European division and Central European desk, respectively, Vladimír Hurban, the Czechoslovak Ambassador to Washington, and Dr. Ján Papánek, his country's representative to the United Nations, called the American decision "a grave political mistake." They believed that "failure of the American forces to liberate Prague has resulted in an increase in leftist sentiments, as well as causing great bewilderment among the Czechoslovak people who had always regarded the United States as one of their chief benefactors."[26] Papánek, however, did not think that everything was lost and expressed the belief that "the moderate elements in [the] Czechoslovak government were now in the ascendincy [sic] and that American policy should adopt an active role in Czechoslovakia on the grounds that the balance of political forces made possible at the present time a swing to a pro-western orientation."[27]

The relative calm in Czechoslovak politics during the summer of 1946 temporarily obscured some of the thornier controversies in the country's political life. Even the question of who liberated Prague, a traditional bone of contention between Communists and moderates, seemed to have lost — at least temporarily — much of its drawing power. Thus, at the opening of an exhibit dealing with the rehabilitation and repopulation of the Sudeten regions, Václav Kopecký, the Minister of Information, and Václav Nosek, Minister of the Interior, both prominent Communists, found it possible to acknowledge Czechoslovak gratitude for the Anglo-American help in liberating Czechoslovakia, an admission not readily made by their fellow party members. Reporting on the festivities to the State Department, Ambassador Steinhardt expressed his surprise over the comments of the two ministers.[28]

Such occasions, however, were all too rare, and, in terms of its sheer propaganda value, the Soviet entry into Prague continued to be milked for whatever it was worth by the Communist Party. When, late in 1947, Czechoslovakia's domestic political situation began to deteriorate rapidly, primarily as a result of the situation in Slovakia and the recent overthrow of the pro-Communist leadership of the Social Democratic Party, the Communists, once again, tried to gain political capital from their version of the capital's liberation. They had repeatedly done so before; the moderates' inability to produce sufficient documentary proof to the contrary played right back into the

Communists' hands. This time, the moderates were to fight back and to enlist American help in their counter-attack. Thus, for example, during an Embassy briefing some Czechoslovak journalists, sympathetic to the Western cause, were given an official statement of the American version of the whole story. Chargé Bruins, present on the occasion, was told by the journalists that "the story sounds too simple to be trusted." On January 21, 1948, *Svobodné slovo,* the daily of the National Socialist Party, the Communists' closest rival in the forthcoming May elections, actually referred to the story but, in the absence of any more substantial documentation, failed to make the desired impact. Bruins was well aware of this handicap and now proposed to do something about it. Specifically, he suggested to Steinhardt, then in New York recovering from a recent illness, that getting "actual photostats of documentation would be a sensation and would greatly strengthen the hands of anti-Communists in pre-election days."[29]

As well as all this sounded, it was easier said than done. Back in Washington, Francis Williamson actually undertook the arduous task of obtaining declassification of the relevant evidence. In a personal letter to Steinhardt, he informed him of his progress:

We are now engaged in the most heart-rending, long-drawn out process of getting one document declassified by the Army, by the British, the Navy, the Air Force, the Joint Chiefs of Staff, and possibly many other organizations. The only one apparently not involved is the Democratic National Committee! It is a very simple document (copy of which is now in the British Embassy in Praha), in which the Soviets request that the United States Armed Forces remain on the Budweis-Karlsbad-Pilsen line. The publication of this document would fit in very well with the current line of the Communist press in Praha, and would also be excellently timed to follow the State Department's publication of the Nazi-Soviet documents. However, declassification in this dream world of Washington is a little more difficult than obtaining an appropriation of $20 billion from Congress. The Army promises quick action and says that we possibly can expect an answer within three months. I suspect after my talk with the British this afternoon that we shall authorize "unilateral action" in the publication of this document.[30]

Whether such authorization was actually given could not be ascertained from the available sources. At any rate, and assuming that the Army would indeed have acted within the hoped-for three months, American action would have come too late. A Czechoslovak paper could hardly have published such evidence after the events of February, 1948.

II

Prognoses, Hopes, and Aspirations

The bulk of Czechoslovakia was still German-occupied when, in the spring of 1945, American statesmen and diplomats expressed their first thoughts about the future of that country. On occasion guarded and tentative, but sometimes rather straightforward in language, these Americans depicted Czechoslovakia's future as promising and bright. It was generally believed that once peace would be restored, the Communist influence in the country would be on the wane and Czechoslovakia would settle down into its pre-war, essentially Western lifestyle.

Reporting from London some four weeks before the liberation of the country, Ambassador Winant informed Washington that, according to a recent conversation between Rudolf Schoenfeld, U.S. chargé d'affaires accredited to Beneš' London government, and Hubert Ripka, a close associate of Beneš' and Czechoslovakia's future Minister of Foreign Trade, "the basic conservatism of the people of the country [Czechoslovakia] would prevail." Ripka further opined that it was better to have Klement Gottwald, the leader of the Czechoslovak Communist Party, in the new government than to have him operate behind the scenes. Similarly, other Communist or Communist-oriented members of the new Czechoslovak government were variously depicted as either "loyal to Beneš" (Defense Minister Svoboda) or "fairly moderate" (Interior Minister Nosek). Time, no doubt, would work in the moderates' favor.[1] Barely a week later, however, Schoenfeld had to balance his report with a direct dispatch to the Secretary of State in which he again quoted Ripka himself, a staunch anti-Communist, as saying that "the center of gravity of political power in the restored state must be deep in the heart of the masses." Furthermore, according to Ripka, "mines, key industries and forestry should be administered by the State or by autonomous bodies" and "public financial institutions, including banks should be under public control."[2] While these pronouncements hardly reflected Ripka's personal credo, they were nonetheless indicative of the new realities facing a restored Czechoslovakia, to which even liberal-bourgeois politicians now had to accustom themselves. Stated differently, like it or not, there would have to be some form of nationalization; it was hoped that the gradual introduction of a socialized economy would come about by democratic means.

It was this climate of guarded optimism that greeted Laurence A. Steinhardt, the United States Ambassador to Czechoslovakia, when he arrived in Prague. He had been officially accredited to the Czechoslovak government earlier, but did not reach his post until mid-July, 1945. His new hosts had good reason to take pride in the appointment and to feel flattered by it, since the choice of an experienced diplomat as ambassador to their country was in itself ample proof of the importance assigned to Czechoslovakia by Washington.

Laurence A. Steinhardt — diplomat, lawyer and economist — was born on October 6, 1892, in New York City. The son of a well-to-do family, he attended Columbia University, graduating from there in 1915 with degrees in both law and accounting. The following year he joined the prestigious New York law firm of Guggenheimer, Untermyer, and Marshall, which signified the start of his career as a successful lawyer. Although primarily involved with investments and corporate law, he managed to break the daily routine by handling cases for more than one notable of the day. Thus, Archduchess Maria Theresa, sister-in-law of Emperor Francis Joseph, engaged his services in an effort to recover a Napoleonic necklace. Romola Nijinsky, wife of the famous dancer, Lily Langtry and Franklin D. Roosevelt were also at one time Steinhardt's clients.

After brief service in the United States Army, where he rose to the rank of sergeant, he returned to his law practice and, in 1923, married Dulcie Yates Hoffman, the daughter of a New York banker. It is little wonder, then, that the successful corporate lawyer, now married to a banker's daughter, soon found his way to membership in the Executive Finance Committee of the Democratic National Committee. A lifelong Democrat and admirer of Franklin D. Roosevelt, Steinhardt and members of his family contributed generously to the party's coffers. As a reward for his loyal services, the newly elected President Roosevelt appointed Steinhardt Minister to Sweden, a post he held until 1937. His next assignment, once again as chief of mission, was to Peru, where he served until February, 1939. The world was still at peace, but the two posts, while certainly not unimportant, could hardly be considered prestigious. It was only his next assignment, this time to the Soviet Union, that gave some indication that Steinhardt's star was rising. Although traditionally viewed as a "hardship post" by embassy personnel, there could be little doubt that it meant a promotion in Steinhardt's diplomatic career. It was upon the recommendation of Secretary of State Cordell Hull that he was transferred "to the higher and more responsible post at Moscow."[2]

As it turned out, Laurence Steinhardt obviously did not live up to Hull's expectations: a mere two years later, in 1941, he was once again transferred, this time to Turkey. Admittedly, Ankara, one of the great World War II espionage and counter-espionage centers, ought not necessarily be viewed as a demotion. Still, there must have been good reasons for Steinhardt's removal from Moscow at the very time when the "Grand Alliance" was being forged. If we are to believe the "old Russian hand" Charles E. Bohlen, then a foreign service officer attached to the Moscow Embassy, the ambassador "knew little about the Soviet Union" and was primarily concerned with his own image and reputation.[4] While such a charge might well be construed as a harsh judgment by an aspiring subordinate, other factors must have played their parts as well. By his own admission, Steinhardt had little liking for the Soviets; he distrusted them profoundly and suggested that Washington be firm in its dealings with Moscow, since the Russians were used to a "language of action, retaliation and force."[5]

Since more often than not the appointment of envoys is based on an understanding of, and even a certain sympathy for, the régime to which they are accredited, the choice of Steinhardt for Moscow ought well to have been questioned from the very beginning. While his remarks about the Soviet régime were made only after he had reached his new destination, there was nothing in the man's background, his social and political views, which ought to have made him the most qualified candidate for such a sensitive post. From all this, one may only deduce further that his erstwhile backers for the Moscow embassy, Cordell Hull among them, may have had second thoughts about the wisdom of their choice, once the new ambassador began to report from the Russian capital.

By contrast, the tour of duty in Ankara must have been much more of a success. In recognition of it, and for his role in the rescue of Allied airmen from Yugoslavia and Rumania, Steinhardt was awarded the Medal of Merit.

Even a sketchy perusal of his voluminous private correspondence reveals him as a shrewd and experienced businessman. Undoubtedly, then, the suggestion that it was essentially a businessman's outlook which provided the philosophical rationale for Laurence A. Steinhardt's mode of diplomacy is well taken.[6] By the same token, however, one might question the wisdom of the State Department's decision to accredit him to a government which quite clearly had embarked on the road to socialism and where private enterprise was likely to be severely curtailed. Steinhardt himself acknowledged this decisive trend to the left and prognosticated the important role of the Czechoslovak Communist Party in shaping the future of the country, a task which the Communists would rely on support from the Soviet Union to accomplish.[7]

The welcome to Prague was both cordial and correct, if one is to judge from the clippings of the Czechoslovak press, which Steinhardt sent back to Washington a few days after the presentation of his credentials to President Beneš. The Communist *Rudé právo* limited its headline to a simple mention of the fact that "The U.S. Ambassador Entered Upon His Official Duties" and the Social Democratic *Právo lidu* did likewise in simply announcing that "Ambassador L. A. Steinhardt Presented His Credentials." A much warmer and positive approach to future Czechoslovak-American relations was displayed by *Lidová demokracie,* the daily of the Catholic People's Party, which commented on Steinhardt's audience with Beneš under the headline that "Democracy is the First Law of All Freedom-Loving Nations of the World." Similarly, *Národní osvobození,* the daily of the Czechoslovak legionaires organization, found it possible to headline its report with the statement that "America Has a Deep Interest in the Welfare and Prosperity of Czechoslovakia." Finally, *Svobodné slovo,* the mouthpiece of the Czechoslovak National Socialist Party, quoted Beneš' reply to Steinhardt's greetings in which the Czechoslovak President remarked that "The World Has Become An Inseparable Unity."[8]

But once the niceties of diplomatic protocol were over, and Steinhardt's work begun in earnest, things looked somewhat different. The Prague legation, which had ceased its official functions in 1939 although the Americans continued to occupy the premises until 1941, had to be re-established. The seventeenth century structure, once the seat of Bohemian nobility, was in almost a complete state of disrepair. Street fighting during the final days of the war had taken its toll on the once elegant aristocratic residence. As late as October, 1945, Steinhardt, in a detailed report to the State Department's personnel division, outlined some of the tasks ahead of him. He mentioned the lack of readily available labor and complained that "materials [were] as scarce as hen's teeth."[9] Some of the most rudimentary facilities, like plumbing and heating, were lacking. But the physical neglect of the

Embassy's structure seemed minor when compared with the problem of severe understaffing, a strain further magnified by the tremendous workload to which scores of issues, still related to the war, had now been added. Such "additional burdens," as Steinhardt would call them, were the various duties related to the continuous presence in the country of the American Army, the dozens of "visiting firemen," as well as government officials and businessmen, which the Embassy "frequently [had] to house and feed" and who had to be provided with various other services. It required the services of two or three employees to attend to all these matters, and Steinhardt resented his Embassy as "being looked upon as a combined tourist agency, hotel association, transportation agency — and delicatessen store."[10] Nor did the Ambassador appreciate the instances of nepotism which must have occurred at one time or another, since as early as June, 1945, even before he had reached his Prague destination, he let the State Department know that he was interested in qualified personnel only. "I have for many years opposed the quaint notion," he wrote to Francis Williamson, the Assistant Chief of the State Department Central Europe Division, "that because someone once visited a country, had business connections there or speaks the language, he or she is of necessity the proper individual to send to that country to serve in the American Embassy — or to represent an American Government Agency."[11]

In spite of some improvements, especially in respect to clerical personnel, Steinhardt, as late as September, 1947, continued to fret over the insufficient size of the U.S. diplomatic representation in Czechoslovakia and over the quality of some of the foreign service officers assigned to serve there. Once again, it was Francis Williamson who found himself the recipient of the Ambassador's complaints. This time, the issue concerned the opening of an American consulate in Bratislava. Steinhardt had repeatedly pointed out the desirability of American representation in the Slovak capital, but it was only in the late summer of 1947 that the consulate had been authorized by Washington. Steinhardt was elated: "I want to express my thanks and congratulations at the miracle performed by you in blasting the Bratislava consulate out of the Personnel Division. This was a real feat, of which you have every right to be proud and which has pleased us here no end, as we have become increasingly worried concerning our ability to cover Slovakia adequately from Prague." But even this "real feat" was tarnished by the proposed appointment of a consul considered utterly unsuitable by Steinhardt.[12] He contrasted the opening of the Bratislava consulate and his difficulty of getting proper staffing with "the expansion of our missions in the American republics — without rhyme or reason — and the way we have had to battle in a few European countries to get an adequate staff." He singled out the Peruvian capital of Lima, a mission he had previously headed, and which, for no good reason, he thought, had been increased from a staff of "about 15 or 18 in 1938 . . . to about 150 today."[13]

So much for the problems of his Embassy. They were severe indeed, but the situation was gradually improving. As for the future of the country to which he was now accredited, Steinhardt at first seemed more optimistic. Shortly after his arrival in Prague, he expressed the conviction that "the Russian occupation unquestionably has done more to cure them [Czechoslovaks] of any Communist leanings than all the preachings and propaganda we could amass."[14] Then, appraising American political opportunities in the country, he predicted an uphill, but by no means hopeless, battle: "Prague is the one capitol [sic] in Eastern Europe where we have a fighting chance to recover lost ground and to stop the westward tide of Communism. It is the one capitol [sic] where if we succeed in holding the line against further Communist penetration it may be that in a year or two the position in Warsaw, Vienna, Budapest and Bucharest can be materially improved."[15] To help bring about such a desired turn of events, the American public had to be made aware of Czechoslovakia's geopolitical importance, and Steinhardt, who had many close acquaintances among leading newspapermen of the day, did his best to spread the word. To Henry Luce, publisher of *Time,* he wrote that Americans simply did not realize "the political and geographical importance of the country — being on the line where the Russian-American armies meet — [a factor which] is far beyond the recognition being given at home at this time." To remedy such American shortcomings, Steinhardt suggested to Luce that the American press "keep a careful eye on Czechoslovakia because it is [his] guess that in a few months from now the country is going to be recognized as the one place which has come back and should be regarded as a model for some of the bigger fish in Europe."[16] While one can only speculate about the exact identity of Steinhardt's projected future target, contextual evidence, based largely on the ambassador's essentially conservative views, would clearly point to Germany.

Convinced that the United States and the Western cause in general were "gaining ground slowly but steadily" and that the tempo was in "our favor," the American Ambassador was by no means the only prophet who predicted a return to democratic conditions.[17]

In retrospect, although the optimism of American diplomats seems unjustified, it was not without foundation at the time. Czechoslovak politicians themselves, both Communist and democratic, voiced high hopes for a happy symbiosis of the two political camps. So, for example, Zdeněk Fierlinger, the left-wing Social Democratic Prime Minister, and Klement Gottwald, the Communist Deputy Prime Minister, welcomed their traditional political opponents, the Catholic People's Party, into the newly-formed coalition government and praised its "excellent record during the war."[18] Not to be outdone by these unexpected compliments from the left, Mgr. Šrámek, chairman of the Catholic People's Party and one-time Prime Minister of Beneš' exile government in London, reciprocated in kind; on the occasion of a major speech in the Moravian capital of Brno, he claimed to be "convinced by his [recent] stay in Moscow that Czechoslovakia would have an absolute sovereign state and need fear nothing from the U.S.S.R."[19]

Although the overall composition of the cabinet was distinctly to the left, with the Communists and their Social Democratic allies occupying many of the key positions, some important portfolios remained in the hands of the non-Communist parties. Similarly, many ranking civil servants and almost the entire middle echelon of the civil service were non-Communists, as was the majority of the officer corps.

Different attempts at strengthening the democratic camp were undertaken by the Czechoslovak Ambassador in Washington, Juraj Slávik. He thought that more Czechoslovaks who had spent the war years in the West, particularly in Great Britain, should be brought back to Prague at once to counterbalance the presence there of the pro-Russian elements. With this in mind, he wrote to U.S. Ambassador Sawyer in Brussels, asking him to facilitate the transport of these people from Brussels via Würzburg and Plzeň, one of the few functioning railway connections. Sawyer correctly guessed the nature and purpose of Slávik's request when he cabled home that "the real basis of [Slávik's] request is to secure return of some more conservative elements now in England preparatory to elections to counterbalance radical elements whose return is being facilitated by Russians."[20]

These, to be sure, were statements for public consumption and, while in some instances they may indeed indicate the true feelings of their authors, they may equally frequently obscure them. However, when balanced with reports of a more confidential nature, they bear up reasonably well. An informant of the Office of Strategic Services who had gained access to Jan Masaryk reported that the Czechoslovak Foreign Minister sounded mildly optimistic when he declared that "he [Masaryk] now felt less uneasiness about the country's future than he did while abroad" and predicted that "democracy's chances for survival in Czechoslovakia [were] steadily improving, because the Communist leaders show[ed] increasing moderation."[21]

Rarely a week passed without further optimistic prognostications on Steinhardt's part. Both in his official reports to the Department of State, as well as in his correspondence with American business leaders, the Ambassador continued to depict Czechoslovakia's future as one of gradual return to its pre-war, Western lifestyle. Reporting to the State Department's Central European desk, whose chief and deputy chief, James Riddleberger and Francis Williamson, respectively, were close friends of his, Steinhardt expressed the feeling that "we are gaining ground slowly but steadily and that tempo in our favor is gradually picking up speed." It was important, however, to convince the Czechs of American good will and cooperation in the question of the expulsion of the Sudeten Germans, a key issue in Czechoslovak politics, lest "the trend in our favor be reversed."[22] He exhorted the American press to "take an optimistic line" in its reporting on Czechoslovakia, since he was "certain that things here are going to work out alright." President Beneš' popularity tended to strengthen the pro-Western forces, while, contrariwise, the "presence of the Soviet Army [in Czechoslovakia] made the Communists extremely unpopular." Some months later, Steinhardt wrote to George Van Slyke, his friend in the editorial department of the New York *Sun*, assuring him that "in having brought about the withdrawal of the Russian Army from Czechoslovakia American prestige is higher than it has ever been and probably higher than in any other country in Europe today."[23] As for the prospects of economic recovery, the Ambassador was equally optimistic, predicting "that within two or three years Czechoslovakia's economy and commerce will once again be geared to the West," since he considered Russian economic assistance to Czechoslovakia insufficient and temporary.[24]

Steinhardt would soon get his first samplings of economic relations between American capitalism and a Czechoslovak economy increasingly oriented toward socialism and state ownership. Two specific issues gave him a foretaste of things to come. The export of American films to Czechoslovakia and the compensation, by Czechoslovakia, of United States citizens who had lost their properties in that country during the war were to show the Ambassador that factors other than economics, such as political ideology, had to be considered in commercial relations with the new Czechoslovakia. In the first of these, the question of the export of American films to Czechoslovakia, Steinhardt displayed much sensitivity for the altered state of affairs; in the second, he espoused the more traditional and legalistic position. American films had enjoyed much popularity in pre-war Czechoslovakia, when that country's motion picture industry was in private hands. Although the structure of the Czechoslovak film industry had changed after 1945 — it was now a state monopoly and, as such, an important instrument of ideological control — the tastes of Czechoslovak moviegoers remained essentially the same. Although, on occasion, a Soviet film of high artistic quality would indeed reach Czechoslovak screens, more often than not the Russian showings were ill-disguised propaganda pieces and technically inferior productions in comparison with those of Western countries or, for that matter, Czechoslovakia's own highly developed film industry. The additional fact that the population was plain tired of reliving the experience of the recent war (a favorite topic of Soviet film makers) and longed for the not always profound but usually entertaining American plots only served to increase the demand for American movies. This desire, in turn, was counteracted by the Communist-controlled Ministry of Information, into whose jurisdiction the recently nationalized Czechoslovak film industry had been placed. Currency matters, such as Czechoslovakia's almost chronic dollar shortage and American demands for compensation in U.S. funds, only tended to further complicate matters.

Thus, while Czechoslovak non-Communist voices called for the abolition of the ridiculous quota system according to which 60 out of every 100 imported films had to be of Soviet manufacture,[25] Ambassador Steinhardt, on his part, tried to impress upon American motion picture executives the significance and potential consequences of the new state of affairs. When American film makers balked at the idea of doing business with a state monopoly, Steinhardt openly upbraided them. He was particularly critical of the attitude of Harold Smith, the representative of the Motion Picture Producers and Distributors of America, for his refusal to do business with a "state monopoly," an attitude which Steinhardt considered both ill-advised and unrealistic. In a series of letters, the Ambassador attempted to convince Smith that while it was a legitimate function of American film makers to depict their own country in the most desirable fashion, it ought not to matter to them whether Czechoslovak importers were private corporations, as used to be the case in pre-war times, or a state monopoly.

In Steinhardt's view, such an attitude could only result in a tarnishing of the American image, apart from the fact that it would ultimately lead to losses for American business, since the Czechs were importing British, French and other foreign motion pictures. Steinhardt reminded Smith of the attitude of the Western Allies vis-à-vis the newly-constituted Soviet Russia during the 1920's; the Allies refused to take an initial Soviet offer of, first 50% and then 20%, in payment of Czarist debts, and eventually wound up with nothing. Steinhardt warned that the same fate might well overcome the fortunes of the American film makers who resented the 60% import quota allotted by the Czechs to the Russians.[26] The Ambassador was, of course, less interested in the financial ramifications of the arrangement; what did matter to him was the propagandistic value which could be derived from a few carefully chosen American motion pictures. Just what he meant by a careful choice he never made clear. Presumably, some agency in cooperation with the U.S. government would see to it that the right kind of films, those depicting America at its best and influencing Czech viewers accordingly, reached the Czechoslovak public.

Attempting to enlist the good offices of the State Department in bringing about a change of attitude on the part of Hollywood, Steinhardt sought the advice of both Riddleberger and Williamson and, in return, offered his own. "If we stay out," he wrote, "we lose one of the best instruments to offset Soviet propaganda."[27] Regarding the whole question as one of "vital importance in the struggle between Communism and Democracy that is now taking place" in Czechoslovakia, he considered it in the best interests of both Czechoslovakia and the United States to come to terms, a move which seemed a vastly more desirable and workable solution to him "than to stay out in the hope of coercing a pretty radical government into abandoning the monopoly."[28]

Yet, and in spite of the Ambassador's best efforts, the whole question of the importation of American motion pictures to Czechoslovakia continued to be a thorny problem between Hollywood and the Czechoslovak government. While Steinhardt could report home that the showing of *Wilson,* a documentary on the life of the United States President who lent his support to the establishment of the Czechoslovak state in 1918, was an "outstanding success" with President and Mme. Beneš among the first night patrons, he found it necessary to speak about some less favorable impact resulting from the showing of American films as well. This time, the film in question was

John Steinbeck's *Tobacco Road*. He quoted excerpts from *Rudé
právo* which, under a headline of "America as she is," suggested to its
readers that "attendance should be compulsory for the pro-Americans
in Czechoslovakia," since in the picture some of the "seamier sides" of
American life might be seen.[29] One could hardly expect from the
Communist Party daily an additional comment to the effect that
Steinbeck's critique of life in the American South was at the same time
a classic example of the freedom enjoyed by Americans in exposing
their own shortcomings and injustices. Although American motion
pictures continued to appear on Czechoslovak screens, the difficulties
between Hollywood and Prague persisted, and Steinhardt's efforts did
not meet with success. Still, to the end he attempted to reconcile the
two opposing points of view and, by his own admission, his dislike for
state monopolies was no less than that of the Motion Picture Producers and Distributors for such institutions.[30]

The Ambassador espoused a more traditional line when it came to
the question of compensation for United States war losses, but even on
this thorny question his attitude remained optimistic; his hopes for an
eventual mutually-satisfactory settlement continued almost to the day
he left Prague for Ottawa, in 1948. Despite his traditionalism, a
different philosophical approach on the part of the Ambassador can
readily be discerned. No doubt his past training as a corporate lawyer,
as well as his background and station, played an important part in it. A
former partner of John Foster Dulles' in the prominent New York law
firm of Sullivan and Cromwell, Steinhardt used all his influence with
the Czechoslovak government to secure the return, or at least the
partial compensation, for United States citizens who had lost their
property on the territory of Czechoslovakia as a result of events
connected with World War II; at issue were claims totaling some $35
million. Except for the properties of large U.S. corporations with pre-
war business interests in Czechoslovakia, the claims, for the most part,
were those of former Czechoslovak citizens who had sought and found
refuge during the war in the United States. Having acquired American
citizenship, they now sought compensation for their losses from the
government of Czechoslovakia. In order to induce Czechoslovakia at
least to consider such claims, United States representatives, in their
various negotiations with Prague, held out the prospect of assorted
economic concessions and direct loans, if, in return, Czechoslovakia
would set aside a fixed amount to be distributed among the claimants.
The morality of this type of arrangement on the part of both partners is
undoubtedly open to question: ought not the Czechs compensate

citizens of a friendly power which had given them assistance during the war? ought not the Americans, traditionally generous and magnanimous, extend loans and credits to a war-torn country without attaching strings to such aid? Less debatable is the legality of the matter. No doubt, a country that had had such a good international reputation as did Czechoslovakia, was under strong obligation to honor such an essentially basic commitment. But, pitted against this tradition of her democratic past and her high legal standards was the new ideological orientation of her régime: why compensate foreign factory owners if, at home, Czechoslovakia had just expropriated and nationalized her key industries? While many of the claimants were deserving people of moderate means, not a few among them were great property owners of pre-war Czechoslovakia. The fact that, on occasion, a former German citizen of Czechoslovakia was on the list of claimants added fuel to the fire; loyal and devoted to the cause of a free Czechoslovakia as such individuals may have been, the tide of anti-Germanism in the recently liberated state was far too strong to consider such subtle shades of meaning. Furthermore, there were hundreds of thousands of war victims right at home; ought they not be compensated first, ahead of those who were fortunate enough to escape and to start a new and frequently good life abroad? Such an other considerations complicated the whole question of settlement.

It is difficult to see to what extent American negotiators realized some of these factors which, from their point of view at least, ought not to have complicated an issue that was essentially economic. The Czechs, on their part, tried to play down the economic aspects of the whole question, attempting to inject political and humanitarian overtones into it. In part, no doubt, both attitudes were quite genuine, simply reflecting the different past and experience of the two partners. But there was also an element of cunning and craftiness on both sides and, to complicate the situation further, the matter soon came to be an issue in Czechoslovak domestic politics.

What normally would be considered a question of international law and conventional procedure soon became one of party politics. The Communists, for the most part, opposed American claims while their opponents were willing to grant, or at least to discuss, them. In view of this, the U.S. claimants and their legal representatives began to take a keen interest in the forthcoming Czechoslovak elections, to be held in May of 1946.[31] John Foster Dulles, the future U.S. Secretary of State who then represented some of the best-known and wealthiest of the claimants,[32] kept in close contact with Steinhardt, who would inform him about the course of the negotiations and the chances of compensation for his claimants. In a letter to Dulles, Steinhardt minced no words. If the Communists should win an absolute majority in the forthcoming elections, he wrote, they will repudiate previous property settlements and further claims, simply declaring them "nefarious Wall Street attempts by American imperialists and war mongers." If, on the other hand, the moderate parties were to win the elections, the United States would have no trouble working out a satisfactory agreement.[33] While the Communists did not win the 1946 elections outright, they did emerge as the strongest single party and, together with the Social Democrats, held a slight majority in the National Assembly and most of the key posts in the newly-formed government. Although the democratic forces managed to obtain some important cabinet appointments, the thrust of the new coalition government was clearly to the left. All this boded ill for future negotiations concerning American claims against Czechoslovakia. It is noteworthy, and says much for Steinhardt's diplomatic skill, that he managed to obtain at least partial settlement for some of the largest and most prominent claimants, the Petscheks among them. He admitted that "the claimants will receive much less than the value of what has been taken from them. On the other hand, the percentage of the claim payable under the settlement is about the same as that which will be received by Socony Vacuum, Vitkovice,[34] and other large British and American claimants."[35] He regarded the fact that any kind of settlement had been achieved at that time as "somewhat of a feat in view of the deep-seated animosity entertained by the radical element in the government against the Petscheks, which has not been apparent in other negotiations." Steinhardt also felt that, under the circumstances, "the terms were the best obtainable without jeopardizing a prompt settlement."[36] He urged acceptance of the settlement, in spite of its shortcomings, since he greatly feared "the risk of changed conditions to [American] disadvantage or a change of heart on the part of the [Czechoslovak] government."[37] As it turned out, Steinhardt was no mean prophet, since most of the American claims have yet to be settled.

III

Troop Withdrawal

One of the first major issues which confronted the newly-arrived Ambassador and which, at the same time, provided some indication of United States influence in post-war Czechoslovakia was the question of the withdrawal of the Allied occupation forces. Steinhardt's own diplomatic skill, as well as the extent to which the United States would throw its weight behind a democratic Czechoslovakia, were to undergo an important test in this particular issue. Given the fact that by far the greater part of the country was under occupation by Soviet troops, with only a small part being occupied by U.S. forces, Steinhardt eagerly seized the occasion to instantly work to bring about the simultaneous removal of Soviet and U.S. forces of occupation.

Once civil order had been guaranteed, and as soon as the country returned to some degree of political normality, there no longer seemed any need for Allied occupation troops in Czechoslovakia. Their early departure was desirable not only for psychological and financial reasons, but even more so for reasons of a political nature. While the presence of the Soviet Army provided an invaluable support for the Communist Party of Czechoslovakia, the U.S. forces, numerically less than one-tenth that of the Soviets', hardly provided an appropriate counterweight for the democratic parties. With elections only months away,[1] there was no time to be lost. It was obviously impossible to insist on a unilateral withdrawal of Soviet forces, who largely lived off the land and whose behavior towards the civilian population frequently left much to be desired;[2] consequently, attempts were being made for simultaneous withdrawal of both Soviet and American troops. From the Czechoslovak side, such attempts were, at first, limited to the more moderate members of the government; eventually, though, the government and President Beneš himself threw their weight behind the request for withdrawal. For reasons all too obvious, the United States government supported such a move.

Withdrawal had been considered by the Americans even before Steinhardt's arrival in Prague. As early as July 6, 1945, the then chargé d'affaires Klieforth urged the Secretary of State to prevent a unilateral

U.S. withdrawal from Czechoslovakia because such a move would "seriously weaken [the] U.S. image and position of democratic forces there."[3] According to Klieforth, the Czechs would deduce that the Americans were withdrawing under a Soviet pressure that the United States was unable to counter. Such a belief, he concluded, already existed in their minds as a result of the liberation of Prague by Russian soldiers.[4] Assistant Secretary Grew replied that no unilateral American withdrawal would be undertaken and that the Department of War had agreed to the Department of State's recommendation for such a course of action. Only a "token withdrawal," proportionate to similar Russian action, would take place.[5] Ten days later, Klieforth could report that President Beneš had sent word through a "responsible intermediary" that he was pleased with the State Department's reply and that it would ease the pressure to which he was exposed by Prime Minister Fierlinger et al.[6]

As soon as Ambassador Steinhardt arrived in Prague, he almost at once began to immerse himself in the whole question of troop withdrawal. The available correspondence on the subject makes clear the Ambassador's continuing insistence on simultaneous withdrawal and his awareness of the political ramifications connected with the question.[7] By September, matters got into high gear, when General Svoboda, the Czechoslovak Minister of Defense, and Vladimír Clementis, the State Secretary in the Ministry of Foreign Affairs, went to Vienna to discuss the matter with Marshal Koněv, commander of the Soviet occupation forces. Simultaneously, the Czechoslovak chargé d'affaires in Moscow, Hnízdo, obtained an audience with Stalin and presented the matter to the Soviet leader. Stalin (and Koněv) at first promised no more than to limit the Soviet occupation forces in Czechoslovakia to "eight small divisions." Nevertheless, Beneš told Steinhardt that he felt Stalin would be willing to withdraw his troops from the country, but that this might be a more difficult task than originally envisaged since both Soviet generals and ordinary Russian soldiers "liked it there." Beneš knew Stalin too well to attach too much significance to such a remark — the personal likes and dislikes of Russian troops and their officers were hardly likely to influence official Soviet policy. If the remark is significant at all, it is to be viewed as an indicator of the then still considerable caution in Beneš' relations with Steinhardt, relations which grew closer and more intimate as time went on. At any rate, in the course of the President's discussion with the American Ambassador, Beneš asked Steinhardt to prepare a plan for the withdrawal of American troops with which the Russians might be confronted.[8]

From the American point of view, the issue was further complicated by both domestic and foreign political aspects. Thus, Averell Harriman, the United States Ambassador in Moscow, was highly skeptical about a unilateral American withdrawal from Czechoslovakia and strongly warned against it. If American troops withdrew from Czechoslovakia without similar action on the part of the Russians ". . . it would have an adverse . . . effect on our relations with Russia. Any move on our part which is interpreted by them as a sign of weakness or vaccilation [sic] with respect to anyone of their actions often finds reflection on their attitude in numbers of other fields not immediately affected by [the] action in question as Russians are extremely sensitive to considerations of prestige."[9]

Essentially, domestic considerations now had to be added to these purely international ramifications of the troop withdrawal question. Back in the United States, things looked different. In a joint meeting of the Secretaries of State, War and the Navy, the Secretary of War expressed the view that failure to bring the boys home "might be subject to some criticism." Although Secretary of State Byrnes was sympathetic to Secretary of War Patterson's suggestion, he keenly felt the foreign political implications of the matter, arguing that the United States should "suggest to Marshal Stalin that Russian and American troops should be withdrawan simultaneously." This, he thought, was the way the Czechs wanted it, since the "Russians live off the land." Should Stalin disagree with the American proposal, the United States would still have a free hand in the matter. For the time being, Secretary of War Patterson consented.[10]

At almost the same time, Robert Murphy, the President's political adviser for Germany, and major-General Bull, Eisenhower's Chief of Staff, visited Plzěn (Pilsen) and Prague to view the situation for themselves. In a report to General Eisenhower, a copy of which was forwarded to the Department of State, they advocated that two United States divisions should remain on Czechoslovak soil to protect the orderly transfer of the Sudeten Germans, and that the Americans eventually withdraw their troops irrespective of any Russian action. Should the Russians fail to do likewise, Murphy and Bull proposed to resort to "appropriate publicity." They suggested that the United States tell the Russians that neither U.S. nor Soviet troops were needed in Czechoslovakia any longer and that a simultaneous withdrawal should be effected.[11] Late in October, Secretary Patterson again approached Byrnes and, with reference to Murphy's and Bull's recommendations, proposed to withdraw the United States troops from Czechoslovakia by November 15th, since there was no longer any military necessity for the continued American presence in the country. Remaining after that date could be justified only by non-military considerations. If Byrnes thought that American troops were needed in Czechoslovakia for political reasons, the entire matter should be referred to the President and a decision made by November first.[12]

Nothing in Secretary Patterson's view suggested any lack of sympathy for the Czechoslovak cause. Still, his priorities naturally were not those of President Beneš. Only if President Truman would override Patterson's purely domestic concerns and give precedence to the foreign political aspects of the matter would American troops remain. Yet, the expense of maintaining them was a heavy political liability. As in the matter of personnel and appropriations for the Prague Embassy, where the State Department's administrative division frequently prevailed over its own political arm, it was for a long time a neck-and-neck race between those who wanted simply "to bring the boys back home" and thus please Congressmen and their constituents, versus those who had the less popular, but vastly more responsible, task of making politically necessary decisions.

Eventually, President Truman telegraphed Marshal Stalin to suggest simultaneous withdrawal by December 1st, because neither American nor Russian troops were any longer needed. Steinhardt was authorized to show a copy of Truman's telegram to Beneš.[13] Truman's proposal met with almost instant success;[14] shortly after, the Czechoslovak President could inform the American Ambassador that instructions for Soviet withdrawal had arrived and that Colonel-General Zhadov, commander of the Russian troops in Czechoslovakia, had requested General Svoboda to arrange for him a farewell audience with General Harmon, the commander of the United States occupation forces. All during November, troops of both powers were being withdrawn and, on the last day of the month, a contented Steinhardt reported to Washington that, as of November 30th, only five American officers and five enlisted men were left on Czechoslovak territory. He added that the Soviets were also evacuating and that the completion of their move was expected within a week.[15]

The simultaneous withdrawal of the occupying forces from Czechoslovakia was the high-water mark of Ambassador Steinhardt's career in Prague. Hubert Ripka, one of Steinhardt's confidants among Czechoslovak politicians, and who at the time was Minister of Foreign Trade, refers to Steinhardt's "initiative" in the matter and compli-

ments him for his skillful negotiations.[16] While Steinhardt was by no means the only United States official responsible for the mutual troop withdrawal, the available evidence clearly attests to his major part in it.

The withdrawal of American and Soviet troops was important for the Czechoslovaks, and it could not have come at a more opportune time. Elections were scheduled for the forthcoming spring, and the presence of foreign military forces could easily be interpreted as undue influence. Charges to this effect were leveled rather frequently, and while they were always directed against the Soviets, none other than Steinhardt himself opined that the continued presence of Russian troops on Czechoslovak soil might well work to the benefit of the moderates. On July 24, he cabled Washington that

> nothing could have done more, from a political point of view, to stave off the threat of Communism in Moravia and Bohemia than the few months [sic] stay by large Russian forces in this part of the country. In my opinion, their indiscriminate seizure of agricultural products, household possessions and livestock, the carting away of personal effect [sic] factory equipment, and an excessive number of cases of personal assault coupled with the stupidity and ignorance of individual Russian soldiers and officers and the delays attendant upon referring the most trivial matters to Moscow has cured the broad masses inhabiting Moravia and Bohemia of any inclination to Communism. I will inform the Dept [sic] as to whether or not the same conditions prevail in Slovakia as soon as I have had the opportunity of visiting there.[17]

To an extent, Steinhardt was quite right. The often indiscriminate behavior of Soviet occupation troops needlessly alienated numerous Czechs and Slovaks otherwise well-disposed towards Russia and things Russian and grateful for the part played by the Soviet troops in their liberation. But while the criticism of the Russians was common in everyday conversation, it did not manifest itself in the forthcoming elections. As their results indicated quite clearly, nowhere nearly enough voters in Bohemia and Moravia were sufficiently alienated to cure themselves of Communism. Contrary to the Ambassador's election predictions,[18] Bohemia and Moravia gave the Communist Party impressive support and enabled it to emerge as the strongest political force in the country.

IV

Post-War Recovery

As was the case after World War I, when the United States came to the aid of war-ravaged Europe, American assistance to devastated Europe after the Second World War was once again requested of and provided by the victorious United States. Among those who sought immediate post-war relief was Czechoslovakia. Although not nearly as directly affected by the ravages of war as many of the other belligerents, it had been heavily plundered by the German occupants because of its exceptionally high pre-war industrial output. The Germans had appropriated pre-war Czechoslovakia's vast and modern military stores and the resuscitated state now found itself in dire straits in its attempt to equip its army. As for the Czechoslovak forces which had fought abroad, side-by-side with their allies, the problem had been alleviated when Americans and Russians donated arms and stores to the returning units which became the core of the reconstituted Czechoslovak Army. Although elite troops, they were but a fraction of the number which the Czechoslovak government intended to mobilize and to equip. The government was now faced with the difficult task of equipping a force of some 200,000 with the remnants of arms and matériel left behind by the fleeing Germans and occasional pieces of equipment remaining from the now disintegrated Slovak Army. In 1945, the sight of a Czechoslovak recruit wearing a tunic of the ill-fated German *Afrika Korps,* civilian pants, a former Czechoslovak helmet kept as equipment by the Slovaks during World War II, and other make-shift equipment was common. There was an equal scarcity of weapons of all kinds.

In this predicament, the Czechoslovak government approached the United States for assistance. The Minister of National Defense, General Svoboda, known for his Communist sympathies, thought it wise to channel his request via Foreign Minister Masaryk, who was well-known and well-liked in the West. On October 20, 1945, Masaryk relayed Svoboda's needs to the American Embassy.[1] Within ten days, Steinhardt promised to help and asked for a list of various requirements.[2] Svoboda promptly furnished a detailed statement of all the needs, and attempting to stir the United States into quick action, reminded Steinhardt that the Soviet government had already delivered and continued to supply "equipment for several Czechoslovak Units, according to the earlier agreement, dated March 1945." However, neither "ordnance matériel and equipment for men" nor signal equipment, of which the Soviets themselves experienced a shortage, was included in these deliveries. He also pointed out that the British were providing military aid to Czechoslovakia, and would deliver 100,000 battle dresses and other pieces of clothing. From the Americans, Svoboda concluded, Czechoslovakia would require military clothing, shoes, underwear, tobacco and various spare parts for motorized equipment.[3]

The size of the request and, conceivably, its veiled political innuendo, prompted Steinhardt to consult the State Department. Secretary Byrnes obviously chose to ignore the pique and replied in business-like fashion. The American Ambassador was instructed to suggest to General Svoboda that he deal directly with the Office of Army Liquidation in Paris; only if the latter could not furnish what Svoboda requested would the State Department intervene. It was also to be brought to Svoboda's attention that payment for such surplus was expected in dollars, although it could be spread over a span of thirty years at an interest rate of 2 3/8 per cent.[4] The records show no evidence of any large-scale U.S.-Czechoslovak transaction relating to American war surplus. Although the Czechoslovak Army did receive occasional pieces of equipment from the U.S. forces, most notably after the latter's withdrawal from Czechoslovakia in November of 1945, the bulk of what was needed eventually was delivered from the Soviet Union or produced by the Czechs themselves.

American assistance to Czechoslovakia manifested itself on a different and much wider scale in the supplies which the Czechs received through the United Nations Relief and Rehabilitation Administration (UNRRA). Although, as an agency of the United Nations, UNRRA was international in the character and composition of its personnel, the bulk of supplies channelled to the various war-ravaged countries under its auspices was of American origin. The direction of the organization in Prague was under a Soviet citizen, R. I. Alexejev. Even though the labeling of many of the goods which reached Czechoslovakia via UNRRA was clearly recognizable as American,[5] and although the Soviet Union participated in the project as a donor, able Communist propaganda convinced at least a part of the Czech population that "UNRRA deliveries are gifts from the Soviet Union." These, at any rate, were the reports that reached Washington, sufficiently disturbing to the State Department as to prompt an inquiry. Acting Secretary Acheson instructed the ambassador in Prague to take the matter up with the appropriate Czechoslovak authorities and to correct such an erroneous impression. There were even suggestions from Acheson that Alexejev would have to be replaced as head of the Prague office of UNRRA.[6]

Some four weeks later, Washington followed up on its initial expression of displeasure with more specific instructions. Steinhardt was to protest to Alexejev about the misrepresentation concerning the origins of the UNRRA supplies and, if Alexejev rejected such a demarche, the Ambassador was to ask the Czechoslovak government to "rectify the facts publicly." If this too was refused, Steinhardt should then advise the State Department about any desirable future course of action.[7]

Steinhardt, in response to Washington's first note, acknowledged the existence of the rumors, but stressed his own helplessness in counteracting them in view of the Communists' control over radio and the press. Nonetheless, he deemed it "politically inadvisable to replace Alexejev as chief of the UNRRA mission at this time."[8] It seems clear from the Ambassador's reply that he blamed the Prague government rather than Moscow for this unsatisfactory state of affairs, and that he hoped that he might achieve remedial action more readily by contacting the Soviet representative directly than via Czech government agencies. He eventually took the matter to Alexejev, who seemed to have assuaged the Ambassador's fears sufficiently to permit him to reply to Washington that the Prague UNRRA mission chief promised to help correct the situation and that an American citizen, Richard Brown, would be put in charge of UNRRA distribution facilities for Czechoslovakia. Furthermore, another American, J. Hitchcock, would be appointed as the organization's press officer for Czechoslovakia. Both moves now permitted Steinhardt to conclude that progress in the right direction was being made. When, subsequently, Alexejev was invited to the United States to see UNRRA operations from the other end, Brown became acting chief of the Prague mission and, for official purposes at least, the matter was now closed. As is the case with most misleading press reports, the damage had already been done; subsequent publication of *errata* and rectifications did little to repair it. Also, by the time the initial misleading statements about the origin of the UNRRA supplies were set straight, the role of UNRRA in the post-war rehabilitation of Czechoslovakia had all but come to an end.[9]

Washington drew the proper conclusion from these attempts to present UNRRA supplies, largely supplied and paid for by the United States, as "brotherly" Soviet help. The State Department, in order to prevent repetition of such practices, now decided on a different approach. In response to an urgent plea by the Lord Mayor of Prague, the pro-American Dr. Petr Zenkl, it suggested that the necessary supplies should be channeled directly to the Czechoslovak capital. Steinhardt, who had transmitted Zenkl's original request, was gratified.[10]

Immediate post-war relief from military stores and all the economic assistance provided by the United Nations Relief and Rehabilitation Administration were of signal importance to Czechoslovakia. It permitted the Czechoslovaks to return to a large degree of economic normality relatively soon after the war. It provided effective help in time of need. Continual relief, however, could not become a permanent substitute for regular and healthy international trade, where the traditional laws of the marketplace prevailed. The Prague government was aware that an early restoration of the conventional channels of international trade would alleviate the country's economic plight and would make transition from the rather artificial UNRRA-supported economy to more normal conditions considerably easier.

With this in mind, the Czechoslovak government was eager to restore economic relations with its trading partners, among which was the United States. Although Czechoslovakia's pre-war trade with the United States did not constitute a major part of its overall foreign trade volume, the dramatic shift in economic conditions all over the world had now changed the picture. Great Britain no longer occupied the preeminent position it once had, and France found it even more difficult to recapture the prestigious role it had previously played in international life. The Americans were now both politically, and even more so, economically, the undisputed leaders of the Western world; although the U.S.S.R. could successfully compete with the U.S. for political primacy, it was no match for its rival in economic matters. It was now the United States dollar rather than the British pound which had become the "hardest" and most sought after currency; international rates of exchange were quoted and pegged to the American rather than the British monetary unit.

The picture had changed even more dramatically in industrial production. A war-ravaged, out-dated and exhausted British industrial establishment could no longer successfully compete with American production, which had established itself as the undisputed leader in the field. In short, it was to the Americans that war-scarred nations looked for salvation. In turn, the United States was just as eager to either resume pre-war economic ties or to establish new ones in newly-opened markets. The enormous changes in post-war politics were accompanied by similar drastic shifts in the world's economic picture, and now was the time to dislodge the old European economic powers and to enter their markets on a large scale.

American economic penetration into post-war Europe has been variously described as "diplomacy of the dollar," "Yankee economic imperialism," and has similarly been taunted as some form of rather ruthless exploitation by a strong and aggressive United States of a weak and devastated world. More charitable critics of the American economic efforts have seen in it simply a return to normality. While the United States did indeed exploit the new opportunities, it did so in a manner which benefited its trading partners as much as itself, perhaps even more so. Be this as it may, few would dispute the equally frequent assertion that, having left the political field to the Russians, the Americans now tried to gain influence in Eastern Europe by means of economic assistance in that part of the world.[11] It is in this context that U.S.-Czechoslovak economics must be viewed after 1945.

In Washington, it was believed that at least some modicum of political influence could be gained in Prague, if favorable conditions of trade could be offered to Czechoslovakia. Although no such official doctrine had been formulated, Secretary Byrnes' important pronouncement that "we must help our friends in every way and refrain from assisting those who either through helplessness or for other reasons are opposing the principles for which we stand"[12] in reality amounted to just that. Acting Secretary Acheson was even more specific in letting the Czechs know what was expected from them in return for American loans. Foremost on the list was the question of compensation for nationalized U.S. property. Furthermore, Prague was not to engage in activities which, in any way, might impede the "U.S. proposals for Expansion of World Trade and Employment" and, in its turn, should stay out of any Soviet-dominated economic plan. Lastly, Washington demanded full disclosure of Czechoslovakia's international economic dealings. Eventually, the demand for non-adherence to any potential Soviet economic bloc was dropped, when it was discovered that its inclusion in the original American draft was based on the false rumor that Czechoslovakia was to be included in the next Soviet five-year plan.[13]

Under normal circumstances and in a more traditional context of international relations, the American demands would not seem all that unreasonable. But now, things were somewhat different. As much as they might have liked to show understanding for the American conditions, or even desired to comply with some of them, this was not readily possible under the changed circumstances. Like it or not, the Czechs had been relegated to the Soviet orbit in the diplomatic dealings of the Big Three, and one of the results of this decision was the impossibility of the Prague government undertaking international commitments which, rightly or wrongly, would be viewed as hostile by the Soviet Union. The acceptance, by Czechoslovakia, of the American preconditions for economic assistance were simply too much part and parcel of the old capitalist world and its traditional trade practices as to go unchallenged by Moscow. Such a challenge Prague was not prepared to risk, and this even more so since, at that time, a war-devastated U.S.S.R. simply could not compete with the American economic potential, both in general terms and specifically in its capacity to render effective assistance to third countries. Stated simply, insult would be added to injury. From a purely economic standpoint, the apprehension of the Czechoslovak government was frequently criticized by a population accustomed to and craving Western-type goods; politically speaking, the picture was different. Many Czechoslovak non-Communists, whatever their reservations about their country's dependence on Russia, would readily admit that the U.S.S.R. was indeed the Czechs' best guarantor against the resurgence of an aggressive Germany and, for the time being at least, it was still Germany rather than the Soviet Union which worried them in the immediate post-war period.

In turn, Czechoslovak Communists were not inimical to the notion of trade with the United States, provided it was on their terms. Only a few months after the liberation of the country, the Communist daily, *Rudé právo,* wrote that the Czechs were not against U.S. economic assistance, but that it had to be channelled via the state, "which would maintain control of industries." The paper also commented on the "skill and cleverness of U.S. financiers" who came in on the heels of the Army to negotiate business deals."[14] While the reference to American businessmen was not exactly complimentary, it was also not abusive. Coming as it did from quarters not known for their affection for things American, it seemed a sufficiently strong signal for Ambassador Steinhardt to convey it to Washington, together with his own thoughts about the potential American investment in Czechoslovak indus-

tries.[15] Only days later, he could report on yet another Czech overture.
This time, it was Foreign Trade Minister Hubert Ripka, a non-Communist, who, in conversation with the Ambassador, expressed
the hope for an early renewal of mutual trade relations, "as Czecho-slovakia was particularly interested in economic and commercial
relations with the United States."[16] Obviously, trade with the Americans had not yet become a party issue in Czechoslovakia.

While thus conveying the desires of the Czechoslovak government
to re-establish and to expand trade and commerce between the two
countries, Steinhardt cautioned Washington against the granting of
an Export-Import Bank loan to the Czechs. He saw no reason why the
United States should not negotiate some loan arrangements with the
Czechs, although he warned that finalization of any such arrangement
would have to await the official announcement regarding Czecho-slovakia's forthcoming program of nationalization. This latter reservation was of consequence to the Ambassador in view of the potential
effect which Czechoslovakia's nationalization decrees might have on
American investments in the country.[17] Taking the Ambassador's
advice to heart, the State Department one week later informed Steinhardt that it had acted on his recommendation and that it had suggested to the Export-Import Bank the deferment of any definite
commitment regarding a loan to Czechoslovakia until the Czechs had
clarified their position in respect to nationalization.[18]

The Czechs, who earlier in the year had applied for a reconstruction
loan of 300 million dollars, were being warned in no uncertain terms:
they had better tread softly on American interests in the country if they
expected favorable consideration by the United States. Washington
did not, however, intend to close the door altogether. On October 4,
James Riddleberger, from the State Department's Central European
desk, informed Steinhardt about a conversation between Jan Hajný,
Commercial Counselor of the Czechoslovak Embassy in Washington,
and a number of American officials; the possibility of short-term
credits for specific commodities had been mentioned as a temporary
substitute for the 300 million dollar loan. Riddleberger seemed to
favor the granting of such short-term credits and thought that "they
were a good gesture on our part."[19]

On October 28, Czechoslovakia's national holiday, President Beneš
formally announced the nationalization of "key" industries and promised compensation to former owners, unless they were Germans,
Hungarians, or other collaborators with the Nazi régime. The nationalization decrees, more than anything else, indicated Czechoslovakia's

future economic posture. Together with the country's overall political
orientation, they were soon to give the Americans some notion of what
was to come. Seen in this context, the issue of compensation to
American owners of nationalized properties soon came to be the linch-
pin of Washington's economic policy towards Czechoslovakia.

The Americans now implemented their policy of leaving the door
open, and in July of 1946, as an initial "good gesture on [their] part"
granted Czechoslovakia a special credit of 20 million dollars for the
purchase of U.S. cotton; a 2 million dollar tobacco credit for the army
had similarly been extended to Czechoslovakia in May of that year.
But this was the extent to which the administration was prepared to
go, at least until the Czechs could advance some concrete plans for the
compensation of nationalized and otherwise confiscated American
assets.

In early July, Steinhardt could report to Washington that he had
reached an agreement with Foreign Minister Masaryk and his deputy,
Clementis, to the effect that discussions concerning compensation of
U.S. nationalized property would begin a month after the swearing in
of the new Czechoslovak government.[20] This hopeful message, however, was more than counterbalanced by a rather pessimistic report by
the Ambassador less than two weeks earlier. Herein, he spoke of an
"unmistakable though indefinable tendency on the part of some
officials of [the] Czech Govt. to show increasing indifference towards
Western powers." He also mentioned that "satisfactory conditions
that prevail throughout the country which resulted primarily from the
more than sufficient UNRRA shipments of food, gasoline, and other
commodities, coupled with the official seizures of all the property of
the richest one-fifth of the population and the relatively small war
damage sustained" only added to this tendency. This attitude of the
Czechs irked Steinhardt and, as a result of his displeasure, he suggested to Washington that nothing further be done in connection with
a proposed reconstruction loan until the Czechoslovak government
and its officials showed some appreciation of all the other forms of
American aid already rendered.[21]

Steinhardt was not alone in charting this new, hardened course.
Support for his point of view came soon and from the highest quarters.
Secretary of State Byrnes, then in Paris attending the peace confer-
ence, was aroused by the continuous support of the Russian point of
view by the Czechoslovak delegation. In particular, a remark by
Soviet Deputy Foreign Minister Andrei Vyshinski, accusing the United
States of attempting to enslave Europe economically, displeased

Byrnes. The fact that the delegation of a state which currently requested American aid supported Vyshinski and applauded his remarks only added fuel to the fire. Countries with such an attitude were
not to benefit from U.S. economic assistance and, although he did not
wish to renege on previous promises, further aid ought not be given. It
so happened that at this very time, Czechoslovakia was the beneficiary
of a "line of credit up to 50 million dollars . . . for the purchase of
surplus property in Europe." Byrnes now used this occasion to cable
the Acting Secretary, Will Clayton, with the request to "look into the
situation to determine whether there might be any proper way of
preventing the unused portion of this Czechoslovak credit from being
utilized in practice." He informed Clayton that he did "not want to
cancel a contract but merely to see to it that we are not making new
contracts subsidizing the Communist control of Czechoslovakia."[22]

   A second major stumbling block now stood in the way of American
loans to Czechoslovakia. Next to the purely economic issues of
compensating American owners of nationalized or otherwise confiscated properties, there now was the political argument. Byrnes was
"convinced that the time had come when [the United States] should
endeavor by all fair means to assist [its] friends in Western Europe and
Italy . . . rather than to continue to extend material aid to those
countries of Eastern Europe at present engaged in the campaign of
vilification of the United States and distortions of motives and policies. Any other course [Byrnes was] sure will not be understood by the
American people."[23]

   Clayton's reply of September 21 to the then still absent Byrnes
merely lists the various credits already granted and brings him up to
date on the state of the pending 50 million dollar reconstruction credit
negotiations. As Clayton saw it, "while the negotiations have not
reached [the] stage of legal commitment to make [a] loan, [they] do
imply moral commitment if [the] Czechs meet [the] conditions mentioned above."[24] Byrnes' views prevailed, further loans were suspended, and the unused surplus property credit rescinded.[25] James
Riddleberger came out with an even more specific comment on the
state of U.S.-Czechoslovak economic relations. On October 3rd, he
stated bluntly that no further loans would be offered to Czechoslovakia until that country "shows concrete evidence of friendship in
its general foreign policy as well as an agreement on compensation and
commercial policy questions."[26]

   There was, of course, the risk that such an attitude on the part of the
United States might be counterproductive. While it is unquestionably

true that similar object lessons frequently produced the desired change in attitude, this type of traditional diplomacy no longer was the sure-fire weapon it once had been. A contemporary comment by Joseph Kodíček illustrates the point. Only weeks after Byrnes and Riddle-berger had had their say, he wrote: "The decision of the State Department may theoretically be what diplomats of the old school call a 'healthy lesson' but contrary to American intentions and the aim of Czechoslovakia, it may have a much more serious consequence, namely to push Czechoslovakia even further into the orbit of Russia and make her more deeply dependent on trade with the Soviet Union and the rest of the Slav bloc."[27]

Washington's economic policy towards Czechoslovakia was but a reflection of an overall new approach by the United States towards assistance for needy and war-ravaged countries. This change in outlook was reported to Steinhardt by Dean Acheson, then Acting Secretary of State, in a top secret communication of November seventh. In it Steinhardt was informed of a meeting between representatives of the British Embassy in Washington and officials of the State Department during which, among others, the "Secretary [of State] outlined [the] Dept's policy on U.S. economic assistance in Europe (Delsec 986 Sep 24) as follows:"[28] Commenting on "world developments in recent months and their effect upon such earlier plans as may have been under consideration with regard to economic assistance in different forms to various countries in Europe and the Near East," Byrnes now stated that things had changed:

> The situation has so hardened that the time has now come, I am convinced, in the light of the attitude of the Soviet Govt and the neighboring states which it dominates in varying degrees, when the implementation of our general policies require the closest coordination. In a word we must help our friends in every way and refrain from assisting those who either through helplessness or for other reasons are opposing the principles for which we stand . . . The world is watching the support or the lack thereof which we furnish our friends at this critical time and the future policies of many countries will be determined by their estimates of the seriousness or lack thereof with which the U.S. upholds its principles and supports those of like mind.[29]

The previous criteria of "need," "basis to repay," and "general attitude of the recipient country" had now been superseded by new ones, of which attachment to and sharing of American principles was paramount.

Prague was aware that the Americans were displeased with them. In early October, Steinhardt had sought out Prime Minister Gottwald and in a long conversation gave him various reasons for United States suspension of the balance of the surplus property credits and the negotiations for the Export-Import Bank reconstruction loan. Among others, the Ambassador mentioned the Czechoslovak government's inaction in respect to seized American properties and the most recent anti-American campaign in the Czech press: "Gottwald seemed impressed." If the instantaneous actions of the Czech Prime Minister are any indication of his true feelings, he must have been impressed indeed. While Steinhardt was still with him, he telephoned both the Foreign Ministry and the Ministry of Information. The former he instructed to immediately submit to him a complete list of seized or nationalized properties; the latter he directed to cease at once any publication of articles "'hostile to our American friends'" and to report to him any breach of his directives so he could see to it that the culprits be disciplined. Steinhardt abstained from predicting the efficiency of Gottwald's steps. He limited himself to the comment that they would serve as a good barometer by means of which one might observe "the extent to which the leader of the Communist Party in Zecho [Czechoslovakia] . . . exercises control over the Communist press."[30]

One month later, Vladimír Clementis, Deputy Foreign Minister, was received by the British Prime Minister, Clement Attlee. The United States Embassy in London, which had obtained information about the meeting, reported that Clementis expressed to Attlee the conviction of the Czechoslovak government that the American action of suspending loans and credits was "'solely on grounds of Czech attitude at Paris Peace Conference.'" To this, Attlee is reported to have responded, "'Secretary Byrnes and others were displeased with the action of [the] Czechs in Paris.'" He advised Clementis, who was then headed for Washington, "'upon his arrival in [the] U.S. to take steps at once to come to an understanding with U.S. authorities.'"[31]

Byrnes seemed gratified with the Czechs' showing of at least some modicum of remorse for their misbehavior. He told Steinhardt so and, as an initial token of American good will, he now lifted his erstwhile objections to a sale, by Great Britain to Czechoslovakia, of some airplanes which had in part been built from lend-lease materials. While he could not expect that the Czechs or, for that matter, any delegation, would consistently vote the way Americans wished them to, he "should wish to see much more substantial evidence of Czechoslovak independence and friendship towards the United States before resuming any form of economic assistance. . . ."[32]

The picture improved further when Byrnes received news from Steinhardt that the Czechs were now actually in the process of implementing their long-standing promises of compensation for American losses. Jan Masaryk informed Steinhardt that in a recent meeting, chaired by Gottwald, the cabinet had agreed on such a policy and that both Gottwald and the left-wing Vice-Premier, Fierlinger, chairman of the Social Democratic Party, were in full support of it. A special committee to study and classify both nationalized and otherwise seized U.S. property was to be constituted, with instructions to report back within three weeks. Gottwald also told his cabinet that, if necessary, special legislation to meet the American claims would be enacted. Similarly, Steinhardt now found it possible to state that the anti-United States press campaign had ceased. He ascribed both changes in the Czechoslovak attitude to "the action taken by [the] Secretary [of State] and suspending surplus property credit and loan negotiations," a step which "has restored respect of [the] Czechoslovak Government for [the] U.S. . . ." In view of all this, he deemed it "desirable that funds at present reserved by Exim Bank for [a loan to Czechoslovakia] continue to be earmarked for Czechoslovakia."[33]

Negotiations for compensation began in early 1947, and some of the American claims were actually settled. But clearly, neither Washington nor its ambassador in Prague viewed this initial Czech gesture as sufficient in both scope and tempo. On June 12, 1947, Steinhardt wrote a long letter to Riddleberger, falling back on the old, hard-line approach. Toying with the "*temporarily* drag[ging of] our feet" in the whole matter of credits, he now referred to the state of the Czechoslovak economy as satisfactory: "Inasmuch as Czechoslovakia is not threatened with economic collapse — such as has been the case in Greece, Italy and perhaps even France — we do not have to worry that a delay in granting the credits may be fatal." In practice, this policy was to be pursued by first settling "all the matters now pending" and then expressing "to the Czechs our willingness to consider credits — and then drag our feet." Since this was the "technique the Czechs have used with us." Steinhardt saw nothing wrong in turning the tables on them now. On the contrary, promises of credits rather than their actual granting would strengthen the position of the moderates in the Czechoslovak government and convince the Communists that they "*must have* credits from the United States."[34]

Even a subsequent slight modification in Steinhardt's hard-line approach is incomprehensible in the overall contextual concept of the then prevailing state of U.S.-Czech affairs. He wrote to Byrnes on June 19th that, in view of the generally satisfactory situation, "the Department may wish to give consideration to [the] advisability [of] extension of both private and public American credits for Czech privately owned industry while delaying or minimizing for [the] present the extension of credits directly to [the] Czech government with exception of certain commodity credits which are at present under discussion."[35] In favoring aid for private enterprise over state-owned or otherwise nationalized Czechoslovak industries, the Ambassador may well have expressed his own convictions, since no such distinction was made in the official position of Washington.

By late spring of 1947, it came to be increasingly clear that American economic aid to Czechoslovakia had been all but discontinued. In its refusal to come to concrete terms with the United States government in the matter of compensation for nationalized American properties, Prague played directly into the hands of those State Department officials who had opposed credit to Czechoslovakia on political grounds. The systematic and overt support by Czechoslovakia for the anti-American pose of the Soviet Union at various international conferences provided yet another rationalization for Washington's gradual termination of economic aid to Czechoslovakia. This is not to say that the Americans were without blame in the matter. They too contributed their part to the evolution of the whole situation. Their inability or, in the cases of some officials, their unwillingness to appreciate and to properly evaluate the many shadings in the political climate of Eastern Europe were undoubtedly just as much a factor. There was still considerable political freedom in Czechoslovakia in 1946, much more than in the rest of Eastern Europe. This the Americans did not seem to properly appreciate. In view of the subsequent and rather generous economic aid given to Tito's Yugoslavia, Washington's position is not easy to justify.

But the Czechs were just as much of a riddle as Washington must have been to them. The constant divergence in attitude from various Czechoslovak quarters did little to reassure the Americans of the good will of their prospective trading partner; in the matter of compensation for American properties Prague's position was more than an enigma. The frequently professed readiness to negotiate an equitable settlement and the lack of concrete action to do so exasperated the American negotiators — Steinhardt among them — to no end. Not infrequently, representatives of the Czechoslovak Embassy in Washington and

Ministers Masaryk and Ripka themselves led the Americans to believe that things were well under way, only to see their statements repudiated by the Prague government which simply dragged its heels on the whole matter. And, since late May of 1946, Prague had a new government not necessarily any more "anti-American" than the previous one. But this time, the government had been duly elected and the Communist Party had emerged victorious from these elections. This new factor in Czechoslovakia's domestic affairs, in addition to the hardening climate in international politics, now had to be considered by both Washington and Prague in their mutual dealings.

V

The Elections of 1946

In the matter of the country's liberation, as well as in the question of troop withdrawal and immediate post-war economic aid, the United States had a rather direct involvement in Czechoslovak affairs. As conditions improved and returned to normal, the special role Americans had played in the almost daily lives of Czechoslovaks gradually came to an end. The American presence in the country continued to be felt, but routine diplomatic practice began to supersede the various extraordinary and temporary bilateral arrangements concluded during the final months of the war and shortly thereafter. Thus, when Czechoslovaks were ready to hold their first post-war elections in late May of 1946, Americans were observers—interested ones, to be sure—but not much more. Still, the outcome of the elections was clearly of consequence to the future relationship between the two countries: not only did Czechoslovakia's domestic social and political order depend on it, but so, too, did the country's future role in the forthcoming confrontation between East and West. Such a confrontation was already in the making; the days of the "Grand Alliance" of the Big Three were numbered.

The American interest in the Czechoslovak elections was motivated by a variety of factors. Having always regarded pre-war Czechoslovakia as some sort of oasis of order and political stability in a part of Europe where these conditions were all too rare, the United States had high hopes that the country would continue to play such a part. Czechoslovakia's highly developed pre-war democratic institutions, so it was expected and desired in Washington, would continue to provide a good example for other countries in that part of the world, an example even more desirable in the troubled post-war years. There were other factors, perhaps somewhat less nobly and altruistically motivated. A highly industrialized country, with factories largely undamaged by the war and with a skilled labor force, Czechoslovakia would be a most welcome partner in post-war American economic plans. Last, but not least, should democracy prevail in the forthcoming electoral struggle, it would obviously be easier to press United

States war claims and to obtain satisfactory settlement than in the case of a Communist victory. In brief, American interest in Czechoslovakia's forthcoming elections was both ideological and practical.

As early as September, 1945, a good eight months before the actual contest, the American Embassy in Prague began to report on the issue in its dispatches to Washington. It was Ambassador Steinhardt's opinion that the leftist parties wished to delay the election for as long as possible, in order to get better organized for them. This was particularly true in the case of the Social Democrats who, having now given up on their once contemplated merger with the Communists, wanted extra time to strengthen their own party organization.[1]

By the end of the year, obviously still under the influence of the successfully completed arrangement for joint withdrawal of Russian and U.S. occupation forces from Czechoslovakia,[2] Steinhardt, who had previously predicted a decline of Communist influence after the elections, ventured the guess that the Communist Party would only get some 20% of the vote. "If my forecast is reasonably accurate," he wrote to Dulles, "they are almost certain to lose two and perhaps three key posts in the government." Such results, no doubt, would have "a sobering effect" on the Communists, and it would therefore be prudent to press American claims against Czechoslovakia after the elections, when they would stand a better chance of being honored than at the present time."[3]

There were occasional dampers on these optimistic prognostications. In early March of 1946, less than three months before the election date, the Ambassador, reporting on information from a "reliable political source,"[4] deplored the lack of cooperation between the two moderate parties, the National Socialists and the Catholic People's Party, and blamed the latter in particular for failing to assist the National Socialists in their struggle at reorganization of the Communist-infested Ministry of the Interior. The People's Party retaliated by accusing the National Socialists of duplicity, since it sometimes prided itself on being part of the socialist bloc while, on other occasions, it posed as a staunch defender of democracy.[5] Although Steinhardt's informant tended to play down the issue of religion and insisted that the cause of friction between the two anti-Communist parties was "almost entirely political and had little to do with religion," this was simply not so; the Catholic People's Party was the only political party which, apart from emphasizing religion as a factor in the nation's daily life, also had clerics in its leadership.[6] Whether or not Steinhardt fully realized these divergent views between the two moderate parties is doubtful at best. Although his occasional incursions into Czechoslovakia's history bespeak a certain familiarity with its past, they say equally much for his addiction to platitudinous generalizations.[7] If he knew anything at all about the role played by the National Socialists and the Catholic People's Party in either pre-Munich Czechoslovakia or in old Austria-Hungary, he certainly never made use of such knowledge in his political analyses.

Such occasional reservations notwithstanding, Steinhardt continued to be optimistic about the forthcoming showdown at the polls. With the actual elections less than two weeks away, he compiled precise statistics relating to the expected allocation of seats in the future National Assembly. According to these calculations

> a Constituent Assembly so constituted would be controlled by the Moderates with 171 votes out of 300 as against the Radicals, including 39 Social Democrats, with 129 votes of which not more than 20 Social Democrats could be relied upon to support Radical measures. In this connection it is important to note that probably at least one half of the Social Democrats who will be elected should be regarded as just as moderate as the National Socialists in view of the fact that the Social Democratic Party consists of Left Wing and Right Wing factions.[8]

These were the most favorable results the Communists and leftists in general could expect, for, admitting that his prediction might be "inaccurate," Steinhardt "should not be surprised if the Communist vote [was] less than [his] prediction, in which event . . . the National Socialists would be the gainers."[9]

Just how the Ambassador arrived at his figures is difficult to say. Neither his reports to Washington nor his private correspondence provides any clue to his calculations. Conceivably, his Czech and Slovak contacts, almost entirely from the ranks of the anti-Communist parties, might have led him to these over-confident expectations. Wherever they came from, Steinhardt remained optimistic to the end. On the eve of the electoral contest, the Ambassador had some more encouraging news. He wrote Secretary Byrnes that President Beneš' and Foreign Minister Masaryk's successful intervention with Soviet Marshal Koněv brought about a postponement of Russian troop movements through Czechoslovakia until after the elections were held, a move which no doubt would tend to strengthen the democratic element. At the same time, he already speculated on some changes in the future Czechoslovak government, voicing the opinion that General Svoboda, the Minister of Defense,[10] would probably be replaced by a civilian.[11]

So much for Steinhardt's prognosis. The actual results of the elections conveyed a substantially different picture. Shown next to each other, the statistics of Steinhardt's predictions and those of the actual results clearly expose his serious miscalculations:

Steinhardt's Predictions[12]

In Bohemia and Moravia:

Communists	72 (73?)
National Socialists	65
People's Party	55
Social Democrats	39

In Slovakia:

Communists	16
Democrats	50
Freedom Party	1
Labor Party	2

Actual Results[13]

In Bohemia and Moravia:

Communists	93
National Socialists	55
People's Party	46
Social Democrats	37

In Slovakia:

Communists	21
Democrats	43
Freedom Party	3
Labor Party	2

Thus, the total Communist strength for all of Czechoslovakia amounted to 114 seats, rather than the 88 or 89 envisioned by Steinhardt, whose inaccurate guesses were just as noticeable in the lack of strength among the moderates. The National Socialists received only

55 seats against the 65 anticipated by him, and, similarly, the Catholic People's Party fell 9 seats short of the 55 he predicted. Only the Social Democrats finished below the Ambassador's expectation, by two seats; since he viewed them as allies of the Communists, which, indeed, in most cases they were, the actual results in this one instance were slightly better than anticipated by Steinhardt. But this was the one and rather insignificant exception, since in Slovakia the results fell similarly short of his expectations. There, the Communists, although clearly outvoted by the Democrats, gained 21 seats instead of the projected 16, while the victorious Democrats garnered a mere 43, a full 7 seats short of the 50 Steinhardt projected. Thus, in a National Assembly of 300, the moderate parties now had 51 seats less than originally envisaged by Steinhardt.[14]

All this must have been rather disappointing to the Prague moderates and to their American backers. No radical shift away from the left, as they had hoped for, did occur; all they could do now was to accommodate themselves as best as possible to the new order of things.

The composition of the new government did not provide too much consolation for them either. As required by parliamentary procedure, Klement Gottwald, leader of the now strongest single party, the Communists, became Prime Minister; Communists occupied a number of other key posts, the Ministries of the Interior, Information, Finance and Agriculture among them. While the importance of the first three portfolios is rather obvious, the Agriculture post was also of great consequence, inasmuch as its head controlled the distribution of land confiscated from the Sudeten Germans in the border district and, quite naturally, could use it in best political pork-barrel fashion. The National Socialists had to console themselves with the Ministries of Justice and Education, significant posts to be sure, but ultimately nowhere nearly as important as the departments of government headed by the Communists.

Having miscalculated rather badly, Steinhardt, in transmitting the results to Washington, expressed his surprise at the strong Communist showing, but refused to give up. He clung to his previous contention that the democratic parties would have the edge since the Social Democrats would split their vote: "Perhaps the most interesting, while at the same time the most important result of the election, will be the struggle for control of the Social Democratic Party, in which there is a strong difference of opinion between the left wing and the right wing."[15] Mistaken as the Ambassador was in his estimate of the election figures proper, he correctly foresaw the upcoming developments in the Social Democratic Party, culminating in its congress of December, 1947.[16]

Two days later, he sent a more exhaustive and analytical report to his government which he based on conversations "with several persons prominent in Czechoslovak political life." Obviously attempting to tone down his previously voiced optimism and to shift focus, he now claimed that the Communist failure to obtain a majority of the 300 seats in the Constituent Assembly vindicated previous predictions, although he admitted that the somewhat higher than anticipated percentage of the Communist vote came as a surprise. While he stressed the fact that the limitation of the number of political parties marked a significant departure from pre-war Czechoslovak political practice, he pointed out that the election "was held in an atmosphere of order and relative calm . . ." and "it cannot be said that the rather strong Communist trend is attributable to intimidation by the Communists nor to its control of the election machinery. Leading persons [were] convinced that it was a secret and fair ballot, having been controlled at the polling place by representatives of all the leading parties." Again, he latched on to the prospect of a forthcoming "*rapprochement* between the National Socialists and the right wing of the Social Democratic Party."[17]

Various American observers, diplomats and others in different parts of the world, expressed a slightly more somber picture about the outcome of the Czechoslovak elections and the reasons for the weak showing of the moderate parties. Thus, Averell Harriman, writing from London, conveyed the views of the British Foreign Office, which appear to be more critical and more to the point. While officials there seemed equally surprised over the strength of the Communist vote — they expected the party to poll in the vicinity of 31% rather than the 38% which it actually got — they did not hesitate to point out what they thought to be the single most important cause in the setback of the non-Communist parties: their own "lack of backbone." They conceded that strong Panslavism and effective anti-American and anti-British propaganda may have played their part; nonetheless, they held the leaders of the non-Communist parties primarily responsible for the poor showing, blaming them for failing to come up with an "effective democratic counterpropaganda." Finally, viewing events in the larger context of world politics, the opinion was expressed in London that since Western democracies were headed for a depression, Czech labor and business classes were attracted by the closed economy of the Soviets and by the prospect of continuous employment resulting from it.[18] While one might take issue with such a view in respect to business-men, there is undoubtedly much truth in it when applied to the working classes, among which, even in pre-war Czechoslovakia, the Communist Party had its most solid basis.

The weakness of Beneš' leadership was similarly criticized by out-side observers. Thus, a report from the U.S. Office of Strategic Services, compiled in Prague only days after the election and based on intelligence gathered from a "prominent member of the National Socialist Party," criticized the Czechoslovak President rather severely. It stated that

> bitter disappointment over the outcome of the elections has increased the sharpness of criticism of the leadership of President Benes[sic] on the part of the National Socialists and the People's Party.
> Even at the cost of the vitally needed leadership critics hold that Benes has elevated the presidency to a mere political symbol. Since the liberation, he has never utilized his great following among the people to give positive direction and leadership.[19]

Whether the non-Communist losers of the election accepted its results quite as stoically as Steinhardt seemed to believe is, of course, debatable. His observation that "there [did] not appear any violent reactions by the Moderates . . . [who now] console themselves with the thought that as there will be another general election in two years, it [was] preferable that the Communists be responsible at this time rather than during the succeeding five year term" is, however, quite correct.[20]

John Bruins, Steinhardt's Counselor of Embassy, and next to the Ambassador, the ranking United States diplomat in Czechoslovakia, seemed somewhat less convinced that there were no outside influences in the Czechoslovak elections. Contrary to Steinhardt's view, which was based on his conversations with prominent Czechoslovak poli-ticians,[21] Bruins did admit to the possibility of "outside pressure on the voters" in the form of "the announcement one week before the elec-tions that units of the Red Army would pass through the Republic from Austria to the Soviet Zone of Germany." While, as previously mentioned, the Russian troop movement was eventually postponed until after the elections, Bruins thought that "the announcement may have served as a reminder to the people that their country was virtually surrounded by Soviet military forces and thus may have caused some timid voters to cast their ballots for the Communist Party."[22]

Subsequent embassy dispatches relating to the elections deal primarily with the behind-the-scenes negotiations over the formation of the new cabinet. On the whole, it would seem, the embassy was well-informed about the political manoeuvering. One typical dispatch referred to "the Moderate parties [now] despair[ing] of gaining the Ministry of Interior . . . concentrating their efforts in trying to get the Ministry of Agriculture, the political importance of which was greatly underestimated [by them] during the recent election campaign."[23] Such steps bespoke a belated, but nonetheless good, understanding of actual political conditions in the country. Indeed, such was the case, and the United States Embassy was not the only one to point its finger on this key ministry, of which only the Communists foresaw its intrinsic importance at the right time.[24]

After some discussion of the Slovak situation, Bruins expressed the view that the new Prime Minister, Klement Gottwald, would invite the Slovak Democrats to participate in the new government, in spite of his intense dislike for some of their leaders, whom he repeatedly accused of having links with the former Fascist government of the Slovak State.[25] Gottwald would do so, Bruins opined, because the Democratic Party of Slovakia had emerged by far the single largest party in that part of the country and its cooperation was necessary to obtain passage of important constitutional changes sought by the Communists. Consequently, Bruins concluded, "the dominance of the Communists makes it far from certain that the results of the election will be translated fully into a government of the National Front or into a redistribution of local control in accordance with democratic principles."[26]

As for the leaders of the moderate parties, they were of two minds about their estimate of future Communist strength in Czechoslovakia. While some thought that the Communists were now at the peak of their power and would gradually decline, chiefly as a result of economic difficulties stemming from the recent nationalization of major industries, others viewed the present strength of the Communist Party as a propitious moment for that party to consolidate its gains. Bruins, in reporting this conflict of opinion among the Czechoslovak moderates to the State Department, stated further that the "more judicial" minds among them refused to predict which way the pendulum would swing since they were convinced that developments outside Czechoslovakia would influence events there. They urged the Western powers not to abandon them by adopting "an attitude of indifference and non-cooperation towards Czechoslovakia," although they recognized that in view of their poor showing at the polls, the Western powers now "may well adopt a cooler attitude towards humanitarian relief and loans to Czechoslovakia as long as [the] present degree of Communist control continues."[27] Continued rumors about increasing internal conflicts in the Social Democratic Party remained one of the few post-election consolations to the Czechoslovak moderates and their American and other Western sympathizers. Thus, Steinhardt could report, a mere two weeks after the Communist victory at the polls, that "there are evidences of increasing cleavage within the Social Democratic Party of which the less radical wing . . . is said to muster about 22 of the party's 36 mandates, and may more often vote with the moderates than with the Communists."[28] Some further comfort for the non-Communists could be derived from the fact that with the help of President Beneš, they managed to regain the reinstatement of one of their deputies, Jožka David, as speaker of the National Assembly. As for gains in the cabinet proper, only the replacement of the Communist Zdeněk Nejedlý as Minister of Education by the National Socialist and distinctly pro-American Jaroslav Stránský could be wrested from the victorious Communist Party. The Ministries of the Interior, Finance and Agriculture, considered crucial in the pre-election campaign, remained in Communist hands, as did the Ministry of National Defense, under General Svoboda, whom the moderates rightly accused of pro-Communist sympathies.

In spite of their triumphs, however, the Communists were as yet most careful not to overreach themselves and to give the impression that the Western-type parliamentary system was on the wane. When their opponents captured two hotly contested mayoral contests in Plzeň and Olomouc,[29] respectively, and local Communist leaders attempted to undo the election results by pressure tactics, they were instructed by their fellow party member, the Minister of the Interior, Václav Nosek, to abide by the election results. To be sure, Nosek acted under orders from the cabinet, and did so grudgingly, but he obeyed them nonetheless. This action of the Interior Ministry became even more significant when compared with a similar order given him by the cabinet early in 1948 which he refused to honor, and which brought about the government crisis of 1948 and the subsequent Communist coup.

Equally, the leadership of the Communist Party made it clear that it did not intend to resort to any radical changes in most other aspects of government and daily life. In a declaration to its executive committee, the party's chairman and now Prime Minister-designate, Klement Gottwald, pledged continued adherence to the Košice Program,[30] although he pledged the introduction of a two-year economic plan, some reforms in public administration and taxation, and some further nationalization. Only in one respect did Gottwald's blueprint clearly reveal elements of radicalism: it referred to the carrying out of a thorough purge, presumably among those in government and other high stations in public life, who, by Communist standards, were deemed "reactionary."[31]

Such professions of continued adherence to democratic principles contrast rather strangely with an earlier statement of Gottwald's on February 4, almost four months before the elections; obviously less confident of a Communist victory at the polls, his assurances were of a different nature. Addressing a gathering of Communist Party district secretaries and representatives of the party press, he assured them that means other than weapons, parliament and "mechanical voting procedures" were available to insure the triumph of the workers. There were plenty of ways to force results favorable to the working class.[32]

Ambassador Steinhardt was either unaware of Gottwald's speech or simply chose to ignore it. Seemingly satisfied with this relatively moderate program of a victorious Communist Party, he called Gottwald "a man of common sense and native shrewdness willing to learn, a thorough Czechoslovak patriot, as a person unlikely to embark on further extremist ventures . . . and more reliable than Fierlinger." He also seemed to console himself with the thought that the "new government will concern itself primarily with [the] execution of the programs of nationalization of industry and other liberal economic measures already begun rather than with [the] initiation of additional radical moves."[35]

VI

The Transfer of the Sudeten Germans

Already in late 1945, by the time the last Allied forces were leaving Czechoslovakia, but even more so during the election campaign, an issue of singular importance confronted the people of Czechoslovakia. Unique in character, complex in nature, and enormous in its dimensions, it also directly affected the government of the United States. At stake was the fate of the German population of Czechoslovakia, those former Czechoslovak citizens known as Sudeten Germans who, after the Munich Conference of 1938, had become citizens of the German Reich while the region in which they lived became an integral part of Germany. Now with the Reich defeated and in shambles, the *Sudetenland* was once again Czechoslovak territory and its inhabitants Czechoslovak citizens. But would the new Czechoslovakia permit those Germans who, in their vast majority, had betrayed and deserted it at Munich to remain within its boundaries and to escape the consequences of their past actions? This was the question which, ever since Munich, had played an important part in the thoughts and decisions of those Czechs and Slovaks who directed Czechoslovak affairs from their places of exile. It was also a paramount concern of those who remained behind and had experienced the consequences of Munich and Hitler's resulting "new order" first hand. Since the United States, together with Great Britain and the Soviet Union, had agreed to the Czechoslovak request to resettle the majority of the Sudeten Germans after the war, the Americans *ipso facto* became parties to the transfer. This even more so, since the bulk of the expellees found new homes in U.S., Soviet and British occupation zones of Germany.

As expected, neither exile politicians nor resistance groups at home evinced much sympathy for those former German fellow-citizens whom they held primarily responsible for the tragedy that had befallen Czechoslovakia in 1938-39. On the other hand, during the earlier stages of the war at least, there was also the realization that not all the Sudeten Germans had behaved disloyally. Mindful of the great risks which Germans devoted to the Czechoslovak cause had taken, the London-based Czechoslovak exile government, at first, approached the Sudeten German question with caution and with an initial attitude of limited compromise. But as the war went on, and as the pace of German persecution in the former Czechoslovakia quickened, the Czech attitude towards the Sudeten Germans hardened perceptibly among the exiles. Similarly, whatever clandestine dispatches the exile government received from the then Protectorate of Bohemia and Moravia left Beneš and his ministers with little doubts about the feelings of the people at home. They demanded a stern and swift punishment for those whom they held responsible for their sufferings. It was all very well to rationalize, from the safe distance of London or Washington, that not all Germans were evil; it was vastly more difficult to impress the persecuted population at home with such unquestionably true considerations. Thus, largely under pressure from home, Beneš and his government adopted an increasingly radical attitude towards the question of how to deal with the Sudeten Germans once Czechoslovakia would be liberated and restored.[1]

This Czech attitude, from initial limited compromise to ever increasing intransigence, frequently perplexed Western observers familiar with Czechoslovakia's high pre-war standards of justice and fair play. Americans in particular, and especially those responsible for civilian and military control in the United States occupation zone of Germany, had difficulty comprehending the Czechoslovak urge to expel what seemed to them an essentially peaceful civilian population. Stated differently, an action stemming from what the Czechs considered political necessity and sound judgment was countered by American emotion. Not that the Czechs were devoid of their own sentiments in the matter, but whatever issues might have divided them at the time, they stood firm and united in their desire to deal with the Sudeten Germans once and for all.

It is not the purpose of this chapter to give an account of the *odsun*,[2] nor, necessarily, to comment on its merits and defects. Rather, it is intended to underscore that the issue was one of the most delicate ones between the United States and Czechoslovakia in the immediate postwar years. It is necessary to recognize that in the transfer itself there is an inherent dichotomy. The Czechoslovak position, based on recent experience with these Germans, was that their transfer was a strategic and political necessity. American personnel in Germany, for their part, viewed things differently. To them, thousands of Germans arriving in the United States zone of occupation, loaded into railway cars with a mere one-hundred pounds of personal belongings, must have seemed a piteous spectacle, frequently incomprehensible in view of the vastly inferior living conditions in shattered and bombed-out Germany as compared to those in largely untouched Czechoslovakia. The Czechs, in turn, contrasted this mode of transfer with the forcible deportation by Nazi authorities of their own kin during the war. They had no difficulty concluding that, whatever the shortcomings of the *odsun,* it compared favorably with the methods of those very Germans who now invoked principles of charity and humanitarianism. But to the average American, largely unfamiliar with the most recent past, the Czechs' action of mass expulsion was at its very best extremely ill-timed, in view of the then existing conditions in Germany.

The war was still in progress when Czech and Sudeten German spokesmen made known their views on the post-war fate of the latter. The Czechoslovak government in exile, which earlier in the war had maintained some flexibility on the question, now displayed an uncompromising attitude. Minister of State Hubert Ripka, one of President Beneš' closest confidants, stated officially that "after the experience in the twenty years of Czechoslovak independence, and under German occupation [the Sudeten Germans] . . . had shown that the democratic way of thinking was alien to the majority [of them]." Since they readily fell for the trappings of Nazism and Pan-Germanism, "it [was] therefore only just that these so-called Sudeten Germans should be sent where their hearts belonged — to the Reich." Subsequently, to soothe the tempers and allay the fears of Sudeten German Social Democrats and Communists, Ripka assured them that the Czechs had not forgotten their loyalty during the difficult times of Munich and that these two groups would be excluded from any further transfer and had nothing to fear from the future. But, the minister concluded, "according to all reports from home, the people unanimously want the German population of Czechoslovakia to be numerically as small as possible."[3]

Thus, Ripka made it quite clear that few Sudeten Germans would be allowed to stay in the future Czechoslovakia, should Beneš and his government have their way. Sudeten Germans in exile, while obviously dismayed, nonetheless seemed to acknowledge the reality of the situation when, at this same gathering, they confirmed that even "the German working class in Czechoslovakia, like the working class in the Reich, had betrayed the international proletariat in this war" and stressed the necessity of a thorough purge among the Sudeten Germans after the war. The speakers, Josef Zinner and Gustav Beuer, Social Democrat and Communist, respectively, while of course not representative of all democratic and pro-Czechoslovak Sudeten Germans, undoubtedly represented an important segment of them.[4] As for Wenzel Jaksch, spokesman of another Social Democratic faction in exile, Ripka made short shrift of him when he accused him of having fallen into the trappings of extreme nationalism and thus, unwittingly, having become a tool of German imperialism.[5]

Already during the previous months, Rudolf Bechyňe, elder statesman in the Czechoslovak exile government whose political influence went back to the founding of the Czechoslovak Republic in 1918, had confided some of his thoughts on the Sudeten German problem to an agent of the U.S. Office of Strategic Services. The agent's report quotes Bechyňe as fully in support of the Sudeten German transfer. Even more than that, "those Germans who are considered loyal and are permitted to stay in Czechoslovakia should not be allowed to remain in the Sudetenland, but should be moved away from the German border, preferably in the region of the Austrian frontier." They were to have few, if any, special rights and the schooling of their children in the German language would be limited to the elementary level only.[6]

For the exiled Sudeten Germans, Ripka's and Bechyňe's remarks were a bad omen. Neither could they derive any greater comfort from the then available evidence on the policies of the Western powers, the only potential protectors of their cause. As early as July 18, 1944, the United States government, in a "Memorandum by the Committee on Post-War Programs" had stated its position: "If the transfer of certain minorities from Czechoslovakia is decided upon, the United States should use its influence to have such *transfers carried out in an orderly manner, over a period* of time, under international auspices."[7] While thus taking the necessary precautions to assure a systematic and humane rather than a chaotic operation, the American government clearly admitted that transfer of the Sudeten Germans was very much a possibility.

In April, 1945, the Czechoslovak Ministry of Foreign Affairs, then based in London, addressed a formal note to the American chargé d'Affaires in which it pointed to some of the forthcoming problems in connection with the Sudeten German population in a liberated Czechoslovakia. The Ministry warned the advancing American soldiers not to consider the Sudeten Germans, in view of their pre-war sympathies for Hitler and Nazi Germany, "as people deserving the treatment which should be accorded . . . to loyal citizens of an Allied State." Czechoslovakia considered "the bulk of these Germans as an element dangerous to the State, and would deal with them harshly after the conclusion of hostilities. Only those Germans whose loyalty to the Czechoslovak cause could be proven, would be permitted to remain Czechoslovak citizens."[8] The note further warned the Americans that Sudeten Germans who had resided outside Czechoslovakia during the war and had refused to live up to their duties as Czechoslovak citizens, such as by failing to enlist in the Czechoslovak armies abroad, would be barred from returning to their former country. Hubert Ripka, who, in the absence of Foreign Minister Masaryk, signed the Czechoslovak note, reserved special criticism for Wenzl Jaksch, who, after "a loyal attitude towards the Czechoslovak state until 1938 and during the Munich crisis, radically changed his political trend during his residence abroad and closely approximated the doctrines of Pan-Germanism." As a consequence of this, Jaksch and his followers could no longer be regarded as "satisfactory Czechoslovak citizens" and were to face the consequences of their actions.[9]

As soon as the fighting stopped, the Sudeten German question quickly emerged as one very important, if not the most important, problem of the Czechoslovak government. There seemed little point in planning the rebuilding of the Republic or in arguing over the constitutional changes and the very character of the new Czechoslovakia until the Sudeten German problem could be solved. Alfred Klieforth, in charge of the U.S. mission in liberated Prague, cabled a mere six weeks after the cessation of hostilities that "the outstanding issue in Czechoslovakia, notwithstanding the gravity and importance of Czechoslovak-Russian relations, [was] the solution of the minority problem, involving transfer of about 3,000,000 Czechoslovak nationals to Germany and Hungary, 20 percent of the country's population being involved . . . Until the transfer problem is solved, all reconstruction [was] make-shift."[10]

Klieforth was correct in his appraisal of the situation, best attested to by the domestic aspects of the transfer problem. Czechoslovak political parties were vying with each other in presenting themselves as champions of transfer. The Communists, always the most vociferous, invoked the Soviet Union as the chief Great Power sponsor in the project. National Socialists and Populists, on the other hand, while unable to bring forward Western powers in quite the same light, pointed to their traditionally anti-German past, exalted their national traditions and obliquely accused the Communists of duplicity. After all, good Marxists loudly proclaimed themselves to be internationalists and proletarians who knew no fatherland; there was such a thing as solidarity of the proletariat and German workers were part of it.

As for the Great Powers themselves, without whose express approval the Czechs could not carry out their *odsun,* the situation between the war's end and the start of the Potsdam Conference presented the following picture. Unquestionably, the U.S.S.R. was the only power formally committed to the idea of transfer. The United States and Britain, while sympathetic and agreeing in principle, had as yet not come forward with an official point of view. The reasoning behind the respective positions of the Big Three was clear enough: the Soviet Union, having suffered by far the most at the hands of the Nazi invaders and being by tradition less concerned with the purely humanitarian aspects of the matter, readily gave its assent to a policy dear to the hearts of the Czechs. Irrespective of the intrinsic merits of the whole Sudeten German question, Moscow could derive useful political capital from it. The Western powers, on the other hand, while unencumbered with such sterile intellectual baggage as "proletarian solidarity," looked at the problem primarily from a technical point of view, both in terms of the machinery necessary for the transfer-proper and the resources available for the subsequent resettlement of the displaced population in the occupation zones of Germany. The long and savage first-hand exposure of Russia to invading German armies, as compared with the relatively short period of time during which the U.S. had been exposed to combat with the Germans, was one important reason why Washington felt less hostile to the defeated Nazis than Moscow. Western tradition and various other factors in both the political and the human past of Americans were equally responsible for America's different approach.

U.S. diplomats soon realized the potential pitfalls of the situation, and the Prague Embassy repeatedly warned Washington that failure to recognize Czech feelings on the question of transfer and to give its speedy consent to them would seriously, perhaps irreparably, damage the American image.[11] In turn, the Czechoslovak government literally bombarded both Washington and London with requests to put the issue on the agenda of the forthcoming Postdam Conference and to give consent to the transfer. On July 3rd, Acting Foreign Minister Clementis wrote to Chargé Klieforth to ask him to prevail upon his government to accede to the Czechoslovak request. Specifically, Clementis wanted the Great Powers, in agreement with Czechoslovakia, to determine the number of Germans to be expelled into each zone of occupation. As for the technical arrangements, he proposed that Czechoslovak coordinating missions be attached to the appropriate staffs in each of the zones of occupation. He reiterated the urgency of the whole matter and pointed out the impossibility of the Czechoslovak government's proceeding with systematic reconstruction and rehabilitation of the country until this question was disposed of.[12]

Assistant Secretary of State Grew replied on July 16th and, that same day, Chargé Klieforth transmitted the essence of the American response to the Czechoslovak Foreign Ministry. Grew's remarks gave some satisfaction to Prague, although they fell short of full compliance with the Czech request. The United States government, the Acting Secretary said, "appreciated fully the injuries suffered by Czechoslovakia at the hands of the Germans and the German minority during the past decades, and, in an effort to arrive at a satisfactory solution, was prepared to examine the question." Having said this much, Grew however insisted that "the solution [to the Sudeten German question] must take into account the broader aspects of the problem in relation to Europe's future security and peace . . . as well as the particular problems which face governments responsible for the military occupation in Germany itself."[13]

There is good reason to believe that Grew's remarks did reflect the true feelings of the United States government, rather than being simply an attempt to placate Prague. Like the Soviet Union, the United States was committed to punishing those Sudeten Germans who were guilty of collaboration with Fascism; unlike Moscow, which correctly realized the propagandistic value derived from support of Prague's position, Washington seemed more concerned with an orderly and humane transfer than ideological gain. It is important to keep this in mind, since it constitutes a crucial factor in the whole Sudeten German question, the consequences of which left indelible marks on Czechoslovak domestic and foreign policy.

On July 31st, Grew cabled the U.S. Embassy in Prague to apprise it of the decisions relating to German minorities made by the Big Three, by now meeting in Potsdam: "The three Govts, having considered the question in all aspects, recognize that the transfer to Germany of German populations, or elements thereof, remaining in Poland, Czechoslovakia, and Hungary, will have to be undertaken." The Acting Secretary added "that any transfers that take place should be effected in an orderly and humane manner."[14] The Allied Control Council for Germany, acting on instructions of the three occupying powers, was to assure equitable distribution in the various zones of the displaced Germans, to report on those who had already arrived, and to submit estimates of time and rate of future transfers. In so doing, they were to take into consideration existing conditions in Germany. Finally, in informing the governments of Poland, Czechoslovakia, and Hungary of the Potsdam decision, the Big Three requested these countries to abstain from further *ad hoc* expulsions of Germans from their countries "pending the examination by the govts concerned of the report from their representative on the Control Council." The Embassy was requested to coordinate communication of this preliminary report with the embassies of Great Britain and the U.S.S.R. and to treat it as "strictly secret until an official statement [was] issued by the [Potsdam] Conference."[15]

Acting on Grew's instructions, Ambassador Steinhardt, who had taken up his post in Prague only days before, promptly informed Foreign Minister Masaryk[16] and, to add importance and luster to the occasion, personally delivered the U.S. communiqué to the Czechoslovak Foreign Ministry. The British chargé d'Affaires, with whom Steinhardt had conferred, did so simultaneously. The Soviet Ambassador was still expecting instructions from Moscow, but promised to do likewise as soon as they arrived.[17]

As expected, the Czechoslovak response was one of relief and satisfaction, albeit with some qualifications. President Beneš lunched with Steinhardt on August 2nd and assured the Ambassador that he understood the necessity for humane treatment of the expellees, as well as for some definitive schedule for the whole process of expulsion. At the same time, however, he made it clear that speed was essential if Czechoslovakia were to derive maximum benefits from the whole operation. He did not fail to tell Steinhardt that the "Russian government had already given its formal consent" and that American "agreement in principle" would further strengthen the position of the Czechoslovak government.[18]

Masaryk, Steinhardt confided to Klieforth, was pleased with the agreement, although not with its provision that "further expulsions be suspended for the time being," which he could understand, "but which might cause unrest among the local Czech population." In view of the above, Masaryk thought it unwise to let the Czechs know, at least for the time being, that further expulsions were to be temporarily halted. Only when the formal agreement was made public in Potsdam would the Czech press carry its full text.[19] That Masaryk, even in this hour of Czech triumph, would find it necessary to qualify his expressions of joy and to temper them with such considerations is in itself the best indication of the feelings harbored by the Czechoslovak population vis-à-vis its one-time German fellow-citizens.

Thus, at the very moment of its triumph, the Prague government experienced its first difficulties with the transfer of the Sudeten Germans. Czech passions and emotions, the desire to get even with those whom they blamed for their country's misfortunes, ran head on into traditional Anglo-American concepts of legality and morality. Then, too, domestic politics in England and the United States were to have their effects on the degree of support and cooperation which Czechoslovakia could expect from these countries. On July 27, 1945, Under Secretary for Foreign Affairs Clementis expressed concern to Steinhardt that Prime Minister Churchill's recent electoral defeat in Britain and the resulting establishment of a Labour government were potentially injurious to Czechoslovak interests. The Labour Party had a record of close connections with Social Democratic parties on the continent, including the Sudeten German organization.[20] The first signs that the new Czechoslovakia was steering a political course which was well to the left of the mainstream of American political thinking did not endear the Prague government to the American electorate. Similarly, reports of mistreatment by the Czechs, sent by Sudeten Germans to their American friends and relatives, provoked a certain amount of sympathy for their plight. The Czechs, while admitting that transgressions of various sorts might have occurred during the months immediately following liberation, nonetheless resented what they considered the maudlin and misplaced sympathies of Americans and Englishmen for people who hardly deserved them. Even the usually pro-Western *Lidová democracie,* the daily of the Catholic People's Party, accused the United States military and civilian authorities of too much friendliness towards the Sudeten Germans; they explained that while this, no doubt, was due primarily to the Americans' lack of knowledge about the Sudeten Germans' past, it was nevertheless undesirable.[21] American authorities seemed to take such criticism to heart, for shortly thereafter special instructions were given to American military and civilian personnel as to how to deal with Sudeten Germans in their daily contacts; these instructions discouraged fraternization.

Nonetheless, the acceptance of the principle of population transfer at the Potsdam Conference by the Big Three marked the successful climax of Beneš' systematic efforts to settle the problem of the Germans in Czechoslovakia once and for all. The Czechoslovak public-at-large, as reported in the daily press, was equally gratified by the approval of *odsun* by the Big Three. While the Communist daily *Rudé právo* gave sole credit to the Soviet Union,[22] *Práce,* official organ of the Communist-controlled trade union movement, credited all three Great Powers with supporting the Czechoslovak request.[23] The National Socialist daily, *Svobodné slovo,* under the signature of Dr. Prokop Drtina, a close associate of President Beneš and, subsequently, Czechoslovak Minister of Justice, called Potsdam "the greatest diplomatic and political victory which our nation has ever obtained in the long history of its eternal struggle for existence against the German nation."[24] Even Prime Minister Fierlinger, no friend of the United States, conceded with satisfaction that Czechoslovakia now had the approval for transfer of her Germans by all three Great Powers.[25]

The official Czechoslovak attitude came in a formal note from Clementis to the U.S. Ambassador. The Acting Foreign Minister expressed the gratitude and satisfaction of the Czechoslovak government and people for the support which the Great Powers had given to their cause and predicted that the resettlement of the German minority would greatly add to the future peace and stability of Central Europe. He assured the sponsoring powers that their desire to have the transfer effected in an orderly and humane manner was as much the desire of Czechoslovakia as it was their own. Clementis then asked for all deliberate speed in the actual implementation of the scheme, pointing out, once again, that rehabilitation and the return to normality of the country could come about only after the Germans were gone. He expressed satisfaction that the U.S. government had already created special organs within the Allied Control Commission to deal with the problem and offered to send a Czechoslovak liaison mission to assist the Americans in their task.[26]

The first concrete step by the Big Three towards implementation of the Potsdam decision was the directive issued by the Allied Control Authority's Directorate of Prisoners of War and Displaced Persons, which stated that 2.5 million Sudeten Germans would have to be moved from Czechoslovakia. Of these, 1.75 million were to be reestablished in the United States zone of Germany. The directive further said that "it [was] considered possible . . . to proceed with the admittance of [the expelled] population immediately after the confirmation of this plan," and that 10% of the total number should be transferred during December, 1945.[27]

During the next few weeks, the positions of Americans and Czechs crystalized. With ever-increasing frequency, the date of the beginning of the transfer became a central theme in U.S.-Czechoslovak correspondence. The Prague government reiterated its desire to start the transfer at once, and repeated its previous arguments linking the transfer to the reconstruction of Czechoslovakia. The American authorities, in turn, tried to impress upon the Czechs the importance of making the necessary physical arrangements for the accommodations of such a large number of newcomers into Germany, where living quarters and the barest necessities of life were already at a premium. The Czechs, on their part, while not underestimating the magnitude and complexity of the whole operation, accused the Americans of false priorities. What mattered most to them were the psychological and political effects of the transfer. They wanted, so to speak, to rid the new Czechoslovakia of Germans almost overnight.

Under these circumstances, it was easy to interpret the American stand as one of lack of cooperation. Sterner critics of the American performance — and these were not necessarily limited to members of the Communist Party — saw in it a willful attempt at sabotaging the Potsdam decisions concerning the Sudeten Germans. While it is difficult to sustain such a view from available documentation, the potential danger to America's reputation was clearly there. Still, to the observer unfamiliar with these different criteria, the initially not infrequent refusal by U.S. authorities to receive their allocated quota of expellees lent itself to the basically incorrect but nonetheless understandable accusation that the Americans were intentionally hampering the transfer.

Thus, by early October, Steinhardt had to report to Washington that "the Czechoslovak Govt has been endeavoring to approach the Allied authorities in Berlin with a view to arranging for an orderly and humane transfer ever since the Potsdam decision approved the transfer of the Germans from Czechoslovakia to Germany."[28] Not only had the Americans failed to initiate action on the whole matter, but, to make things worse, the Prague government so far had not even been permitted to submit its plan for the operation. It appeared to Steinhardt that the Allied authorities were trying to delay matters until the spring without as much as having given the Czechs a hearing. The Czechs could see in such tactics little else but an attempt to shift onto them the burden of feeding and otherwise caring for the Sudeten Germans during the forthcoming winter. More than that, even those Germans who were not indigenous to the Sudeten regions, but who were now in Czechoslovak territory, having fled before the advancing Soviet armed forces, were now to be thrust on the economy of Czechoslovakia.

This situation caused the Ambassador considerable concern, for he readily foresaw an outbreak of anti-German demonstrations. Moreover, he would not be surprised if the Czechs, "considering the inhumane treatment [they] suffered at the hands of many of these same Germans for over six years and the extent to which their patience is now being strained by refusal of the Allied authorities to permit them to expel even the worst offenders" would resort to open violence.[29]

Another important consideration was the attempt by the Soviets and their Czech disciples to put the blame on the United States. This, from an American point of view, was doubly damaging at this particular moment when Czechoslovak public opinion, rather pro-Soviet right after the end of the war, was now shifting in favor of the West and the United States in particular. Failure to recognize this propitious momentum and to take full advantage of it would be a grievous political mistake.

It therefore appeared to Steinhardt "that overdue arrangements for orderly and humane transfers might well prevent further alleged mistreatment of German elements in Czechoslovakia," an opposite opinion of the United States Political Advisor to Germany, Robert Murphy, notwithstanding. In view of all this, and having in mind the unfavorable consequences which further delays might do to both America's image and to the cause of the Czechoslovak moderates, transfer should begin at once.[30]

The carefully worded, strong note of the American Ambassador to his government reveals two things. First, it shows that Steinhardt, particularly sensitive on this question, had brought himself fully to share the state of mind of the citizens of the country to which he was accredited. But more than this, Steinhardt's dispatch also reveals an instant and correct comprehension of the international aspects of the Sudeten German problem, a phenomenon lacking among some of the unimaginative soldiers and civilians who, on behalf of the United States, sat on the Allied Control Commission.

Pursuing his policy, Steinhardt next addressed himself directly to Murphy. The two were well acquainted, and Steinhardt felt free to speak his mind. In a letter of December 7th, he warned him that American failure to accept a quota of expelled Sudeten Germans would seriously jeopardize the American effort "to bring Czechoslovakia back into the fold." The Ambassador, comparing the U.S. and Russian positions towards the Sudeten German transfer, remarked that "the Soviet military authorities have been far more adroit in recognizing the political importance of Czechoslovakia," and Americans, in order to compete successfully with the Soviets in gaining Czechoslovak sympathy "*must* have at least one train a day."[31]

The U.S. posture was harmed by irresponsible reporting in the American press. On October 2nd, *The Washington Post* had claimed that the "Czechs [were] engaged in mass expropriation and mass deportations of 3 1/2 million Sudetens," which caused Steinhardt to complain to Francis Williamson, head of the Central European desk in the State Department. The Ambassador accused various American journalists, John MacCormack among them, of having fallen prey to a few ill-informed and pro-German U.S. officers, and thus of having harmed the cause of the United States.[32]

In spite of all this friction between Americans and Czechs during the next few months, and in spite of the steadily worsening relationship among the big powers, much of the transfer was eventually achieved with a minimum of trouble and in an essentially humane fashion, an observation formally conveyed to Prague by the American authorities responsible for the operation.[33] It was not until late in 1946 that the Sudeten German issue once again caused problems between the two governments. None other than President Beneš, unwittingly as it no doubt was, was responsible for creating a major misunderstanding. In a radio address to the Czechoslovak people on the occasion of the country's Independence Day, he clearly conveyed the impression that the transfer of the Sudeten Germans from Czechoslovakia was all but completed: "It is now that the last trains are leaving the territory of the Republic, bearing the former German inhabitants of this State."[34] The same day, the Minister of the Interior, Václav Nosek, at another Independence Day ceremony said that the transfer "will be completed within a few hours."[35] While it is now clear that both remarks were made for their propaganda value and were mixed with the euphoria customarily dispensed by politicians on festive occasions, General Lucius Clay, the U.S. Military Commander in Germany, and Murphy, his political advisor, took Beneš and Nosek at their word. They felt no need to resume transfer operations, halted in December of 1946 on account of the cold weather until spring of 1947, as previously agreed. The Czechs, in turn, insisted on resuming the still unfinished transfer, and invoked the appropriate agreement reminding Americans of their pledge.

From all available evidence, it seems clear that the Czechoslovak case was well founded, since there was a formal written agreement between Prague and the United States that, after a temporary suspension during the winter, the transfer would be resumed April 1, 1947. It was further explicitly laid out that preliminary discussions about such resumption were to commence not later than February fifteenth. Clay and Murphy, however, all but ignored the formal agreement, and pointed to the statements of a number of Czecho-slovak politicians to good advantage.[36] Transfer operations were resumed eventually, but not until a rather heated exchange between Prague, Washington, and Frankfurt had taken place.

As previously stated, the merits of the transfer are not at issue here. Nor are some of the criticisms of the United States to be construed as being indicative of any moral disapproval of American actions in the whole question of the expulsion of the Sudeten Germans. What is intended is more of an appraisal of American tactics in the whole matter. The United States, which contributed so greatly to the defeat of Nazi Germany, failed to derive concomitant political capital from its victory. With a finely honed sense of justice and fair play, and removed from the scene of the atrocities committed by Germans against Czechoslovaks during the past years, some Americans found it difficult to comprehend why such harsh, summary treatment should be inflicted on a whole group of people who, by the time the U.S. came into direct contact with them, looked rather peaceful, if not outright innocent. The occasional excesses committed by vengeful Czechs against these Germans only strengthened the American conviction that a wrong was being perpetrated.

But this is about all that can be said in defense of the American attitude. Well-meaning but largely ignorant of the long history of German-Slav conflict in the region, the current Washington govern-ment was, by its essentially humanitarian and apolitical position, to give the impression that it favored the Germans over the Czechs. This Czechs simply could not comprehend, in view of the long and gallant struggle of the United States against Germany and on behalf of justice and freedom.

A second injurious legacy of this particular issue arose from its timing. It came at the very moment when the Czechs, who had been infatuated by things Russian in the months immediately succeeding their liberation, had begun to see things from a different perspective and to approach the whole question of their liberation by the Allies in a less pro-Russian frame of mind. Thus, at the very moment when American political stock in Czechoslovakia began at last to rise, the United States, by an act which reflected some of its own best political traditions — fairness to the vanquished — alienated an important segment of Czechoslovak public opinion which, paradoxically, at this very moment was in the process of abandoning its uncritical pro-Russian attitude and throwing its sympathies towards the United

States. Herein then, is at least a partial explanation of an American attitude that the Czechs had such difficulty comprehending and another instance of how Americans, who had won the war, were now failing to make use of their victory.

VII

Czechoslovakia and the Marshall Plan

The transfer of the Sudeten Germans was but one of many issues which the new post-war Czechoslovakia had to face. It was a matter of signal importance for the country's future, with ramifications in almost every facet of daily life. For the average citizen the economic consequences of the transfer were ultimately just as significant as the sheer political impact. A substantial part of Czechoslovakia's industries were located in the Sudeten regions; its management and staff were recruited almost exclusively from the local German population. In pre-war times the output of these enterprises, many of them highly specialized, had constituted a substantial part of Czechoslovakia's exports and a valuable source for foreign currency. Apart from these important economic considerations, the excellence of the products had contributed significantly to the country's good name and solid reputation as a trading partner. Bohemian glass, custom jewelry, Bohemian lace, toys, musical instruments and last, but not least, the excellent Bohemian hops, were known staples on international markets.

It was in this sphere that the exodus of much of the German population was felt most keenly. The Czechoslovak government had the satisfaction of having solved the Sudeten German problem politically, but at the very moment of its triumph, it now had to cope with the resultant economic consequences of its own actions. While it was relatively easy to send workers' and soldiers' brigades to the abandoned farms and to harvest the produce — although this, too, was frequently done in rather haphazard ways — it was next to impossible to immediately staff the abandoned factories and to resume production. To be sure, the government had made provisions to retain some of the indispensable managerial staff and some of the expert workers to keep the factories open, but the general disruption of the whole economy, going back to the war years, was simply too great as to be readily remedied by such hastily improvised measures. In turn, the new settlers, who were now given title to the abandoned farms of the Sudeten Germans and who were to take their places at the working benches in the factories, lacked both know-how and proper incentive. The "gold diggers," as they were called, wanted to get rich and to reap the rewards for having sold their souls to the right political party: in this case, the Communist Party which, by virtue of its control over the Ministry of Agriculture, the government agency largely responsible for resettlement policies, controlled the resettlement process in the Sudeten territory.

In brief, there was neither the necessary expertise nor sufficient skilled labor to revive production on a desirable scale; the once-thriving industries in Sudeten German territory were either abandoned, mismanaged or greatly understaffed. In addition to all this, the momentous economic changes brought about by the recent nationalization of the country's key industries, to which the economy had barely begun to adjust, did nothing to alleviate the strained situation. In view of the fact that Czechoslovakia's industries experienced little damage during the war in comparison with many other European countries, the inability of the Czechs to get back on their feet seemed even more paradoxical and lamentable. Although the overall economic picture improved somewhat by the second half of 1946, a full-scale economic recovery was yet to come.

The conditions affecting Czechoslovakia's international trade were equally unsatisfactory. Czechoslovakia's principal ally, the Soviet Union, was as yet not in a position to give substantial aid. The enormous destruction which the Russians experienced at the hands of the invading Germans precluded any systematic relief efforts on the part of the Soviets, who were busy rebuilding their own industries. Even in supplying raw materials to Czechoslovak factories, such as cotton and crude oil, the Soviets were of little help. More often than not, the staples offered proved unsuitable for processing in Czechoslovak factories, whose machinery was usually geared to raw materials of a different and higher quality grade.

Trade and economic exchange with the West was hampered for different reasons. Some of the highly industrialized Western countries, like Great Britain, were in the midst of their own economic recovery with only limited possibilities of assistance to others. Germany, an important trading partner of pre-war Czechoslovakia, was in shambles. The United States, as already seen, often attached special conditions to its willingness to grant loans or other credits, conditions which the Czechs were either unable or unwilling to meet. The steadily worsening political climate among the Big Powers did nothing to improve matters in the field of international economics. In the spring of 1947, two years after the devastating war had come to a close, the hopes for large-scale revival of world trade with Czechoslovakia as one of the participants looked anything but promising. It was into this climate of limited hope but continuing distrust that, in the summer of 1947, George C. Marshall, the newly appointed Secretary of State, introduced the plan that bears his name. Since, in his invitation to participate, Marshall made no distinction between the various areas of Europe, it must be taken as evidence that the United States was now ready to aid all needy European nations, irrespective of their political orientation. At any rate, on July 8th the Prague government accepted the invitation to come to Paris for preliminary discussions, only to rescind its acceptance two days later. This change of heart by Prague has ever since remained an issue of some dispute among historians. More than that, since, as some of them claim, it came about as a result of direct pressure from Moscow, it has also been portrayed as the specific time when Czechoslovakia ceased to be a sovereign agent for all intents and purposes. Available sources, both American and Czechoslovak, convey the following picture.

The Czechoslovak government initially discussed the question of participation in the Paris Conference as early as June 24th; by July 4th, the government had decided in principle to take part. An important factor in the decision seemed to have been Jan Masaryk's opinion, which was given at a press conference in Oslo, where the Foreign Minister had been heading a Czechoslovak cultural delegation. Masaryk favored the Marshall Plan if its aim was to unite Europe; he was against it if it acted as a divisive force.[1] It is worth mentioning here that the decision to accept was taken in spite of an important attack against the Plan in *Pravda* on June 22nd, and in spite of the fact that the Soviet Foreign Minister, Molotov, had left the Paris Conference already on June second. Hence, it would appear that the Prague government, including its Communist members, was familiar with the negative reaction by Moscow, yet decided on acceptance in spite of it.[2] Back in Prague, Masaryk consulted the Soviet chargé d'affaires, Bodrov, who familiarized him with the reasons for the Soviet withdrawal. The Soviets withdrew, Masaryk reports him as saying, because they saw in the Marshall Plan an instrument of American interference in the internal affairs of European countries by means of the Plan's "steering committee." But, having said that much, Bodrov then discussed with Masaryk the participation of others at the Paris Conference and *three times* reiterated that he had nothing to say and that he had not received any instructions about it.[3] "This verbal and private pronouncement by Bodrov greatly toned down the warning character stemming from official Soviet pronouncements, and Czechoslovak Foreign Minister Masaryk understood it to mean just that and reported in this sense to the Czechoslovak government."[4] Two other factors played a part in Prague's initial decision to accept. The first was an understanding reached with the Poles, arrived at during the visit of a Polish delegation in the Czechoslovak capital shortly before. The second was the realization of the Prague cabinet, including its Communist members, that Czechoslovakia was faced with an unusually poor harvest and that a major food shortage was in the offing. The question, in spite of its ever-increasing political overtones, had not yet lost its purely economic character. It was only when a Czechoslovak government delegation arrived in Moscow on July 9th that the Soviet influence on Prague came into the open.

To keep the record straight, it must be said that the visit of the delegation had been arranged well in advance of any Marshall Plan problems. The Czechs were to discuss with the Russians a proposed Franco-Czechoslovak treaty and various economic questions. Hence, it would be incorrect to say that the Czechs were simply called on the carpet. Once there, however, Stalin used the occasion to impress upon Gottwald, Masaryk and other members of the delegation the dim view which the Soviet Union took of their proposed participation at the Paris Conference.

In a telegram hastily dispatched from Moscow, the Czechoslovak Ministers reported to Prague that once the Soviets had familiarized themselves with the Czechoslovak position and their decision to accept the invitation to Paris, Stalin and Molotov had expressed surprise. This even more so, since the Yugoslav, Polish and Rumanian governments had all consulted with Moscow prior to their refusal.[5] It was obviously bad enough to have decided on such a weighty question without prior consultation with the Russians, but it was even worse to have made the wrong decision. The Russians then told the Czechs that the real intention of the Marshall Plan was the formation of a Western bloc and the isolation of the Soviet Union, and that the Plan itself was merely a vehicle to influence the politics of its participants. While no one in the Soviet government doubted Czechoslovakia's friendliness to Russia, Czechoslovakia's participation in Paris would prove that the Czechs had permitted themselves to be used as instruments against the U.S.S.R. This neither the Soviet government nor the Soviet public would tolerate and, consequently, Czechoslovakia should revoke its participation. The message then asked the president to call the remaining members of the government into session at once and to rescind acceptance of the invitation to Paris. It suggested to him the ways and means that this could best be done, such as by mentioning that other Slav and Eastern European nations did not participate, and that under these circumstances the Czechoslovak presence in Paris could readily be construed as an act hostile to the Soviet Union and other allies of Czechoslovakia.[6]

Even more interesting are the protocols of the cabinet meeting, which had been hastily convoked by Beneš upon receipt of the telegram from Moscow. From the excerpts available, it would appear that the ministers present split essentially on party lines, although even the non-Communist members could no longer dare to insist upon acceptance of the invitation to Paris. The way in which they differed from their Communist colleagues and Fierlinger was chiefly in their insistence to get to the root of the matter rather than to blindly accept the message from Moscow. Specifically, the National Socialist Minister of Education, Jaroslav Stránský, insisted upon a "thorough consideration of the whole matter," in view of the fact that the original decision to accept had been taken *after* Molotov had left the Paris Conference and that "nothing had prevented the Soviet Union to make known its own point of view."[7] He was concerned about the loss of prestige which the government would suffer from such an abrupt volte-face, expressing the view that, as of today, the world was indeed divided into two blocs. In conclusion, he posed the rhetorical question as to what might have happened had Czechoslovakia gone to Paris. Had there been political conditions incompatible with the participation, the delegation could always have come home; otherwise, there were things to be gained. He believed that the American intention "'to put Europe on its feet'" did indeed exist.[8]

This spirited defense of the original decision was countered by the remarks of Vice Premier Fierlinger, who took it upon himself to defend Bodrov's rather cryptic behavior vis-à-vis Jan Masaryk. Obviously, "Bodrov could not tell us 'don't go there.' This would have been offensive." On the contrary, he saw in Bodrov's behavior "the carefulness and tact of the Soviet Union."[9] Václav Kopecký, the Communist Minister of Information, advocated a categorical reversal of the original decision. He expressed doubt about the economic importance of the whole conference, hoping that Czechoslovakia's non-participation would be an effective weapon against the attempts to isolate the U.S.S.R.

Of interest also are the remarks of Vice-Premier Ján Ursíny, who spoke for the Slovak Democrats. He recalled that the government's original decision had been based on both economic and political considerations. Since Czechoslovakia's situation, as an industrial state, was vastly different from Yugoslavia, Bulgaria and Poland, then still largely agrarian, "commercial contacts with an industrialized West were a necessity" for the Czechs; but, he also recognized the political ramifications of the question, which "[it was] necessary to respect." The question now remained to find a suitable form of explaining to the people at home and abroad what had happened.[10]

Finally, speaking for the Catholic People's Party, Minister of Transport Jan Kopecký thought that the Czechs should have gone to Paris and that such an action was not inconsistent with their treaty with the U.S.S.R. On the contrary, he opined, their going there might have been of use to the Soviets since, in this way, they would have been kept well-informed. Yet, he too found it necessary to add that since Moscow had not agreed to Czechoslovakia's participation, it was important to find "a solution 'with honor.'"[11]

The debate in the cabinet, heated at times, is ample proof of genuine divisions of opinion within that body. It is, however, just as much proof that certain basic tenets of Czechoslovak politics were beyond dispute and, so to speak, in a dialectically unassailable position; one of them was Czechoslovakia's special relationship with the U.S.S.R. The debate of the Czechoslovak cabinet on that fateful July 10th was more reminiscent of the medieval church, where one was permitted to engage in learned disputations within an *a priori* conceptual frame of reference rather than the deliberations of a democratically constituted body in our own times.

In his assessment of the significance of the Prague government's most recent action, Steinhardt listed a dozen factors which he considered "powerful instruments of persuasion over Czechoslovakia now in possession of [the] Soviets." Among them were the surrounding of the country by Soviet troops, except for a small part bordering on Bavaria; the leading position of the Communist Party in Czechoslovak politics and its subsequent control of the key ministries; control of the police; considerable influence in the army and local governments; control over many newspapers; "preponderant" influence in the trade union movement; an increasing Czechoslovak dependence · on Soviet trade; and, finally, the ever-present fear by the Czechs of a resurgent Germany against which the U.S.S.R. provided the best protection. It was precisely because, up to now, the Soviets had only "in very rare instances taken explicit advantage of these powerful instruments of pressure" that the moderates had so far been able to hold their own and even experience some success "in maintaining and strengthening democratic liberties under difficult conditions." Whether the uses of these instruments of Soviet dominance would now increase, Steinhardt was not certain. For the time being, however, "there [were] no visible signs as yet that [the Soviets] intend[ed] to tighten control over Czechoslovakia at this time." In conclusion, the Ambassador promised that his Embassy would be particularly vigilant in watching for any signs of increased Soviet pressure on Prague, especially in respect to the "more thorough" carrying out of "Communist policies within [the] framework of [the] present National Front Government," the Communist attempts to weaken their opponents and to purge their ranks, and finally, in any attempt "to prepare ground for [a] Communist coup d'état."[12]

A careful reading of Steinhardt's dispatch leaves the impression that the Ambassador more or less expected the reversal of the Czech government's initial decision to attend the Paris Conference, given the impressive array of factors which made such a reversal almost inevitable. Such a view is only strengthened by another of his dispatches of the following day, addressed to James Riddleberger. Designed as "personal," it told the Chief of the Department's Central European Division point-blank: "Suffice it to say that the Czech reversal, insofar as it concerns attendance at the Paris Conference, was not exactly a surprise. The surprise was the prompt initial acceptance." At any rate, he promised Riddleberger to come up with suggestions for "a review of [U.S.] policy towards Czechoslovakia and setting a new course for the near-term future."[13]

Six days later, he made good his promise and advised the State Department to take the following course in its future policies towards Czechoslovakia: 1) propose to Prague the conclusion of a cultural convention, similar to the one which the Czechs concluded with Great Britain only weeks before; 2) prevail upon the War Department that "for political reasons" it should adopt "a conciliatory attitude" in the upcoming negotiations concerning Czechoslovak payments in dollars for its exports and imports across the U.S. Zone of Germany. Both these gestures were to show the Czechs that the United States had "not abandoned" Czechoslovakia and that it was not necessary for Prague to "rely economically on [the] Soviet Union."

These two signs of continued good will, however, were to be accompanied by a much more impressive show of strength. The United States should "avoid making any contribution towards protecting the economy of Czechoslovakia from deterioration, as long as [the] Government of Czechoslovakia continues to permit itself to be used as [an] instrument of Soviet policy, and continues to stake the maintenance of improvement of [the] country's economy on Soviet promises to deliver necessary raw materials. . . ." Similarly, the State Department, then pondering over whether it should bring the recent Hungarian coup d'état before the United Nations Assembly, should do just that and by all means possible, since such a move would impress upon "many Czechs that [the] fate of eastern European countries continues [to be] a matter of concern to the U.S. and the American Government has no intention of limiting its concern to mere notes to offending governments." Such action, irrespective of its outcome in the debates of the Assembly, "might well have the effect of inducing Czech Communist leaders to proceed in Czechoslovakia with greater caution than they might otherwise be disposed to do." An interesting sidelight to Steinhardt's recommendations for the new American policy towards Czechoslovakia is provided in the very opening sentence of his dispatch. In it, he expresses the view that the "situation within Czechoslovakia has not thus far changed so radically as world press has represented." What he thought had happened was that "a condition believed by well-informed to have long existed has been removed from the realm of doubt of irrefutable evidence and publicly disclosed."[14]

Late in July, Dr. Hanč, Counselor of the Czechoslovak Embassy in Washington, conferred with Francis Williamson and Harold Vedeler from the State Department's Central European Division; among other matters, he dealt at some length with the reasons for the Czechs' withdrawal from the Paris Conference. Hanč told the Americans that "the Czechoslovak Government was not to be blamed entirely for the withdrawal of its acceptance of the invitation to . . . Paris. . . ." He also "implied that Soviet pressure on Czechoslovakia was so great that it could not be withstood." Some good, however, might yet come of it, or so, at least, Hanč thought, since "this action, along with other developments within Czechoslovakia, would decrease the Communist influence at the next election."[15]

However, in an interview given to James H. Long of the Associated Press, printed in the *Daily Review* of the Czechoslovak Ministry of Information, Jan Masaryk seemed to have absolved the Soviets of exercising undue pressure on Prague in the whole question; at any rate, the title of the article, "Any Talk of Ultimatum Against ČSR [Czechoslovakia] is Silly," suggested that much.[16] Steinhardt, who

sent a verbatim text of the article to Washington, was not convinced
that Masaryk's story rang true. The fact alone that what "must be at
least the twentieth public statement on this subject issued by a
prominent member of the Czechoslovak government should appear at
this late date [was] in itself significant." He then went on to criticize in
detail some of Masaryk's explanations, calling them "disingenuous."
What seemed to have vexed Steinhardt particularly was Masaryk's
assertion that he and Gottwald "'realized'" even prior to their talks
with Stalin and Molotov "that under existing circumstances their
original decision to go to Paris must be reverted." He commented,
rather angrily, that this "realization had not dawned upon them before
they left Praha."[17] Not only was there no evidence that Masaryk was
actually telling Long the truth, on the contrary, Steinhardt went on,
originally neither Masaryk nor Gottwald was even scheduled to go to
Moscow; only Hubert Ripka, Minister of Foreign Trade, was to
journey to the Soviet capital to discuss Soviet-Czechoslovak economic
relations. It was only when the issues of the Franco-Czech treaty and
Czechoslovak participation at the Paris conference came up that
Gottwald and Masaryk came into the picture.[18]
    Some of Steinhardt's strongest words, however, were reserved for
Masaryk personally. He chided him for his ". . . inexcusable . . . contribution to the Communist thesis that the central plank of the
Marshall Plan and Paris platform is the building up of Germany's
industry more or less — and mostly more — in the hands of German
capitalists." Upset by this particular remark by the Czechoslovak
Foreign Minister, Steinhardt could "only conclude that Mr. Masaryk
has gone 'overboard' in his efforts to convince his Communist colleagues, still skeptical, in spite of his long record of faithful service, of
his loyalty to the Soviet alliance."[19] In view of the fact that Masaryk
and Steinhardt were personally on friendly terms and on a first name
basis, the Ambassador's remark about the Foreign Minister would
appear doubly serious.
    Of equal interest are Steinhardt's reports on the reactions of the
Prague non-Communist parties. He characterized their initial reaction
as "one of shocked surprise and humiliation which in a few cases
verged on panic." Some prominent National Socialists and members
of the Catholic People's Party "immediately began formulating plans,
to be implemented in case of eventual need, for leaving Czechoslovakia and setting up [a] national committee or government in
exile." But once the initial panic had passed, Petr Zenkl, Vice-Premier
and Chairman of the National Socialist Party, predicted a return to

some degree of normality, inasmuch as he anticipated that the Soviets, "while keeping a tight grip on Czech foreign policy, [would] not interfere in Czech domestic affairs." He even believed that Russia's behavior in the whole matter might cause some defections within Communist ranks, a prediction contradicted by other moderates who thought the opposite. According to them, now was the time for opportunists to join the Communist Party in view of an "ultimate victory of Communism." But whether this "more sanguine mood of [the] moderate leaders [would] persist . . . depend[ed] largely on whether [the] Soviet Union [did] in fact refrain from future interference in Czech domestic affairs." Should the opposite happen, it would, in view of the most recent Soviet interference "recreate [a] mood of panic."[20]

As for the American reactions, Steinhardt received two excellent first-hand reports in early August. One was from his Counselor in Prague, John Bruins, then on home leave in New Jersey, who wrote him that "the Czechs were very much in the headlines when the Prime Minister went to Moscow, but since then the papers have completely dropped that angle."[21] The other was from his friend in the State Department, Harold Vedeler, who told him that the recent developments in Prague "produced a great impact on certain divisions of the Department . . . who seemed to attach as much importance to this as to Munich." Vedeler seemed to think, however, that the two divisions of the State Department which had made such a comparison, the Division of Research for Europe and the Division of Investment and Economic Development, had somewhat exaggerated the importance of Czechoslovakia's withdrawal from the Paris Conference. Perhaps things were not as bad as Munich, or such, at least, was the predominant opinion of the Central Europe Division, if only because

(1) the Czechs had hedged from the beginning their acceptance of the invitation . . . making it possible for them later to withdraw if it should appear advisable; (2) the Czech action was in keeping with the previous submissive character of their foreign policy; (3) the retraction was a logical corollary sooner or later of the Soviet withdrawal from discussions of European economic cooperation and (4) it seemed a natural accompaniment to the increasing number of mutual aid pacts, cultural agreements and comprehensive economic agreements which apparently are binding Czechoslovakia ever more closely to the Soviet Union and its satellites.[22]

Complimenting Steinhardt on his "outstanding reports . . . on the subject," Vedeler assured him that the State Department had taken most of his suggestions to heart and would implement many of them. However, Vedeler reported that Washington was less enthusiastic about some of them, particularly Steinhardt's proposal to bring the Hungarian coup before the United Nations as a deterrent to further Soviet actions of a similar nature. To do so, Washington feared, might not only be inopportune, but might also invite Soviet countercharges regarding the U.S. administration of Japan under General MacArthur.[23]

In mid-November, Jan Masaryk came to the United States to discuss with the State Department officials a variety of issues, such as the Czechoslovak claims for its share in the Gold Pool,[24] and various other economic matters. Secretary of State Marshall participated in the talks, and Masaryk used the occasion to tell him, face to face, why Prague withdrew in its initial acceptance to the Paris Conference. "Czechoslovakia was not always free to adopt the kind of position she would like to take," Masaryk told Marshall, and "Czechoslovak policy frequently had to cut across that of the U.S." In his reply, Marshall assured Masaryk that he "appreciated the fact that Czechoslovakia had originally wished to join the European Recovery Plan," and expressed the hope that normal trade relations between the two countries would soon be established. He explained to the Czechoslovak Foreign Minister some of the objectives of his Plan which, among others, were "that U.S. assistance would get normal trade circulation started again and would promote an increasing volume of exchange between east and west." What seemed to be preeminent in Marshall's mind was "a reestablishment of European confidence" which was "essential."

Marshall also shed some interesting light on the questions raised previously by the Polish Ambassador to the United States as to "why Russia had not been consulted in the original plans for the recovery program." To this, Marshall replied that neither had England or France, who merely "immediately acted upon [Marshall's] general proposal." This was true, although Marshall "recognized that it might have been difficult for the Polish Ambassador to understand in view of Soviet propaganda against the program."

In a question which must have proved embarrassing for his visitor, Marshall then asked "whether [Masaryk] could account for Soviet Russia's actions since the end of the war, which seemed incomprehensible in the effect they had produced in destroying the good-will which Soviet Russia had enjoyed with all the world in 1945." Masaryk attempted to explain the Soviet position as one emanating from "suspicion of the outside world and from Soviet obsession that the U.S. [was] bound to suffer an economic collapse, which will withdraw it from world affairs and leave the fate of Europe to Soviet decision."

Up until now, the discussion between the two statesmen was essentially routine; both said what they were expected to say, given the political orientation of their respective governments. Only in his farewell words to Marshall did Masaryk reveal some of his own feelings towards the Secretary of State's recovery plan and, indirectly, towards the United States. He told Marshall that he personally greatly admired the American effort to assist Europe and expressed regrets that Czechoslovakia could not participate in his program.[25]

There is no reason to believe that Masaryk's remark about his personal feelings in the matter was anything but frank and sincere. What mattered, however, were not his personal views but his inability to apply them to official Czechoslovak foreign policy. This in itself was an excellent indication of Communist strength and of the real political power of their opponents. And it was in this political frame of reference that the country now approached its immediate future.

It was not only Czechoslovakia's future that had been decisively influenced by the whole Marshall Plan question. The Czechs became a pawn on the larger chessboard of international politics. As is often the case with small countries, and as had been the case with the Czechs before, they were caught between two great powers. One year before their show-down over Berlin, the United States and the Soviet Union had decided to make Czechoslovakia an early testing ground for what came to be a new phase of the cold war. The Soviet pressure on Czechoslovakia, as well as the American decision to consider Prague fully in the orbit of Moscow after the Czechs had withdrawn from the Marshall Plan, put things into perspective. It was unfortunate for Czechoslovakia to have been drawn into this confrontation at such an early date. Conceivably, had it been able to resist the Soviets longer, the Americans might have come to see that Prague and Moscow were not necessarily synonymous. After all, and only shortly thereafter, Washington managed to distinguish between Yugoslav and Soviet Communism and to come to the aid of the former at the crucial moment. By mid-1947, the Prague régime may have been Communist-dominated and may have given in to the pressure of Moscow in an important foreign policy matter, but it was nowhere nearly as mono-lithically Communist as Belgrade.

This is not to absolve Moscow of its share of the blame, but merely to point out that things being what they were, the United States might have shown more flexibility in the given situation. Since it was not likely that the Soviet Union would permit a country in its sphere to act independently on important questions of foreign policy, the United States could not possibly have helped matters by slamming the only door which remained open. In so doing, Washington not only decisively weakened the position of the non-Communist forces in Czechoslovakia, but effectively aided in bringing the country even further under the domination of Moscow. Presumably, this was not the aim of the United States' foreign policy, but its response to the Czechoslovak refusal of Marshall Plan aid contributed immeasurably to the further and more intense division of Europe on ideological grounds. A unified Europe was now more distant and more difficult to achieve. Czechoslovakia was no longer considered significant, and Beneš' hopes of making the country "a bridge between East and West" were shattered almost overnight as the Cold War escalated into confrontation in Germany and Yugoslavia.

VIII

Political Parties

One of the more common criticisms of Czechoslovak political life during the year 1945 — a criticism not necessarily limited to the observations and analyses of the American Embasssy in Prague — was focused on the non-Communist parties and the whole structure of the National Front. The former, it was charged, suffered from timid leadership and did not live up to the expectations of many of their members in terms of true political independence. The National Front concept of government, in turn, was chiefly blamed for this inability of the individual parties to play roles truly in conformity with what is only expected from a genuinely independent political party. In this unusual juxtaposition, where supposedly independent political parties with socio-political orientations vastly different from each other are part of a larger governmental bloc and operate within its conceptual framework, there appears the unique compromise which the non-Communist parties had to pay as a price for their political survival. While it is undoubtedly true that all parties, including the Communists, could readily make common cause in a variety of matters, such as the expulsion of the Sudeten Germans from Czechoslovakia and the just punishment of war criminals, the philosophical foundations, past traditions and the very nature of the composition of their membership made it next to impossible for them to jointly subscribe to others. For example, National Socialists, Slovak Democrats and Populists[1] were strongly opposed to further nationalization of industry; the latter two parties, heavily dependent on Catholic membership, must have had some difficulties in reconciling themselves to the avowed atheism of the Communists. The cleavage between Marxists and non-Marxists was equally deep when it came to defining civil liberties, which the former recognized only insofar as they did not interfere with the "rights and sovereignty of the toiling masses" while the latter adhered to a more traditional, Western-style concept and definition. Similarly, Communist and non-Communist views on the holding of private property, radically different from each other, provided additional ground for friction and confrontation.

In matters of foreign policy, the incompatibilities between the two ideological blocs were equally pronounced. The Communists wished to base Czechoslovakia's foreign policy almost entirely on an alliance with the U.S.S.R., with occasional vague reference to progressive forces in the West. Non-Communists, on their part, while recognizing the Soviet Union's new and important role in Czechoslovakia's political life, were unwilling to break with the West. A host of other issues, from highest governmental policy down to the most common everyday activity in a citizen's life, were almost daily subjects of contention between Communists and non-Communists. In many ways, then, it is remarkable that the parties cooperated as long as they did within the framework of the National Front, in view of their diametrically opposed orientation on so many matters.

In order to appraise the role of the non-Communist parties in the political life of Czechoslovakia from May, 1945 until the events of February, 1948, it is necessary to tread a delicate path between the theoretically established rights and privileges of political bodies and individuals and the political reality of a functioning government. Only a reader familiar with the unique Czechoslovak post-World War II milieu, where Masaryk's pre-war democracy had been restored with the new shadings of a people's democracy, can gain some understanding of the actual possibilities of the non-Communist parties in their attempts to preserve political independence for the country. For the historian, this question poses a particularly delicate problem, since it requires him, to an extent far greater than usual, to use circumstantial evidence and to relegate traditional documentation more and more to the overall framework and the whole façade of the story. For example, a solemn proclamation by the leadership of the National Socialist Party, on the anniversary of the liberation of the country, to "stand forever with the U.S.S.R." is to be taken no more seriously than an occasional friendly reference by the Communist leaders to the United States and its part in World War II. The situation tends to become more complex when spokesmen of parties did indeed state their credos. Here the question arises as to what extent one may stand up for one's ideals and aspirations without shaking too severely or destroying altogether the all too artificial bulwark of the National Front. Although the nearly three years of post-World War II politics in Czechoslovakia were marked by a variety of political climates, with "liberal" periods alternating with severe crises, it is important to keep in mind the degree of artificiality in the country's political structure during that time.

In terms of a traditional political scale wherein Marxists are on the far left and conservatives and clericals are on the other end of the political spectrum, the Czechoslovak People's Party found itself on the far right. This, however, is not to say that it was an extreme rightist party in any sense of the word: apart from its liberal democratic tradition going back to pre-war Czechoslovakia, the Populists resented more keenly than any others among the non-Communist parties the atheism and anti-clericalism of the Communists. Under the leadership of two clerics, Mgr. Jan Šrámek, the party's chairman and a Vice-Premier of the government, and Mgr. Hála, vice-chairman of the party and Minister of Posts and Telegraphs, the Populists were an amalgam of some of the older Czech conservative circles and a young and more secular membership. Curiously, it was this younger wing, led by Dr. Adolf Procházka, Minister of Health, and Dr. Ivo Ducháček, Chairman of the National Assembly's Committee on Foreign Affairs, that stood in the forefront of the anti-Communist struggle.

In comparison with this younger and more progressive wing of the party, Šrámek and Hála were rather timid and ineffectual in the arena of daily politics. The former, a respected politician of pre-Munich days and one of the few dissenters in the crucial vote of ceding the Sudeten territories to Germany in 1938, had served as Prime Minister in President Beneš' exile government in London, only to be replaced by the Social Democrat Zdeněk Fierlinger during the final weeks of the war. In his mid-seventies by now, Mgr. Šrámek was more of a venerated symbol than an active fighter when he returned to the liberated homeland. Hála, in turn, was a shy and reticent man who, even as a cabinet officer, was apprehensive to go on a visit to London for fear that travel by a Czechoslovak cabinet member to a capitalist country might infuriate the Communist Prime Minister Klement Gottwald. It should come as little surprise then, that in its fight against Communism and its attempts to preserve Czechoslovak democracy, the People's Party was ill served by its leadership. The brunt of the struggle rested squarely on the shoulders of Procházka and Ducháček who in their efforts were ably seconded by a group of younger journalists clustered around the party weekly *Obzory*,[2] a publication frequently attacked and occasionally banned by the Communist Ministry of Information.

The limitations inherent in this state of affairs were manifest from the very beginnings of the resurrected state. Thus, in June of 1945, Party Chairman Šrámek, while calling for a "legislature constitutionally elected by secret vote" also demanded reform in Czechoslovakia's pre-Munich constitution and referred to Czechoslovakia's treaty with the U.S.S.R. as a pact "far more significant than the usual inter-state treaty," since it would influence Czechoslovakia's internal life as well and would ultimately lead to an integration of Eastern and Western cultures in the country.[3] Some months later, echoing a similar note, Mgr. Hála, at a party rally in the Moravian city of Znojmo, referred to Czechoslovakia's alliance with the U.S.S.R. as its "main alliance." The prelate added that the country would even prefer to temporarily break its traditional friendship with Great Britain "rather than suffer the loss of unity with the Soviet Union."[4] Undoubtedly, the statements of the Chairman and Vice-Chairman of the People's Party reflected the sentiments of many Czechs and Slovaks during the immediate post-war months, since they expressed gratitude to the Soviet Union for its part in Czechoslovakia's liberation. At the same time, they were just as indicative of the limitations of Czechoslovakia's post-war democracy. Above all, they mirrored the new political realities in Eastern and Central Europe, where Western democracies had now left the field to the Soviet Union.

While in June of 1945 Russian stock in the country was still at an all-time high, it fell considerably during the months thereafter. Thus, the fact that Hála, as late as February of 1946, still found it necessary to pay compliments to the U.S.S.R. in a pre-election speech in which he aimed at strengthening the chances of an avowedly anti-Communist party, is in itself the best proof of the circumscribed character of what is commonly referred to as freedom of expression. Ambassador Steinhardt, commenting on Hála's speech, put it bluntly when he said that the People's Party simply had to do these things in order to protect itself from Communist criticism.[5]

On occasion, Šrámek and Hála would stiffen and strike a more pro-Western note,[6] but the party, supposedly the most "anti-Communist" in post-war Czechoslovakia, did not really live up to its reputation. Only Helena Koželuhová, one of the editors of *Obzory* and a member of the party's more progressive wing, and a few younger functionaries clustered around her openly opposed Communism and, on occasion, the Soviet Union itself. It was Koželuhová and her group who saw in the party's political Catholicism more a hindrance than an effective weapon against the Communists. She also feared that the party's official platform, a reformist Christian socialism based on papal encyclicals of the nineteenth century, no longer provided the necessary counterweight to the highly effective Marxian socialism. In *Obzory* and in party caucuses, Koželuhová tried in vain to convince the leadership that the time had come to give the party a more modern and more secular look. In *Obzory,* she also attacked the Communist Party, especially those of its organs which committed illegal acts, such as unlawful imprisonment or mismanagement of confiscated property. To the clerical and conservative leadership she was too much of a maverick; eventually, she was expelled from the leadership of the party.

"The People's Party," the American Ambassador wrote, has been "reduced to a cipher." Those of its prominent members (Health Minister Dr. Procházka in particular) who showed themselves more independent were kept "under a tight lid" by Šrámek and Hála. According to Steinhardt, the National Socialists and the Slovak Democrats were now "left alone to fight the anti-Communist battle."[7]

Criticism of the political ineffectiveness of the Catholic People's Party came from yet different quarters, those from which its leadership least expected it. A report from President Truman's Vatican representative, in late 1947, confirms the opinion held by Steinhardt and by many of the party's members themselves that its clerical leadership was weak and ineffective. J. Graham Parsons, Assistant to the President's Representative to the Holy See, informed Washington that in a conversation with Mgr. Domenico Tardini, a senior Vatican officer subsequently to become the Holy See's Secretary of State, he was told that much. While the Vatican continued to be interested in the party's fate, it did not in any way direct or influence its activities; the blame for the party's showing must rest squarely on Šrámek's and Hála's shoulders.[8]

This criticism of the People's Party by both Steinhardt and the Holy See may seem somewhat harsh, although not entirely without merit. None other than Dr. Jaroslav Pecháček, one-time chief of Mgr. Šrámek's cabinet and a ranking functionary of the party's Prague district bureau, readily admits some shortcomings within its ranks. In particular, he points to Šrámek's insufficient contacts with foreign diplomats, his age and his chronic illness. The first may well be responsible for some of Steinhardt's comments about the life of the party: one has only to compare it with the excellent and frequent contacts which existed between Dr. Petr Zenkl, chairman of the National Socialist Party, and the American Embassy. The latter two, in turn, accounted for Šrámek's frequent absences from often important cabinet meetings. But Pecháček does not share Steinhardt's general and often platitudinous assertions that religion and ideological differences between Populists and National Socialists mattered all that much. Rather, he contends, the failure to make common cause between them was due more to the rivalry for votes, which he views as a natural and healthy phenomenon in any democratic society. Addressing himself to the question of the National Socialists' adherence to the Socialist Bloc within the government, Pecháček concedes that cooperation among its members was not always effective, but at the same time points to frequent cooperation of National Socialists with Communists and Social Democrats on lower levels. In one instance, in particular, does Pecháček criticize the behavior of the National Socialists. The point in question was an editorial in *Svobodné slovo* which expressed satisfaction with the election results of 1946. Obviously, Pecháček contends, the almost 40% of the Communist vote "must have given the shivers" to each and every true democrat.[9]

At the eleventh hour, it seemed that the People's Party was undergoing a change of heart. Only days before the February coup of 1948, the Central Intelligence Agency, basing its news on a "Czechoslovak source with excellent contacts in People's Party circles," reported that Šrámek, who had regularly been absent from cabinet meetings, had now returned and was about to launch "a frontal all-out attack on the abuses in the Czechoslovak [Communist controlled] secret police system." This was an attack which he intended to carry "through to the end, even at the risk of disrupting the National Front." The rationale behind Šrámek's proposed move was a firm belief that in an eventual showdown with the Communists over this issue, the Social Democrats would desert and leave the Communists isolated. Thus, President Beneš "would be compelled to request new elections immediately." The CIA sources speculated that such a projected move on the part of Šrámek might "at least in part" be based on an understanding reached with President Beneš, who conferred with František Hála, People's Party Deputy Chairman, on January twenty-ninth.[10] As the next days were to prove, this change of heart on the part of the People's Party leadership and its potential effect on Czechoslovak politics never came to the test.

The Czechoslovak National Socialist Party, the second opponent of the Communists in the Bohemian lands, was of a somewhat different mold. Numerically stronger than the People's Party, it pulled the second highest number of votes in the 1946 elections, after the Communists. Although from a theoretical point of view National Socialists and Communists had at least some common denominators in their political platforms vaguely covered by the socialist label, National Socialist resistance to communism was more vociferous and more effective than that of the People's Party. The origins of the party went back to Austria-Hungary and, traditionally, the party prided itself on its "Czechness:" Communists and Social Democrats owed at least part of their allegiance to the alien gospel of Marx; the Populists had their connections with Rome. Only the National Socialists were a "truly Czech" party with no foreign links. When, prior to elections, the other parties protested their allegiance to the Republic, the National Socialists could always reply that their "Czechness" was a permanent feature rather than just an attribute to be paraded before the voters at the appropriate time.

The party derived additional strength and esteem from the fact that many of its ranking members had either been victims of Nazi persecution during the war or had served with distinction in President Beneš' London exile government. Furthermore, and contrary to the People's Party, National Socialists held politically sensitive portfolios in postwar governments, of which the Ministry of Justice was by far the most important. Similarly, in terms of popular appeal, the National Socialists, with their frequent parades and rallies, were more of a visible symbol of resistance to Communism than the equally strongly opposed but more conservative and timid Populists.

In the person of Dr. Petr Zenkl, the former Lord Mayor of Prague, the party had an experienced politician as chairman. Both he and the party's Secretary-General, Dr. Vladimír Krajina, a well-known professor at Prague's Charles University, were hardened fighters who had spent much of the war in Gestapo jails. The latter, in particular, was a frequent Communist target because of his knowledge of the often questionable conduct of Communist Gestapo prisoners, information considered sufficiently dangerous by the Communists for them to attempt to remove Krajina from the scene by the use of force.[11] Dr. Jaroslav Stránský, who was to replace the Communist Zdeněk Nejedlý as Minister of Education after the 1946 elections, Dr. Prokop Drtina, Minister of Justice, and some of the younger National Socialist members of the National Assembly, such as Dr. Milada Horáková, chairman of the Assembly's Security Committee, and Ota Hora, minced no words when it came to parliamentary duels with their Communist opponents. Less visible than the ministers, but more important in the formation of the party's platform, was another member of Parliament and the party's political secretary, Dr. Julius Firt. All said, and even though they, like the Populists, ultimately lost out in the fight against unlimited Communist power in Czechoslovakia, the National Socialists nonetheless constituted the most vociferous and significant opposition to Communism during the years from 1946 to 1948.

They, too, however, had an influential wing which, while opposed to the Communists, did not wish to provoke an open conflict with them. Mindful of the new division of Europe into spheres of influence and aware that Czechoslovakia had definitely been left in the Soviet orbit, they acted accordingly. There was, furthermore, the very real fear of a resurgent Germany against which the Soviet Union was by far Czechoslovakia's best protector. Jožka David, old-time party member and Chairman of the National Assembly, and the younger Hubert Ripka, Minister of Foreign Trade, were the chief advocates of a working arrangement with the Communists which, in turn — or so at least they hoped — would prevent direct interference in Czechoslovak affairs by the Soviets.

The election results of 1946 had proved somewhat disappointing to the National Socialists. Although they did not expect to emerge as the strongest single party, they had hopes of a larger popular vote than they actually received. They did not take their defeat lying down and, during the remainder of 1946, closed ranks and gave every impression of gaining in numbers. Thus, by early 1947, John Bruins, then in charge of the U.S. Embassy in Prague, could report that the National Socialists were "at present the strongest and best-led of the non-Communist parties and [had] the largest representation in the National Assembly after the Communists."[12] Like many Czechs themselves, Bruins noted the frequently-repeated declarations of the "party chiefs'" continued support of Czechoslovakia's "present foreign policy and of a socialist or 'socializing' program." He also observed the National Socialists' "very forthright stand against further nationalization, against domination by the Communists of the Army, Secret Police, Information Ministry, trade unions and work councils, and against totalitarianism in general." Although not unaware that the party's "concentration on resistance to Communism" might detract from its own "constructive features," he nonetheless expected it to take "an increasingly stronger line in the future." Commenting further on the "unwarranted influence" of the Communists in the country's affairs, Bruins pointed to the lack of cooperation between the non-Communist parties who, much to the joy of the Communists, accused each other of various shortcomings.[13]

The following day, focusing his dispatch to Washington on some of the causes of friction between National Socialists and Populists, he singled out the latter's clericalism as opposed to the former's anti-clericalism, Vaticanism and "[the People's Party's] connections with other Catholic parties abroad" against the National Socialists' "Czech nationalism," "personal rivalries" and "Šrámek's dislike for Jan Masaryk" as some of the main problems between the two. Since, broadly speaking, National Socialists and Populists frequently appealed to the same classes of potential electoral support, the lack of unity among them was all the more regrettable.

But, as had been the case with Steinhardt's views on the People's Party, the Embassy's opinions about the strengths and weaknesses of the National Socialists would appear equally open to question. This time, Julius First replies to the charges. Making light of the remarks of the American diplomats and calling them "a naive search for an alibi for the hazy and foggy American politics towards Czechoslovakia," he indicts the Embassy for its frequent and lighthearted exhortations to anti-Communist politicians — Zenkl in particular — to make a radical stand against the Communists. This attitude seemed doubly irresponsible in view of the subsequently demonstrated fact that Washington had no intention whatsoever to get tough itself.

As for the charge of lack of cooperation between the two non-Communist parties, Firt attaches little significance to them. Pointing to Czechoslovakia's *modus vivendi* with the Holy See, an arrangement reached in 1929 and signed for Czechoslovakia by the then Foreign Minister Edvard Beneš, and the Populists' subsequent support for Beneš' candidacy for the office of President of the Republic, he sees in both of them the effective ending of the one-time rivalry between the two parties. He admits that the subsequent joining by the National Socialists of the Socialist Bloc did bring about a "certain ill-feeling" between the two but, by late 1945, when National Socialists ceased to attend the Bloc's meetings and insisted that "everything should be discussed within the National Front, in the presence of the Populists," this animosity subsided. In spite of local differences, prompted by a healthy quest for electoral votes, "there was complete trust and cooperation between the leadership of both parties."[14]

Some three months later, the Embassy now seemed more encouraged by the party's performance. This time it was the Ambassador himself, describing a special rally of the National Socialist Party on the occasion of the party's fiftieth anniversary, who noted the "distinctly anti-Communist character" of the proceedings. Furthermore, he purported to have detected a similar vein in the remarks by the main speaker, party chairman Zenkl. All this encouraged the Ambassador and led him to believe that it "would bolster the confidence of moderate parties."[15]

Subsequent dispatches only strengthened the American observers' impression of a growing cleavage between National Socialists and Communists. Their opinions were based largely on an important editorial by Ivan Herben, editor-in-chief of the National Socialists' daily *Svobodné slovo,* in which he spoke of an increasing realization by the Communist Party chiefs that they were losing their hold on the people and of a cleavage within the ranks of the Communist Party, with "radical agitators" on one side and "realistic politicians" on the other.[16]

By late summer, events such as the original acceptance and subsequent rejection by Prague to take part in the initial Marshall Plan talks left additional scars on the Czechoslovak political fabric. They were bound to add fuel to the fire and, in increasing measure, brought about Communist attacks against the National Socialists. Whether such a Communist drive would "be confined to propaganda and parliamentary channels or will eventually assume more sinister form [was] the decisive question of current Czechoslovak politics." The Embassy obviously thought that such a drive was indeed in the offing, detecting in the denunciation of the National Socialist leadership by the Communists the "first straw in the wind of Communist strategy in Czechoslovakia."[17]

Whether or not this was so, the National Socialists were not going to give up easily. In a speech by Zenkl, their chairman reaffirmed the party's allegiance to the Czechoslovak-Soviet treaty, calling it the best guarantee for Czechoslovakia's security; at the same time, he took care to refer to it as "a treaty of the whole people with the people of the U.S.S.R., and not the treaty of a party with a party in the U.S.S.R." The inference was clear, but the careful wording of Zenkl's speech made it just as clear that non-Communist parties in post-war Czechoslovakia had to be extremely careful in their criticisms of Communism in order not to offend the Soviet Union. Irrespective of the intrinsic merits of such a step, it obviously severely circumscribed the National Socialists' radius of action. Charles Yost, First Secretary at the Embassy and one of its ablest political officers, readily saw the danger inherent in such a limitation. To him, the Communists would simply refer as "traitors" to persons daring to criticize the Czechoslovak-Soviet alliance or any of the actions taken under its cloak; this was to suggest to him "the manner in which the Communists will endeavor to deal with such persons if opportunity occurs." In the same dispatch, Yost pointed out that "the Communists had recently been criticizing the National Socialist leadership for [such] attempts to undermine the Soviet alliance."[18]

The Embassy's First Secretary, then acting as chargé d'affaires, next reported on the National Socialist counterattack. This came in the form of a bold proposal by Krajina, who called for either the fusion or total elimination of no less than seven ministries of the Czechoslovak government. Basing his appeal on grounds of economic necessity, the move did not conceal its essentially anti-Communist character, since Krajina's first choice fell on the Communist-dominated Ministry of Information, whose agenda, he suggested, could readily be taken over by the Ministries of Education and Foreign Affairs. Although chances of success for such an action were limited indeed, the Secretary-General of the National Socialist Party clearly displayed considerable courage in proposing it.[19]

One of the high points of National Socialist resistance to Communist pressure came in an important speech delivered by Dr. Jaroslav Stránsky, the Minister of Education. On August 31, in the Moravian mining capital of Moravská Ostrava, Stránsky took the bull by the horns in publicly faulting the government for reversing itself on its stand towards the Marshall Plan. Carefully distinguishing between the interests of Czechoslovakia and the international political situation in general, Stránsky bluntly stated that it would undoubtedly have been to the benefit of the country to have accepted the invitation to Paris; furthermore, the original acceptance and subsequent rejection of the invitation was clearly the result of subordinating Czechoslovakia's interests to those of the U.S.S.R. Such behavior, the Minister went on, was shameful: while Czechoslovakia obviously could neither exist nor conduct her foreign policy in a political vacuum, "first of all [Czechoslovakia] should see everything through Czechoslovak eyes, and only then through the eyes of our Allies, because only in this way will [Czechoslovakia] be a valuable ally and not a worthless satellite."[20]

Rarely, if ever, during this difficult and complex period of Czechoslovakia's post-war history had one of its politicians evinced similar courage in openly questioning the wisdom of blindly following each and every Soviet move. It was an outright provocation of Czechoslovakia's Communists, and Yost's remark that Stránsky's speech "constitutes one of the most forthright statements which has been made in recent months by a responsible Czechoslovak political leader in opposition to the foreign policy of the Czechoslovak Communist Party" is well taken.[21] Together with Stránský, Krajina was easily the most outspoken of the anti-Communist critics. As early as September, 1946, he attacked them openly, this time treating a major subject about which Czechoslovak Communist politicians were particularly sensitive: the administration, by Communist officers, of Czechoslovak prison camps for former Gestapo officials. It had long been rumored and suspected that Communist officers in charge of such camps were granting favors and even freedom to former Gestapo men in return for the latters' silence about the conduct of some Gestapo-held Czechoslovak Communists during the war.[22] Obviously, the disclosure of such behavior would severely damage the otherwise good reputation of the party during the Nazi occupation. Krajina, himself a Gestapo prisoner at the time, now charged that the Communists were trying to hush up the deeds and misdeeds of some of their comrades. Furthermore, one Staff Captain Pokorný, commander of such a camp, was inducing former Gestapo men to give false testimony against democratic leaders, Krajina included. This was a serious accusation, since the Communists derived much of their strength from the reputation that, unlike the bourgeois pre-Munich parties, they had never made any deals with the capitalists and fascists and, consequently, had no part in Munich and later Czechoslovak catastrophes. This lily-white reputation was now about to be tarnished, and the Communists were going to do their best not to permit it. Krajina, who had impeccable evidence for his charges, thus became their prime target.[23]

As late as December, 1947, member of Parliament Ota Hora, chairman of the National Assembly's Security Committee, openly attacked the Communist Minister of the Interior in an article entitled "Do we live in a police state?" He accused the Minister of interfering with some of the basic tenets of freedom, even the freedom of listening to non-Communist views. Comparing existing conditions in supposedly liberated Czechoslovakia to those prevalent in the Nazi-created Protectorate, Hora called for a return to Czechoslovakia's pre-Munich democratic way of life.[24]

In a sense, then, the National Socialist Party put up a good fight, but, like most other traditional bourgeois parties, it too was outdistanced by superior Communist organization and by the Communists' ability to appeal to the masses by means of clever and effective propaganda. As was the case with other non-Communist parties, it too failed to heed the age-old lesson that strength comes through unity. Instead of arousing either Populists or Social Democrats into common action with them against the Communists, the National Socialists went their own way and only occasionally put up a united front against the common foe. During the final weeks preceding the coup of 1948, there appeared to be some effort on the part of the National Socialists to draw closer to the Social Democrats, who had recently[25] declared their independence from Communist tutelage. In early December, an article in the party's weekly, *Svobodný zítřek,* made a spirited defense of the policies of the Minister of Food, Social Democrat Václav Majer, who had just been attacked by Gottwald for the unsatisfactory state of the nation's food situation.[26]

As for the National Socialists' cooperation with their most powerful potential ally, the Slovak Democratic Party, the situation was much the same. Little, if any, effective cooperation between these two strongest non-Communist parties in the country was in evidence. Even Julius Firt, who had previously dismissed similar charges of lack of cooperation between non-Communist parties as excuses given by the Americans for their own lack of a firm policy, had to acknowledge that "a real weakness existed." He sees the reason for this lack of cooperation between National Socialists and Slovak Democrats much less in the frequently cited differences between the secularism of the former and the clericalism of the latter than in the lack of understanding for Slovak national identity on the part of the Czechs. Slovak Democrats took pride in their achievements during the Slovak National Rising of 1946, while the Czechs, led by President Beneš, attempted to play them down. Paradoxically, Communist and non-Communist Czechs made common cause in this denigration of Slovak accomplishments, much to the dismay of the Slovak Democratic Party.[27]

At least, and literally only days before the whole crisis of 1948 came to a head, the two parties reached an agreement which, among other things, stipulated non-interference of the partners in each other's territories (the National Socialists were not to expand into Slovakia and vice-versa) and "mutual support in the event of pre-election attacks by the Communists."[28] Commendable as such a move was, it came rather late and only after the effectiveness of the Slovak Democrats had been all but destroyed as a result of the recent purge of its ranks by government action. In other words, the unquestionable courage and moral rectitude of many a prominent National Socialist often came to naught since it simply was not supported by systematic and concerted efforts by the party. Under the circumstances, the Communists were bound to be the chief beneficiaries of this almost chronic disunity among their opponents; they certainly did not fail to exploit this situation to the fullest.

So much for the non-Communist parties in the Bohemian lands. Things were different in Slovakia: there only two parties vied for electoral favor and, contrary to the situation in Bohemia and Moravia, the Communists found themselves decidedly in the minority. But, within less than eighteen months the Slovak Democrats, who scored an impressive victory at the polls in 1946, saw this victory literally disintegrate before their own eyes. The party's membership was heterogeneous in composition: the majority consisted of members stemming from the now-dissolved Agrarian Party, representatives of Slovak political Catholicism, and Slovaks of a genuine Czechoslovak political orientation. It was this very ability to attract to its ranks people from the former parties and organizations which were now either formally proscribed or otherwise politically compromised which got the party off to its very impressive start. Similarly, and more than anything else, this vast and varied reservoir of members and sympathizers accounted for the Democrats' success in the elections. In brief, almost everyone who was anti-Communist, from old-time Social Democrats to former sympathizers of the separatist Tiso regime, sought and found haven in the Democratic Party. Under the leadership of the young agrarian, Dr. Jozef Lettrich, the party now tried to provide at least some political counterweight to the Communist-dominated Bohemia and Moravia.

Paradoxically, with the passing of time this initial strength of the Democrats which came from their ability to be the party of many men and many minds, also proved to be a major drawback. Once political conditions in Czechoslovakia returned to some degree of normality, all those who had originally joined the party for either lack of other choice or merely to hide their "Hlinkist" past under a new political umbrella, now began to manifest centrifugal tendencies. This was particularly noticeable among the representatives of the party's Catholic wing and even more so among those who, at one time, had political ties to the now discredited "Slovak state."

The presence in the Democrats' ranks of a small number of former separatist politicians provided the Communists with precisely the kind of ammunition which they needed for an attack on their opponents. Although the Communists themselves continued to shelter in their ranks former Fascist fellow travelers and informers,[29] both in the Bohemian lands and in Slovakia, they now left no stone unturned in order to expose the Democrats for doing the same thing. At first, the Democrats paid little heed to the various accusations, but the Communists' ability to muster mass support from various workers' and partisan groups soon added momentum to their cause. Belatedly and under pressure, the Democrats began to purge their ranks. Failure to take such action on their own and in good time greatly impeded the political effectiveness of the Slovak Democrats and, ultimately, all but deprived them of the fruits of their impressive victory at the polls even before their demise as a party after the February, 1948 coup.

Against this backdrop of failure by the non-Communist parties, the record of the Czech and Slovak Communists appears impressive indeed. The Communist Party of Czechoslovakia was founded in October of 1921, largely in the same way as many of its European sister parties, by a split within the ranks of the Social Democrats. Already in pre-Munich days, Czechoslovak communism was a factor to be reckoned with and, by the time of Munich, the Communists ranked fourth among the then two dozen Czechoslovak parties.[30] The party's stand during the Munich crisis, when it advocated armed resistance rather than surrender, and its underground wartime activity on behalf of a restored Czechoslovakia gave it impressive credentials in the post-war quest for voters. Most important, though, was its traditionally pro-Soviet orientation, which, with the new state of affairs in post-war Czechoslovakia, easily proved the Czechoslovak Communists' greatest asset. Only after the immediate post-liberation psychosis had subsided and when it therefore became possible to examine the Soviets' and the Czechoslovak Communists' role in a more critical light, did a realistic appraisal of the party's role make its way into Czechoslovak political thinking.

The Communists were now being chided for their reluctance to join the Czechoslovak underground from its very beginning during the war, and then only after the "capitalist" war had become a legitimate war for the greater glory of the fatherland of socialism in June, 1941, after the German attack on the U.S.S.R. Similarly, one could now question the constant switch from proletarian internationalism to Czech nationalism in the party's political platform. Some bolder spirits might have gone so far as to state bluntly that the Communist Party was more of a Russian than a Czechoslovak one, acting, as it frequently did, in the interests of Moscow rather than Prague. As the post-war popularity of the victorious Soviet Army waned and the harsh realities of everyday Soviet life began to displace its glowing image, the once powerful psychological support which the party derived from them weakened accordingly. It would, however, be incorrect to assume that it was now possible to openly and systematically criticize Communism and the Soviet Union. The latter remained an especially touchy subject and the ability of the Czechoslovak Communists to make their cause synonymous with that of the U.S.S.R. stood them in good stead. An attack on the Soviet ally and its faithful Czechoslovak disciple, the Communist Party, was, in Communist minds, tantamount to treason. It was precisely this extra shield brought about by the international political situation as much as by the country's domestic affairs which protected Czechoslovak communism from the harsh winds of an open political market place.

The first comprehensive summary of Communist strength in the resurrected Czechoslovakia was the enormous influence which the party wielded in the various National Committees. These bodies, functioning on three distinct levels (local, district and regional), were the newly created administrative units into which the country was now divided. Partly due to their excellent organization, but also under the aegis of the Soviet Army, the Communist Party managed to staff the most important National Committees posts with its own members. This was particularly so in the reoccupied former Sudeten regions, where, during the first months after the liberation, the Communists were virtually in full control. Even in cases of numerical parity among the four political parties, the various National Committees were usually dominated by the Communist members. Alfred Klieforth, the American chargé d'affaires and the first ranking U.S. diplomat to arrive in Czechoslovakia after the cessation of hostilities, quoted "a usually reliable source" and reported a "show-down" in this matter between Hubert Ripka, the National Socialist Minister and Klement Gottwald, a Communist and then the Vice-Premier. During the confrontation, Ripka "threatened to create parallel committees if the non-Communist members were not given due attention." Such a show-down was eventually avoided and "according to the same source, Gottwald adopted a conciliatory attitude and agreed to modify matters."[31]

Some weeks later, the newly arrived Ambassador Steinhardt, who had by now taken charge of the U.S. mission in Prague, conveyed the impression to Washington that things were improving for the non-Communist parties. In a conversation with Czechoslovak President Beneš, to whom he had just presented his credentials, Beneš had expressed to him "the conviction that the Communists were steadily losing strength in Czechoslovakia and expressed doubt that they could elect 25% of the members of Parliament."[32] The President may well have been correct in the first part of his statement — there was indeed a decline of Communist predominance once the Russian liberation euphoria had subsided — but he was grievously mistaken on his second prognosis. So was Ambassador Steinhardt, who on a different occasion predicted a similarly rosy future for Czechoslovakia.[33]

For the time being at least, there was some degree of harmony between the parties. Even after the impressive Communist election victory of May, 1946, Gottwald, now Prime Minister, made clear in a press interview that the victory of the Communist Party at the polls would "not bring about any changes in Czechoslovak foreign policy." While the Soviet Union would remain the chief ally of Czechoslovakia, the new Premier hoped that friendly relations with the Western powers would continue, assuming that "the West would accept the results of the general election as a free expression of the will of Czechoslovak citizens."[34] Similarly, Gottwald proved conciliatory on most other major issues which traditionally divided Communist and non-Communist parties. The Communist victory, he said, would not bring about a limitation of personal freedom, nor need tradesmen and artisans fear that their enterprises would be nationalized, since "nationalization had already gone far enough."[35] Thus, and in spite of the mandate which the Communists had gotten by democratic means,[36] the party platform seemed to be one of moderation and cooperation.

Other factors contributed to the relative calm on the Czechoslovak political scene. The Soviet Union's conciliatory attitude at the Foreign Minister's conference may well have set an example for the Czechoslovak Communist Party or so, at least, Steinhardt thought in one of his frequent secret reports. Gottwald's health, seriously impaired by overconsumption of alcohol, and the rather unfavorable impressions of the U.S.S.R. gained by a Czechoslovak parliamentary delegation which had just returned from there undoubtedly left their marks on the thinking of Czechoslovakia's Communist leadership.[37] John Bruins corroborated Steinhardt's view when, in a similar dispatch, he informed the Secretary of State "of a certain weakening in the Czechoslovak Communist Party," a phenomenon which, however, seemed to be offset by increasing militancy among the Slovak Communists who, paradoxically, lost rather badly in the past elections. Simultaneously with the above, Counselor Bruins noticed "a stiffening in the position of the non-Communist parties."[38]

While it would be too strong an expression to refer to this period as one of close and effective cooperation between Communist and non-Communist parties, there indeed existed a political climate conducive to joint constructive work. How seriously all this was taken by Steinhardt is best illustrated in his remarks to Bruins. The Ambassador, on home leave in New York, had been informed that the *New York Times* was about to publish an article critical of Gottwald and Czechoslovak communism in general. Apprehensive that such reporting might do much harm, he promised his best efforts in forestalling its publication: "You are well aware of my high regard for — I might even say my affection for Gottwald — and I would deeply resent any such nasty article about him." The Ambassador asked Bruins to reassure Acting Foreign Minister Clementis that he would use all his influence with Arthur Sulzberger, the *Times'* owner and publisher, to "head off any such article," by requesting the name of the person preparing it, so that he could stop things in good time.[39] It is obvious from all this that Steinhardt, like many Czech non-Communist politicians, did indeed believe that cooperation within the National Front could be achieved, irrespective of socio-philosophical differences; the Ambassador's attitude in this particular matter bespeaks his concern not to create the impression that the United States favored one segment of Czechoslovak political opinion and showed hostility towards another.

The era of good feeling was not to last much longer. By June of 1947, Washington was told about an "increasing cleavage between Communists and other parties."[40] It was a correct reading of the Czechoslovak political barometer. Once again, external and internal matters coalesced to bring about the changed mood. The "Grand Alliance" of World War II had all but fallen apart, and it became increasingly more difficult for Czechoslovakia to remain that bridge between East and West which its non-Communist segment had hoped it to be. Caught between the U.S. position of a speedy economic reconstruction of Germany, a rather frightening prospect for the Czechs, and the spectacle of communization in some of its East European neighbors upon which the Soviets had just embarked in Rumania, Poland and Hungary, Czechoslovak parties and politics split on similar lines. Among the issues which then divided Communists and non-Communists, the controversy connected with Czechoslovak participation in the Marshall Plan was undoubtedly the most weighty and best known.[41] The Communists' publicly stated aim of capturing a straight majority in the 1948 elections did not help matters either. Nor did the suspensions of United States credits for Czechoslovakia and the formation, in 1947, of the Cominform, an institution designed to take the place of the Comintern, dissolved in 1943 as a friendly gesture to Roosevelt and Churchill. The gulf between the Czechoslovak Communists and their opponents widened once again.

By August, the "Embassy [had] learned indirectly from [a] source it believed reliable" about a speech by the Communist Minister of Information, Václav Kopecký, in which he was reported to have claimed that the "Communist Party and ÚRO [Central Trade Union

Organization] [were] the sole powers in Czechoslovakia. If [Commu-
nists and trade unions] wished, [they] could start a revolution at any
time. Whatever Gottwald says is backed by the Russian Army... look
what is happening in Hungary and the Balkans... that process will not
stop at our borders." Asserting that Slovakia was the key to the
Czechoslovak problem, Kopecký suggested that the fomenting of anti-
Communist activities in Slovakia was part of the Communist strategy
of bringing an end to the prevailing political situation in the Republic:
"When we are successful in getting Slovakia to secede, it will be easy to
liquidate [political opposition in] Bohemia and Moravia."[42] Charles
Yost, who informed Washington about Kopecký's remarks, was surprised that even as outspoken and rabid a Communist as Kopecký
would say such things "in the course of an informal speech [on July 27]
at a very secret meeting of young Communist newspapermen." Yost
attached sufficient credence to it to refer to it as the present "policy at
least of Left-wing of Czechoslovak Communist Party to which Kopecký belongs." As additional proof of the authenticity of the remarks,
Yost referred to "Kopecký's well-known indiscretion," a correct opinion supported by other evidence of the period. Yost's own high
standards in his reporting would further tend to support his trust in the
genuineness of Kopecký's speech.[43]

The National Socialists, in the meantime, had become another
target of the Communist offensive. In an article in *Rudé právo* of
August 17, they were taken to task for criticism of the Soviet Union, an
act considered tantamount to high treason by the Communists.[44] By
early September, Yost could confirm that "in a sudden shift of
strategy, the Communists have now decided to make the National
Socialists their chief target of attack"; while this did not mean that
"the attack on the Slovak Democrats [was] over," it did mean that the
Communists viewed the National Socialists as "the most dangerous"
of their political foes.[45]

A special new levy on millionaires, often referred to as the "millionaires' tax," provided another issue of heated argument between Communists and their opponents. The dispute arose over the question of
compensation to farmers who had suffered heavy losses due to
droughts and crop failures. As in the case with similar measures in
other countries — such as social security increases in the United
States — political parties competed with each other in sponsoring the
measure. The dispute arose when it came to finding the necessary
funds for it. The Communists proposed a special tax on "millionaires,"
to which the non-Communist parties objected on the grounds that

such a measure would be discretionary because it singled out only one segment of the population to bear the whole burden of the subsidies and, in so doing, discouraged private savings and investments. This, in turn, enabled the Communists to refer to their opponents as protectors of "speculators, big estate owners and big businessmen," a somewhat ridiculous charge in view of the fact that a Czech "millionaire" was a man of rather modest means by standards of hard currency countries.[46] Even Foreign Minister Masaryk, not known for his outspokenness on touchy subjects, eventually entered into the fray; in a letter to the press, he made it known that, had he been present at the parliamentary session dealing with the "millionaires' tax," he would have voted against it.[47]

An interesting sidelight on the whole controversy is provided by Yost's remark that the Communists never really expected their proposal to pass, but merely used the whole issue as yet another opportunity to "smear leaders of non-Communist parties individually by name as protectors of reactionaries and enemies of the people." This, to him, seemed a clever manoeuver designed to separate the rank and file of the non-Communist parties from their leadership, on the grounds that the latter did not really care for the common man in the street.[48]

Not all the leaders of the Communist Party took a similar hard line. Thus, for example, Prime Minister Gottwald, in an interview with the New York Herald-Tribune correspondents Ned Russell and William Atwood, conceded that the National Front type of government in Czechoslovakia would continue, even if the Communists gained an absolute majority in the next elections. But even in these public remarks, obviously primarily destined for Western consumption, Gottwald predicted the fusion of the whole Czechoslovak working class into one political party, simply stating that "the future [inevitably] would lead to this."[49]

Quite correctly did Steinhardt report that the Communists were "really pressing hard" and refusing to compromise on any issue now. They did so, the Ambassador thought, either "on orders from the Kremlin" or to "hold elections before the expected economic pinch influence[d] the public."[50] Steinhardt's dispatch did not reveal what had caused him to speculate about the "orders from the Kremlin." Since, ordinarily, the Ambassador was in the habit of referring to his various connections, if not necessarily identifying them, one can only conclude that these were essentially thoughts of his own. But in spite of all this, Steinhardt did not think that the moment of decision was at hand. According to him, the Communists had not yet made up their minds as to whether to adopt a compromising attitude vis-à-vis their political opponents or resort to more violent measures. On which course they would eventually embark depended in no small measure on the forthcoming Social Democratic Party Congress, where the leadership of their ally, Fierlinger, hung in the balance, and on the forthcoming "Big Four" Foreign Ministers' Conference in London. If Fierlinger were re-elected, Communists and Social Democrats might merge and this, in turn, would add momentum to the Communist offensive.[51]

Some insight as to the seriousness of the situation may be gained from an exchange of views between President Beneš and Prime Minister Gottwald, as reported to Washington by the Ambassador. Beneš confided in Steinhardt, telling him that during a recent visit of Gottwald's in which the Prime Minister complained that "it was becoming increasingly difficult for him, as Prime Minister, and leader of the Communist Party, to function," Gottwald said that he might have to resort to purges of anti-Communist parties to govern effectively. To this, Beneš is said to have replied, "Then you will have to begin with me."[52] In view of Beneš' still hotly disputed role in the 1948 coup, this statement by the President would appear to be of particular significance.

Four days later, and once again reporting on a conversation with Beneš, Steinhardt claimed to have detected "a more hostile attitude towards [the] Communists than [Beneš] had in any previous talk with [him]" and a strong desire, on the part of Beneš, "for continued friendship with the United States." Beneš felt that "the Communist attack on the government had been beaten off" and took particular delight in the ouster of Fierlinger as chairman of the Social Democratic Party,[53] for which "he readily took credit." Beneš' "optimism reached the point of asserting that the turning point had been reached" and while he anticipated "at least two more Communist efforts between now and the election in May, to intimidate, even terrorize, the non-Communists, and thus influence the outcome of the elections, he [did] not believe that further efforts [would] precipitate a more acute crisis than those just passed." Finally, the President expressed his belief that the non-Communist leaders and the public-at-large "have taken courage from the recent Communist defeats," so that "any future crisis [would] be less pronounced."[54]

There were other indications that the Communist offensive was waning. On November 5, Steinhardt claimed to "have learned of

Gottwald's personal dislike for [Rudolf] Slánský, the Secretary General of the Czechoslovak Communist Party," which "has led to the intimation by the Prime Minister that Frank would be a more acceptable Secretary General." These internal differences within the Communist Party, Steinhardt now thought, "might prompt Gottwald to take a less aggressive position than might otherwise be the case in dealing with the crisis in Slovakia."[55]

Then, in early December, the Embassy's Counselor, John Bruins, who once again headed the mission after Steinhardt's departure for the United States for medical reasons,[56] transmitted results from the recent student elections held by the various branches of Charles University. The rather strong anti-Communist showing pleased Bruins and what seemed to encourage him particularly was the resounding Communist defeat in the University's Philosophy Department, where Communists had previously wielded much influence.[57]

An interview, granted by Gottwald to United Press correspondent V. M. Pinkley and reported on in the Communist-controlled *Daily Review* of the Czechoslovak Ministry of Information, showed the Prime Minister and Communist Party leader in a flexible and conciliatory spirit. While Gottwald sang the praises of the Soviet Union and expressed gratitude for large Soviet food shipments, he also asserted that Czechoslovakia would not become a member of any "bloc" and that "good Communists must also be good patriots."[58]

Bruins, however, seemed equally aware of the unabated actual strength and influence of the Czechoslovak Communist Party. Commenting on an article by Slánský in the Belgrade-published *For A Lasting Peace, For A People's Democracy,* the official publication of that organization, in which Slánský proudly pointed to the numerical strength of his party in the various organs of the Czechoslovak government, Bruins showed full comprehension of the Communists' ability to use this strength to best advantage by means of superior propaganda and political patronage, which he considered "no less important than in the United States."[59] Nonetheless, Bruins did not think it likely that in spite of its recent reversals the Communist Party in Czechoslovakia might resort to illegal means in its attempt to gain an absolute majority. In a brief report, in which he minced no words, he discounted such a possibility on the grounds of "(1) the non-revolutionary character of the Czech people who would probably react to such methods in a manner unfavorable to Communists; (2) Czecho-[slovakia was] only [a] Soviet periphery country with highly developed industry," and since the "Soviet Union greatly need[ed] Czech products, unorthodox Communist election methods would impair Czech ability to get necessary raw materials from the West; (3) President Beneš [was] regarded as [an] 'ace in the hole' who [was] highly popular and respected and who could be counted upon in an emergency to use his position strongly to resist extra-legal action."[60] The prognosis was wrong on all three counts and Bruins was by no means the only one to miscalculate the situation and the Communists' aims. Most of the ranking members of the non-Communist parties seemed to think likewise, or so, at least, their actions in the coming weeks would indicate; if Ambassador Steinhardt correctly reported the President's thoughts to Washington, Beneš was among them.

Steinhardt and his senior officials might have done well to heed the warnings of their recently appointed representative in Bratislava. From there, Vice-Consul Claiborne Pell, in a report on events connected with the Slovak crisis, concluded in no uncertain terms: "I believe it may be possible that the Communists, thwarted in their attempt to gain control within the Parliamentary framework, may decide to stay without it and use force. However, that will be for Praha, if not for Moscow, to decide. And time will tell the result. At the same time, no matter what, I imagine they will step up their anti-American attack."[61]

The Slovak Crisis of 1947

After a relatively uneventful spring, the summer and fall of 1947 marked a number of important events in the political life of Czechoslovakia, events that caused much dissent and open warfare among the political parties. The controversy concerning Czechoslovakia's withdrawal from the Marshall Plan negotiations was still in full swing when yet another issue, this time a purely domestic one, stirred passions anew. It centered on Slovakia.

With the collapse of the "Slovak State" in the spring of 1945, Slovakia, which in 1939 had declared its independence under the aegis of the Third Reich, now reverted to Czechoslovak sovereignty. Although the first units of the Free Czechoslovak forces, in conjunction with the Soviet Army, had liberated some Slovak territory late in 1944, and although Tiso's régime had been severely shaken by the Slovak National rising of that same year, the "Slovak state" had managed to maintain itself in power until March of 1945, when the new Czechoslovak government established itself temporarily in the East Slovak city of Košice.

Compared to Bohemia and Moravia, Slovakia saw considerably more military action during the war and, in spite of its relatively satisfactory food supply, the country suffered heavily during the final months of the conflict. Severely damaged communications, few industrial enterprises and a population thoroughly demoralized made recovery difficult. Contrary to the historic lands (Bohemia-Moravia) where liberation from the Nazi yoke was greeted with unbounded enthusiasm, irrespective of political affiliation, many Slovaks had mixed feelings about the new state of affairs. Suffice it to say that while, in their majority, the Slovaks may well have been satisfied to rid themselves of their German sponsors who had given them life, not all of them welcomed the reincorporation of their territory into a resurrected Czechoslovak state. Apart from the collaborators, who had good reason to expect deserved punishment from the Czechoslovak authorities, there were, as always, the masses of an essentially apolitical population which, after 1939, simply got accustomed to an administration which was paternalistic and authoritarian but native Slovak nonetheless. All this had now suddenly changed. The fact that the first organs of the new Czechoslovak government were accompanied by units of the Soviet Army, not only the official enemy of Slovakia during World War II but an ideological enemy as well, added fuel to the fire.

The Czechs, in turn, viewed the situation somewhat differently. They reasoned that the Slovaks should consider themselves fortunate to be readmitted into Czechoslovakia and, from then on, be counted among the victors of the war rather than share the fate of other Axis satellites, like Hungary and Bulgaria, which now found themselves on the losing side. Historical and cultural differences, of which religion was only one, and which antedated World War II, did not make a Czecho-Slovak synthesis any easier. In the immediate post-war months, however, the resuscitated Czechoslovak state faced other more pressing problems than a re-definition of the mutual relationship between Czechs and Slovaks; yet, before 1945 came to an end, the question of Slovakia once again loomed large on the Czechoslovak political horizon.

From the very moment when Czechoslovak and Russian armed forces set foot on Slovak territory, there almost instantly developed polarization between Communist and non-Communist forces. The former, as always on the initiative, benefited greatly from the prestige of the victorious Soviet Army, whose presence proved a great help in the establishment of an effective Communist Party apparatus in liberated Slovakia. The non-Communists, in turn, drew not inconsiderable part of their support from the cadres of the old Tiso régime, tainted by collaboration with the Germans; although a blanket accusation of rank-and-file party members was frequently unjustified, the stigma nonetheless was there. It was precisely over this issue of individuals compromised by the former Tiso régime and now holding political office in the Slovak Democratic Party[1] that the Slovak crisis of 1947 developed. The decisive victory of the Slovak Democratic Party in the 1946 elections and the trial and execution of Tiso in the following year were its two main components.

When the election results of May, 1946 gave the Slovak Democratic Party a two-to-one majority over the Communists, a vote so completely different from that of Bohemia and Moravia, leaders of the party took over the chairmanship and some of the important portfolios in the autonomous administration for Slovakia *(Sbor povereníkov)*. Although the Slovak Democrats' success at the polls had been resounding, the Communists continued to control the labor unions and the various organizations of partisans and other para-military formations dating back to the war. Added to this was the fact that the composition of the central government in Prague was the reverse of Slovakia's administration. There, as a result of the 1946 elections, the Prime Minister was a Communist and the Communist Party controlled most of the sensitive cabinet posts. Consequently, the Slovak Democratic Party, although impressive at the polls, could never fully capitalize on its victory. Despite the fact that it counted among its leadership a number of men whose individual courage and political acumen can hardly be doubted, as a group the party failed to prove the leadership expected from it as a result of the overwhelming mandate given it by the voters. To further neutralize their defeat in the past elections, the Slovak Communists now reversed their one-time call for a strong and autonomous Slovak administration. More and more, they tended to support the central government in Prague, where, as victors in the elections in the Czech lands, the Communists had assumed a leading role. In their quest to offset the results of the Democratic Party's victory in Slovakia, the Communists had the effective help of various mass organizations, such as labor unions and partisans. In brief, since they were part of a larger whole, the Slovaks could not go their own way in terms of political coloration.

Tiso's trial and subsequent execution provided the Slovak Communists with yet another weapon in their struggle against the victorious Democrats. In the spring of 1945, only weeks before the conclusion of hostilities in the European theatre of war, Tiso and members of his government surrendered to the United States Army in the Austrian town of Kresmünster. In the fall of that year, the former President and his party were handed over to Czechoslovak authorities for trial. The proceedings, which lasted from December of 1946 to April of 1947, and the subsequent death sentence and execution of Tiso pitted Slovak Democrats and Communists squarely against each other. The Democrats, under substantial pressure from their Catholic wing, attempted to spare Tiso's life.[2] The Communists, once again supported by labor unions and various partisans' organizations, insisted on the death penalty; they saw in it not only a symbolic, but also a just, punishment for Tiso's wartime activities. When the Democratic Party formally requested a pardon, Communists and partisans took to the streets and made their views known in no uncertain terms. On April 16, 1947, the Democrats' request was discussed by the Prague government. The petition failed; apart from the Slovak Democrats, only the ministers of the Catholic People's Party voted for pardon. Tiso was executed two days later.

The resounding defeat[3] of the Democrats' attempt to have the death sentence commuted proved most disappointing to them and to their Catholic supporters in particular. Matters only got worse when the Presidium of the Slovak National Council, with the Communists dissenting, attempted to remove the presiding judge, the Communist Dr. Igor Daxner, only to see its attempt overturned by the government in Prague. Irrespective of the intrinsic merits of the legal procedures — Slovak autonomous rights against the constitutional principle of non-removal of judges — the clash further aggravated tensions between Slovak Democrats and Communists, between Bratislava and Prague.

The trial of former President Tiso and the circumstances surrounding the verdict and the request for pardon gave the Slovak Communists a good opportunity to test the effectiveness of mass organizational pressure in politically sensitive situations. They were to do so again, when, in the fall of 1947, they purported to have discovered a conspiracy against the state, led by former members of the one-time Hlinka party who had now found cover and protection in the present Democratic Party. Among other accusations, the conspirators were charged with spreading propaganda hostile to the Republic, various acts of sabotage, and attempting to restore an independent Slovakia. They were further accused of connections with Ferdinand D'určanský and Karol Sidor, two former ministers in Tiso's Slovak state now exiled, respectively, in Latin America and Rome and active in anti-Czechoslovak causes. The Communists immediately called for a thorough purge among the officialdom of the Democratic Party and attempted to strip it of its democratically obtained majority on the Slovak Board of Commissioners. Eventually, the Slovak Commissioner of the Interior, General Mikuláš Ferjenčík, issued an official report[4] which did indeed confirm that some minor officials of the Democratic Party were involved in anti-state activities; however, he stated emphatically that neither the size of the operation nor its supposed contacts abroad, which were to procure foreign intervention, posed any threat to the security of Czechoslovakia. Ferjenčík's explanation notwithstanding, the Communists continued their agitation and through a series of impressive public demonstrations created the impression, among the population, that Slovakia was caught in a major political crisis.

The United States Embassy in Prague kept a close watch over the events and tried to put them into proper perspective. On September 16th, First Secretary Yost reported that while there might be some truth to the fact that former Tiso officials had sought and found refuge in the Democratic Party, most moderate observers in Prague "[were] extremely skeptical that any conspiracy of [the] proportion and character indicated in yesterday's communique exist[ed]."[5] Adding his own commentary, Yost viewed the Communist accusation as simply another aspect of their campaign against the Democratic Party, on a pattern previously tried in other Eastern European countries. He also informed Washington of the forthcoming departure for Bratislava by Claiborne Pell, the Embassy's Third Secretary and Council General-designate to the Slovak capital, to inquire further into the situation.[6]

Subsequent and more detailed reports by Ferjenčík tended to confirm his erstwhile impression as to the relatively minor extent of the whole affair, although there was some truth to the Communist charges regarding the foreign connections of the conspirators. D'určanský and Sidor, the former in his capacity as chairman of the Slovak Action Committee based in New York and the latter, one-time Slovak Minister to the Vatican and now exiled in Rome, had indeed launched various propaganda offensives to discredit the Czechoslovak régime and to accuse the Czechs of subjugating the Slovaks against their will. The Slovak Action Committee addressed a letter to Secretary of State Marshall in which it claimed to have been entrusted by the Tiso government with the safeguarding of Slovak interests and asked Marshall to explain the Slovak situation to the United States government and to intercede on behalf of a free Slovakia.[7] There is no evidence of any action by Marshall; nor did Charles Ross, President Truman's Secretary,[8] or H. Freeman Matthews, the State Department's Director of European Affairs,[9] both recipients of similar pleas from the Slovak Action Committee, evince any great desire to intercede upon a request by Slovak emigrés. The Slovak separatist cause fared no better in its attempts to influence United States policy via the Holy See. There, Karol Sidor had approached H. Tittman, a U.S. Foreign Service Officer and Truman's personal representative to the Pope, with a request to assist him in the exit from Czechoslovakia of Sidor's wife and daughter. Although a personal rather than political matter, the Department of State maintained its correct posture and advised Sidor to address his request directly to Prague.[10] Even the Vatican, in spite of its reputation as a protector of conservative and authoritarian regimes during World War II, washed its hands of the

Slovak cause. In an audience granted Tittman by Mgr. Tardini, the Papal Secretary of State, the latter made clear the Holy See's disinterest in the cause of the now executed President Tiso and referred to him as a "political prelate" for whom the Vatican had little use.[11]

Similar pleas, political and personal in content, addressed to a number of United States Senators and Congressmen by various Slovak organizations in the United States,[12] were either disregarded outright or, at best, politely referred by their recipients to the proper U.S. government agencies. There they met with the standard response that Slovakia was a former enemy of the Allies and that those who claimed to be spokesmen of Slovak affairs and thus wished to influence the course of Czechoslovak politics, do so directly in communicating either with the Czechoslovak government or its representatives abroad.[13] The American position of diplomatic correctness and non-involvement in the internal affairs of another country was a sensible one. The United States may well have sympathized with the cause of the Slovak Democrats, but it was not about to jeopardize its own good name when Slovak Democrats decided to extend cover to elements of a questionable political past.

Still, all was not well in Slovakia. While there is little doubt that the Communists exploited the newly developed political crisis for their own aims rather than in an attempt to give genuine democratic government to the Slovaks, the attempt by the Slovak Democrats to hush things up as best they could and their protestations that the whole crisis was a minor affair proved equally unsuccessful. On September 27th, General Ferjenčík, confronted with an important new piece of evidence, now found it necessary to issue a second report in which he stated that high public personages had been implicated during the investigations of a second plot against the Czechoslovak Republic and had maintained continuous contact with D'určanský and Sidor and other organizations based abroad and hostile to Czechoslovakia. As a result of these new findings, which accused the plotters of an attempt to overthrow the Republic, Ferjenčík requested the special committee dealing with parliamentary immunity in the Czechoslovak National Assembly to lift the immunity of the Slovak Democratic deputies Bugár and Kempný. After a two weeks' tug of war between Communists and the Slovak Democrats on how to go about this and at the same time guarantee a fair hearing to the accused, the National Assembly did indeed lift the immunity of the two Slovak deputies, plus that of a third, Josef Staško, though only with the express proviso that the men would be tried by a regular court in Bratislava rather than by police authorities in Prague. This unusual solution, whereby immunity was withdrawn, but under special conditions only, invited Laurence Steinhardt's remark that this was "a typically Czech compromise" [between Czechs and moderates], a statement somewhat sarcastic, but very true nonetheless.[14]

Matters for the Democrats turned from bad to worse. On October 4th, in a sudden police raid on the offices of the Vice Premier, Ján Ursíny, one of the Democratic Party's top men, evidence was discovered which linked his personal secretary, Otto Obuch, to the Slovak conspirators abroad. The police claimed to have found incontestable proof of Obuch's systematic transmittal of highly sensitive government documents to his foreign contacts. Although it was made clear that Obuch had acted on his own, without the knowledge of Ursíny, the latter found it necessary to resign in order to avoid judicial proceedings against himself.[15]

While heavily implicated, the Slovak Democrats were not about to give up the fight, nor were they willing to be portrayed in the role of being the only Slovak political party which had given shelter in its ranks to former Tiso elements. In a long and carefully written editorial in their daily, *Čas,* of October 5th, the Deputy Chairman of the Slovak Board of Delegates, Rudolf Fraštacký, one of the ablest politicians in the ranks of the party, now went over to the counter-offensive. Fraštacký accused the Slovak Communists of intending to break up the Slovak Democratic Party by force ever since their inability to do so by democratic elections in May of 1946 was demonstrated. Quoting Ladislav Holdoš, a leading Slovak Communist, Fraštacký asserted that such a resolve had taken place only days after the elections, on June 6, 1946, when Holdoš reportedly declared that a definite plan to break up the Democratic Party existed and would be carried out in order to gain power for the Communist Party. It was imperative, according to Holdoš, "to prove an anti-state activity within the Democratic Party and dissolve it on the basis of this accusation." Fraštacký next charged that the Slovak Communists, like the Democrats, had within their ranks numerous members who, during the time of Tiso's regime, had approved of the "Slovak State out of cowardice or conviction." More than that, Fraštacký went on, Slovak Communists had given the shelter of their party to individuals who have "no Slovak national past and no convictions," and who, in pre-war times, considered themselves Hungarians.[16] If necessary, details as to the identity of such Communists would be furnished.

Fraštacký took particular delight in chiding the Slovak Communists for their erstwhile political program of large-scale autonomy for Slovakia. The Communists had sponsored such a program in anticipation that their showing at the polls would be as impressive in Slovakia as it had been in other parts of the country. When this hope failed to materialize, the Slovak Communists now changed tactics and sponsored a centralist administration. Through their deputy, Holdoš, Slovak Communists now proclaimed that "Praha will dictate on the whole territory of Czechoslovakia." This sudden volte-face amused Fraštacký and gave him ample opportunity to accuse the Slovak Communists of a lack of principle. He further accused them of flagrant disregard "for recovery and normalization of post-war conditions;" since they did not take into account the real needs of Slovakia or the interests of the Czechoslovak state, Fraštacký charged that they were interested in power only. The welfare of the state was secondary to them.

The editorial concluded with the warning that "the fate of the Slovak Democratic Party [was] the fate of Czechoslovak democracy," and cautioned that only a genuine purge of Slovak political life irrespective of party affiliation rather than a one-sided, slanderous campaign against one party would give Slovakia the healthy political climate of which she was in dire need.[17]

It was a gallant counter-attack on the part of the Czechoslovak democratic forces, a relatively rare phenomenon in those days, but it did not carry sufficient weight to undo the damage. The fact that courts of law had indeed proven the complicity of Obuch, Bugár and Kempný, along with the well-concerted Communist propaganda, proved too strong to preserve the Democrats' position in Slovakia. After much political manoeuvering behind the scenes, Prime Minister Gottwald was entrusted to go to Bratislava and to open negotiations there for a reconstituted Board of Commissioners.

As was to be expected, the jockeying for position on the new Board was long and tedious, with the Communists now attempting to terminate the Board's Democratic majority once and for all and the Democrats trying to save at least some of their old bastions. They were now willing to concede some of their portfolios to their Communist opponents, but they refused to give up the fruits of an election victory achieved by popular democratic vote by consenting to a Communist majority on the Board. Even before the fighting regarding the Board's new composition got under way, the controversy as to whether members of partisan groups and trade union representatives should be included had to be settled. Since both of these were rather heavily

Communist-dominated, the Democrats refused such a proposal and, in so doing, improved their chances for the eventual composition of the new Board of Commissioners. But, and quite clearly as a concession to the Communists, the leadership of the Democratic Party, on November 22nd, abrogated its one-time agreement with the Catholics.

On November 13th, Steinhardt reported that he had heard from a member of the cabinet that unless there were to be unforeseen developments during the next few days, the "new Board of Commissioners in Slovakia will consist of 7 Democrats, 5 Communists, 1 Freedom Party and 1 Slovak Social Democrat giving a comfortable majority to anti-Communists." The Ambassador had also learned that the Democrats were holding out for the continuation of General Ferjenčík as Commissioner of the Interior, while at the same time they were quite willing to relinquish the portfolio of Justice, though only to a member of the Freedom Party or Social Democratic Party, not a Communist. Finally, according to Steinhardt's information, the Communists had been on the defensive for the past two days of negotiations, "trying to save what they can from the defeat they are about to sustain."[18]

Steinhardt's sources proved fairly accurate. When agreement was finally reached and the composition of the new Board of Commissioners was announced, the Democrats could count six members against five for the Communists, one Freedom Party member, one Social Democrat and two non-party men. The Ambassador, who claimed to be familiar with the political convictions of some of the new members, interpreted this to mean that nine non-Communists now opposed five Communists, with General Ferjenčík "regarding himself as a neutral." What pleased him even more was the Democrats' ability to prevent the sensitive portfolios of Justice[19] and Agriculture from falling into Communist hands and to keep out of the newly constituted Board of Commissioners representatives of partisan and trade union groups, whom they considered little more than Communists in disguise.[20]

The Ambassador's ultimate comment, according to which "the total solution of the Slovak crisis which began with the resignation of the Slovak Board of Commissioners [was] in fact a severe setback for the Communists,"[21] is perhaps somewhat exaggerated in view of the fact that they did achieve the expulsion from the Board of compromised members and actually gained more seats than they had had on the old Board. Also, Gustav Husák, a Communist, was elected chairman of the reconstituted Board. A more even assessment of the outcome would be to say that justice had been done, since unworthy elements had indeed been purged from the ranks of the highest governmental organs of Slovakia without permitting such a purge to become a convenient tool of any one party. The broader implications of the Slovak crisis of the fall of 1947 were yet to come. Already, prior to its final settlement, Ambassador Steinhardt speculated as to "whether the Communists [would] be satisfied with a purge of the Slovak Democratic Party, thereby materially reducing the democratic strength in Slovakia and increasing the Communist prestige, or whether they intend to carry out the purge beyond Slovakia into the Czech non-Communist parties." He offered two replies to his own hypothetical question, an optimistic and a pessimistic one. He suggested that in the former case, "the present Communist drive [was] part of the election campaign to reverse the outcome of the election in May of 1946 by giving the Communists the majority in Slovakia — as a result of intimidation — and that the Communists believe that they will increase their strength in Bohemia and Moravia without completely crushing the opposition." Seen through the eyes of a pessimist, however, "the drive on the Slovak Democratic Party [was] merely the opening gun in a campaign of intimidation which will spread in due time to the leaders of the non-Communist parties in Czechoslovakia. It [would] probably be some time before we [would] know which plan the Communists had in mind."[22]

Present-day historians, writing with the hindsight of some twenty-five years, have no such doubts. Commenting on the ultimate aims of the Communist drive against the Slovak Democrats, Radomír Luža writes that the "Slovak November crisis" simply was a dress rehearsal for the Prague "February crisis."[23] The events of the weeks immediately succeeding the Slovak crisis prove Luža right; Ambassador Steinhardt did not have to wait long to get his answer.[24]

X

The Congress of the Social Democratic Party

Of paramount importance to the political future of Czechoslovakia, and closely watched by the Americans, was the forthcoming Congress of the country's Social Democratic Party. Czechoslovak Social Democracy traces its roots to the Austro-Hungarian Empire, where the party had been active since the last decades of the nineteenth century. It had always had a considerable following in highly industrialized Bohemia and when, in 1918, the old Empire disintegrated, the party continued its existence in the newly founded Czechoslovak Republic. Many prominent inter-war politicians belonged to it, and none other than the founder of the Republic, Thomas Masaryk, had frequently expressed his sympathy for the party's aims, albeit, as Head of State, he had no official party affiliation.

In the early 1920's, Social Democratic parties all over Europe underwent significant changes. Under the direct influence of the Russian Revolution and confronted with the success of the Bolsheviks, most of the parties split, with the left-wingers constituting themselves into Communist parties. Such was the case in Czechoslovakia. In 1920, the left wing of the Social Democratic Party became the Communist Party of Czechoslovakia. While only a fraction of Social Democrats left the party to join the ranks of the Communists, there remained within the party a not insignificant segment of members who, while continuing to adhere to the old label, increasingly veered to the left. These losses notwithstanding, the Social Democratic Party, during the twenty years of the first Czechoslovak Republic, remained a party of democratic and only mildly left political coloring, playing an important part in the political life of the state.

After Munich, the party was dissolved and during the course of the Second World War many of its members were exposed to German persecution. Those fortunate enough to escape went either to London or Moscow. While in London, Social Democrats experienced considerable difficulties in their dealings with President Beneš, then head of the Czechoslovak exile government based in the British capital. The Moscow group clustered around Zdeněk Fierlinger, former Czechoslovak envoy to the U.S.S.R. and a long-time friend and admirer of the Soviet Union. Although numerically smaller, the Moscow group proved far more adroit in the final negotiations for a provisional Czechoslovak government; when this government entered liberated Czechoslovakia,[1] in the spring of 1945, Zdeněk Fierlinger did so as Prime Minister. For the next year, until the first post-war elections in May of 1946, Fierlinger continued his close cooperation with the U.S.S.R. and the Czechoslovak Communists, most of whom had spent their exile in Moscow. It was largely due to Fierlinger's enormous influence in the Social Democratic Party that the party, as a bloc, sided with the Communists on many major issues in the National Assembly; when, in the 1946 elections, the Communists emerged as victors, the Social Democrats, although disappointed with the results in terms of their own following, obtained just enough votes to give the joint Communist-Social Democratic bloc a necessary majority in Parliament.[2]

Many old-time members of the party resented this close cooperation between Communists and Social Democrats and its concomitant erosion of the latter's political independence. They took particular offense with some of the Communists' high-handed methods in their display of government leadership, especially the Communists' handling of the state security organs, which they considered contrary to the democratic process. Nonetheless, like many of their colleagues from other political parties, they did not at first think it opportune to raise their voices in protest, in view of the great popularity which things Communist and Soviet enjoyed in Czechoslovakia immediately after the war. It was only during the latter part of 1946 and all during 1947 that the Social Democratic Party of Czechoslovakia began to reassert its political independence and to recover at least some of its lost ground.

On October 24, 1946, Ambassador Steinhardt, for the first time, reported on the widening rift between Social Democrats and Communists,[3] a topic which was to become one of the major items of Embassy reports for the next fifteen months. In early February of 1947, Chargé Bruins complemented his chief's assessments with further information on the subject. According to information obtained by the Embassy, the left wing of the Social Democratic Party had lost control of the party, a fact attested to by a recent directive to local party units which freed them from their previous obligation to vote with the

Communists on every occasion. Fierlinger, who now tried to stop, or at least to postpone, such a move, was overruled.[4] A further trend in this direction was evidenced in a speech given by Minister of Industry Bohumil Laušman, one of the Social Democrats' more moderate leaders; at a major party rally in the Southern Bohemian capital of České Budějovice, the Minister fondly recalled the memory of Thomas Masaryk, decidedly not a favorite among Czechoslovak Communists. In a rather piqued anti-Soviet stance, Laušman further told his audience that it should not blindly copy any foreign socialism, but instead "should adapt the principles of scientific and Marxian socialism to the Czechoslovak soil." Non-parliamentary rule was alien to Czech traditions, and Czechoslovakia could not "put up for a single minute with dictatorship."[5]

In a follow-up to this theme, this time at a Social Democratic convention in the Eastern Bohemian city of Pardubice, Laušman struck a similar note. Careful not to give offense to the Soviet Union and its Czech friends, the Minister of Industry stressed the Czechoslovaks' sympathies for the East, but he was quick to add that they entertained similar warm feelings for the West. The Czech people would go their own way, according to their own traditions: "they could neither be bought" nor "do they want to become a satellite." All the Czechs desired was harmony and cooperation between the Great Powers, in which they saw the best guarantee for their own happiness and independence. In conclusion, Laušman expressed the hope that the party's new strength would make itself manifest in the elections, scheduled for May of 1948.[6]

Ambassador Steinhardt, commenting on Laušman's speech, was careful not to overestimate its value in terms of an outright anti-Communist stance. While he liked the Minister's references to the Czechs' not becoming anyone's satellite and quite clearly saw in them a thinly veiled reference to the U.S.S.R., he also took note of the "cannot be bought" clause, unmistakably directed against the United States. Similarly, in his comments on a number of other points raised by Laušman, Steinhardt clearly distinguished between their pro-Western and pro-Eastern innuendos. Ultimately, however, the Ambassador seemed encouraged when Laušman, insisting that the forthcoming elections be held as scheduled, clearly showed his lack of sympathy for the recent Communist demands to have them postponed until a new constitution had been adopted. This open challenge, more than anything else, seemed to convince Steinhardt that the Social Democrats had more or less regained their political independence "and will resist intransigently Communist efforts to delay these elections."[7]

In a more specific attempt to assess the relative strength of the anti-Communist forces in the Social Democratic Party, Bruins reported in June that the less radical wing (under the leadership of Majer, the Minister of Food; Němec and Vojta Beneš, the President's brother) "is said to number about 22 of the party's 36 mandates [in the National Assembly] and may more often vote with the moderates than with the Communists."[8]

By mid-summer, it was clear that a split of considerable proportions had developed in the leadership of the Social Democratic Party; diplomatic dispatches during the months of June and July of 1947 kept belaboring the theme of such a rift. Steinhardt spoke of an "increasing tendency of Social Democrats to make common cause with Moderate parties" in order "to weaken Communist influence in [the] government" and predicted that this, in turn, might "oblige less radical Communist leaders to seek a measure of assistance from Moderates." As a result of all this, the Ambassador now concluded that the "Communists have lost [the] initiative [in the National Assembly], and are now on the defensive."[9]

It was an over optimistic prediction, as Steinhardt was soon to discover. The Communists might well have made minor concessions of a temporary nature and, in so doing, given the impression that they were on the defensive. Quite to the contrary, they were very much on the offensive and, by September, they had all but neutralized the initial gains of the moderate wing in the Social Democratic Party. After much hard bargaining behind the scenes and some formidable pressure applied by the Communists, the two parties issued a joint communiqué, according to which they pledged themselves to continue to strengthen their cooperation among "the basic elements of the working people," to continue to work for the establishment of a "Socialist bloc" within the National Front, to press for the enactment of a special law taxing millionaires, and to strive for harmonious cooperation within the National Front.[10] Both the "Socialist bloc" concept and the proposal for a millionaires' tax were projects dear to the Communists which they had propagated for some time and which, until recently, some Social Democrats had resisted. The joint communiqué made clear that whatever the resistance among moderate Social Democrats, it had now come to an end.

There was immense speculation about the sort of pressure applied by the Communists, with threats "of an explicit and drastic character" being mentioned.[11] Be this as it may, the communiqué caused great consternation among the party's rank and file; the relative ease with which the Communists achieved their victory left their opponents baffled. The seemingly unconditional surrender of Blažej Vilím, the Social Democratic Party's Secretary-General, and František Tymeš, another of its leaders of a moderate political complexion, only added to their consternation. Finally, the fact that the communiqué had been extracted from the Social Democrats without even a meeting of their executive added insult to injury. Václav Majer, the Minister of Food and one of the leading lights among the moderates, initially resigned, only to withdraw his resignation a few days later; Bohumil Laušman, the Minister of Industry and heretofore the most vocal spokesman for an independent Social Democratic Party, had equally not been consulted. It was clear that in the first major show-down between the party's left-wingers, led by Fierlinger, and the moderates, the former had carried the day. The moderates' disillusionment was particularly great since they had considered Vilím the strong-man of the party "who might be able to lead it out of the Communist fold," while Tymeš was viewed by them as the most likely candidate to succeed Fierlinger as chairman in the forthcoming Congress of the party, scheduled for November.[12]

First Secretary Charles Yost, who had compiled the information about the struggle within the Social Democrats' ranks, had previously reported with considerable accuracy. In view of this, his suspicions of Vilím's "surrender" is difficult to explain since it was Vilím who turned out to be the guiding spirit of the forthcoming Party Congress in which Fierlinger was unseated. Since, in this particular dispatch, there is no mention of even the "usually reliable source," frequently referred to in Embassy reports, one must surmise that an interested inside source must have misinformed him.

At any rate, the newly created situation brought about a serious crisis within the moderate elements of the Social Democratic Party. It provoked equal doom among the other non-Communist parties, especially the National Socialists who, for some time now, had been toying with the idea of drawing closer to the Social Democrats in an effort to build up resistance against the Communists. Best proof of the gravity of the incident, which by now had easily transcended the confines of mere inter-party politicking, was the sudden return of President Beneš from his summer vacation. This unexpected development made it clear that a crisis of major proportion was at hand.

Charles Yost, at the time the Embassy's chargé d'affaires, claimed to have some inside knowledge of the audience granted to Vilím and Tymeš by the President of the Republic. His report to Washington makes it clear that the two men got a severe dressing down from Beneš. The President reprimanded them for signing the joint Social Democratic-Communist communiqué and "thus creating a bloc within the National Front," an act he considered pernicious to the health of Czechoslovak political life. To leave no doubt in anyone's mind about his own position, Beneš, in a subsequent conversation with Food Minister Majer, changed his stance and "was very cordial with [Majer]" and refused to accept his resignation.[13] As far as Fierlinger, the party's chairman and the *deus ex machina* behind the communiqué, was concerned, President Beneš refused to even receive him, a gesture not altogether unexpected in view of the recent distrust with which he came to regard him.[14]

Prime Minister Gottwald, Fierlinger's Communist counterpart in the drafting of the communiqué, did not fare much better. According to Yost, Beneš confronted his Prime Minister with an outright accusation of "destroying the National Front and subverting [the] normal political life of [the] country." He assured Gottwald that even if the millionaires' tax legislation were rammed through the National Assembly, he would not sign it; he also upbraided the Prime Minister for the Communist tactics employed in extracting the joint Communist-Social Democratic declaration. Then, addressing himself to fundamental issues and revealing point blank his own political views, a rare occurrence during his three post-war years as President, Beneš bluntly stated that "he would not stand for non-Communist parties being eaten up one by one as had occurred in other eastern European countries." Finally, in his perhaps strongest statement ever, "he declared that in case of [a Communist] Putsch he would not ease [the] Communists' way by resigning or leaving [the] country." Nor did he have "any intention of dying for some time to come," although he had been ill.[15]

While the admonition to Vilím and Tymeš and the confrontation with Gottwald must undoubtedly have been humiliating to them personally, politically speaking, Communists and left-wing Social Democrats had carried the day. All that now remained for the moderate Social Democratic wing was to mend fences as best they could. As expected, the process of recovery from the unusually sharp and sudden setback was slow and painful. In their explanations and in the explanations of those domestic and foreign observers who attempted to get to the root of the sudden Social Democratic volte-face, there is constant reference to severe Communist pressure of all kinds. While some sources limit themselves to talking of threats of a general nature coupled with ardent appeals by the Communists for the preservation of socialist unity, other sources accessible to the United States Embassy go as far as mentioning direct intervention by the Soviet Army in Czechoslovakia should the Social Democrats fail to see the imminent danger to which socialism was exposed in that country.[16] Ambassador Steinhardt, in his unusually heavy correspondence on the subject, kept assuring the State Department that he would yet get to the root of the matter; but, neither he nor his First Secretary, Charles Yost, could ever pinpoint the exact cause.[17]

The allusion to direct Soviet Army intervention is by far the most extreme of all the alleged threats and no other source refers to it explicitly. There is one other reference to a talk between Vilím and a "controlled American source," according to which Vilím and Tymeš made the pact with the Communists to prevent instant elections and "something much worse which I [Vilím] won't mention." Vilím then claimed that by signing the agreement with the Communists, the Social Democrats really saved the political situation "and I [Vilím] do not use these words as a phrase."[18] It is conceivable, although by no means proven, that the "something much worse" might have meant an intervention by the Soviet Army; in the absence of any other evidence at this time, nothing further can be said.

The Embassy was more successful in pinning its hopes on the forthcoming Congress of the Social Democratic Party. So, indeed, were those Social Democrats who regretted the initial decisions of their party leaders to join ranks with the Communists and had now begun to raise their voices once again. The Social Democratic Youth Movement and the Social Democratic trade union organizations in the factories became the focal points of the revival of party independence. The former had for a long time resented the leftist leadership of Fierlinger; the latter, although by nature genuinely sympathetic to the cause of socialism, increasingly resented the constant pressure from their Communist fellow workers, to which they were exposed in their places of employment. Considering themselves the historical spearhead of the proletarian movement in Czechoslovakia, whose origins went back to Austria-Hungary and whose members fought for the causes of the working man long before the Communist Party of Czechoslovakia had even existed, they took unkindly to the frequent propaganda barrages by their Communist fellow workers. Finally, there were at least two men among the top leadership of the party who could be counted on to resist the pro-Fierlinger forces. Of the two, Václav Majer, Minister of Food, was by far the more resolute, though Bohumil Laušman, less outspoken in his anti-Communism, was the better politician. If Fierlinger was to be displaced, the more moderate and more politically astute Laušman would be likely to succeed him. This too was Steinhardt's prognosis, in which he was seconded by the British Embassy, which had placed its trust in "three or four well-informed sources." According to them, "chances are better than ever that Fierlinger [would] be removed as chairman of the Social Democrats" at the forthcoming Party Congress and that Laušman would succeed him in the post of party leader.[19]

In spite of these optimistic predictions, the Social Democratic Party as such was not regarded by Ambassador Steinhardt as "a more reliable buttress against Communism in Czechoslovakia than [it has been] in other Soviet satellite countries." Quite to the contrary, the party was "now weaker than ever and continued moreover to be torn by internal tensions." What Steinhardt feared was that "the mood to replace Fierlinger by Laušman" might not last until the November Congress, in spite of the presently prevailing desire by a considerable majority to oust Fierlinger.[20]

Other indications as to the difficulty of redressing the situation, so badly damaged for the moderate Social Democrats by the joint Communist-Social Democratic communiqué, came from Communist quarters. None other than Prime Minister Gottwald, chairman of the party, in an interview with the Prague correspondent of the *New York Herald-Tribune,* gave some indication that the joint pact between the two socialist parties might be a mere prelude to the formation of a single political party of the working class. Since, according to Gottwald, "it [was] evident that aside from the very young and the very old and sick people, there [were] only working people in this country,"[21] and because Gottwald saw fit to so inform the Western press, the spokesmen of the moderate parties now reasoned that such indeed was the Prime Minister's wish. At any rate, they so commented on Gottwald's interview in their own press organs, chiding him that even though he might head the Czechoslovak government, he knew little about the political mentality of Czechs and Slovaks who valued their individual conceptions of public affairs too much as to permit the formation of a single party.[22] Finally, the National Socialist Minister of Justice, Prokop Drtina, in a speech at a rally of his party in the Eastern Bohemian town of Kolín, concluded that the chief reason for the Communist-Social Democratic pact was the apprehension of the

Communists of failing to obtain a 51% vote in the forthcoming election.[23] Late in October, the Embassy claimed to have learned from its previously mentioned "controlled American source"[24] some of the details of the proposed restructuring in the Social Democratic Party and in the cabinet, should the forthcoming Party Congress bring about the ouster of chairman Fierlinger. In regard to the cabinet, there was special interest concerning a proposal for the abolition of two ministries, one of which was the Ministry of Information; it was headed by the rabid Communist, Václav Kopecký, and, ever since its creation in 1945, had caused particular aggravation to the moderates and President Beneš.[25] This proposal in itself led observers to believe that the anti-Fierlinger wing of the party had high hopes for success in the imminent show-down. But, as so often before with hopes of the moderates, these expectations also did not really correspond to the political realities of the day. If anything, they merely bespoke the essential inability of most moderate politicians to get to the root of the problem then prevalent in Czechoslovak politics.

Furthermore, it was clear that all was not well within the party and that the rift created by the September pact with the Communists had far from healed. A major statement of the party's policy, published in its daily press organ, *Právo lidu,* on October 19th, carefully explained some of the reasons for the pact and, in so doing, tried to exonerate its Social Democratic signatories; at the same time, in a move to placate its opponents, it protested the continued independence of the party.[26]

In view of this continued division within the Social Democratic Party, the outcome of the party's Congress, held in mid-November in the Moravian capital of Brno, must be seen as a success for the moderate wing and a repudiation of those members responsible for the conclusion of the Communist-Social Democratic pact two months earlier. As predicted, Laušman did indeed replace Fierlinger as chairman; at the same time, Fierlinger was also deprived of his Vice-Premiership in the government, a post in which he was succeeded by the party's Secretary, Vilím. The U.S. Ambassador, in his initial report on the Congress, stressed the secret ballot procedure in the election for chairman and party executive and, although he did not claim to be in possession of exact figures, gave the approximate final count as 280 votes for Laušman as against 180 for Fierlinger. Fierlinger, so Steinhardt reported, bluntly accused Vilím of working against him and being primarily responsible for his defeat. Although Steinhardt warned that "Laušman should not be regarded as a representative of the right-wing of [the] Party," he referred to the new party chairman as "no Fierlinger" and "by no means a Moscow stooge." While Laušman may well have "to cater somewhat to [the] working classes," the prime importance of his election was "that [the] Communists can no longer rely upon a slavish acceptance by [the] Social Democratic Party of any and every step they desire to take. To this extent [the] balance of power which [the] Social Democratic Party obtained as a result of the last election has been reestablished." He concluded that from now on the Communists would have to find other means of "maintaining their control of [the] government" than automatically counting upon Social Democratic support in any issue which they considered important. As for the person of the deposed Fierlinger, the Ambassador's comments displayed equal satisfaction. He referred to Fierlinger's ouster as "highly gratifying as eliminating from control of the Social Democratic Party an individual who as has now been demonstrated sought with considerable success to make his party an appendage to [the] Communist Party."[27]

Less enthusiastic about the outcome of the Congress, and for obvious reasons, were the pro-Fierlinger forces in the Social Democratic Party and, even more so, the Communists. The former gave vent to their anger and disappointment in an open letter to the party's Congress, in which they pledged their continued loyalty, but protested some of the proceedings and some of the "anti-Soviet" speeches given during the deliberations.[28] *Rudé právo,* the Communist daily which published the letter, added some of its own remarks of protest and disappointment. It deplored the removal of Fierlinger and expressed fear that his disappearance from the party leadership would remove a bulwark against "reactionaries and corrupters." Attempting to connect the deposed leader with the larger interests of Czechoslovakia, it referred to him as one who had played an important part in the "National Liberation Movement," a part for which he was held in "great esteem" by members of the Social Democratic Party. The paper expressed particular bitterness over the positive reaction to Fierlinger's ouster by the French socialists, the "party of Léon Blum which approved Munich."[29] Finally, and almost a month after the Congress, André Simone [Katz], editor of *Rudé právo,* attempted to connect the U.S. Embassy with some of the attacks on Fierlinger, when he quoted Joseph Alsop's most recent articles on Czechoslovakia.[30] Alsop referred to the "creeping terror in Prague" and depicted Fierlinger, the "old patriot" and "young betrayer" as a short, sharp-looking man with shifty eyes and a talent for survival, who "should no longer be regarded as a loyal Czech." Simone wondered who supplied Alsop with all this information about Fierlinger, adding sarcastically, "obviously not the American Embassy."[31]

President Beneš seemed particularly pleased with the outcome of the Social Democratic Congress; he openly confided to Ambassador Steinhardt that he considered it a "major victory"for which he, Beneš, gladly took credit. He assured the Ambassador that he would continue to do his best "towards making the Social Democratic Party as independent and non-Communist as possible."[32] To Beneš, who believed that he had been betrayed by his erstwhile friend and close political associate,[33] the fall of Fierlinger proved especially gratifying. As events turned out, it was a short-lived success for the ailing President.

Embassy spokesmen, rather obviously, were just as pleased with the outcome of events as was the Czechoslovak President. Steinhardt, who had taken home leave in late November to undergo an operation, announced, shortly after his arrival in the United States that, as of now, "the Social Democrats are holding the balance of political power in the country"; his statement was prominently featured in *Právo lidu.*[34] John Bruins, the Embassy's senior Counselor who once again acted as chief of the mission during the Ambassador's absence, reported that "the more moderate elements [in the party] have now taken the initiative" and credited Beneš with a lion's share of their success. As to Fierlinger's political future, Bruins, whose information was based on "recent conversations with several members of [the] Executive Committee of the party,"speculated that the deposed Social Democratic leader might be offered the ambassadorship to France, although it was doubtful that he would accept, since continued absence from the country would further erode his political base."[35]

For the Social Democratic leadership, the explanation of the changes resulting from the recent Congress was somewhat more complex. An editorial in the party's weekly, *Svět práce,* conveys some of the difficulties and complexities of the whole process of Fierlinger's unseating and his replacement by Laušman, a man of the center rather than a right-winger, who would have been unacceptable. It also made clear that "there was no dispute [at the Congress] as far as the party's action program was concerned. Nor about the whole East-West relationship, foreign policy, or the agreement with the Communists of September 12, 1947." The dispute arose among two factions, one of which "swears by democracy and curses socialism, the other swears by socialism and curses all the conventions of parliamentary democracy." What really mattered was the liquidation of all the rumors about the party's loss of independence in the future: "Instead of the outstanding diplomat, the party now puts at its head a robust and firm leader, whose roots are deeply intertwined with those of the party . . . Laušman is young [44 years old] — he also has the talent and possibility to lead the party to greater importance in the struggle for application of democratic and socialist forces in the state."[36]

The careful wording clearly attests to the fact that, although defeated, Fierlinger and his men had not been eliminated as political forces in the Social Democratic Party. Nonetheless, some of the fruits of the Brno Congress could be seen almost immediately. The party, as a whole, drew somewhat closer to the National Socialists; its contacts with the Communists were no longer as frequent as before. Similarly noticeable was the increased stress on democratic procedure and gradual de-emphasis of socialism. The party's left did not take its defeat lying down, however. Some of its leading members organized their own club within the party and began to publish their own periodical. They continued to support the Communists and, if necessary, were willing to split the party over this issue.[37]

Impressive as it was, the success of the moderates was too circumscribed to be of much avail in the immediate future. The fact that it came only three months before the Communist takeover further diminished its practical value. But neither of these observations should detract from the fact that the victory was genuine and convincing.[38] In this sense, at least, it was one of democracy's few triumphs in post-war Czechoslovakia.

XI

The Final Months

Political tension in the country increased considerably as 1947 drew to a close. Although the Communists had made clear their continuous political strength in the recent Slovak crisis, as indeed they had during the Marshall Plan controversy, there were a number of indications of their decreasing popular support. The moderates, who had been dealt severe setbacks in the above-mentioned issues, regained some of their lost confidence from the outcome of the recent Social Democratic Party Congress, as well as from the results of the various university student elections. But in spite of the overall optimistic outlook for more favorable results in the May elections, the moderate parties continued to suffer from lack of effective leadership and little coordination amongst themselves. Thus, notwithstanding the personal courage of individuals within their ranks, neither National Socialists nor the People's Catholic Party gave its members the same clear-cut direction which the Communist rank-and-file got from their leadership. As for the Social Democratic leaders, who had just recently emerged at the top of their party, they were, as yet, rather cautious in order not to jeopardize their hard contested victory by any show of anti-Communism. In short, the cooperation among the parties of the National Front, never ideal, but always sufficient to maintain the political equilibrium, was breaking up. Sessions of the National Front and meetings in the Council of Ministers grew in acerbity, as did speeches in Parliament and polemics in the press and on the radio. In the latter two, the Communists had a distinct advantage. While there was considerable freedom of speech and press, certain topics, such as the Czechoslovak-Soviet alliance and references to Soviet leaders, had to be treated with care and delicacy. Churchill and Roosevelt could be attacked openly, not so Stalin and Molotov. To find fault with the U.S.S.R. and the ideas its leaders professed was, at best, a risky business for a Czech newspaperman or broadcaster; it was better to abstain from criticizing them altogether. Even in the National Assembly, where parliamentary immunity gave the deputies some measure of protection not readily available to the ordinary citizen, it was impolitic to make open anti-Soviet remarks. Moderates could and did attack Czechoslovak Communists, but here, too, great care had to be taken so as not to offend the U.S.S.R. in the process. But when compared with the other "people's democracies," there was unquestionably more freedom in Czechoslovakia than in any others. However, by Western standards, Czechoslovak freedom and democracy were no longer what they used to be in Masaryk's pre-Munich republic.

After the recent purges of anti-Communists in Hungary, and after Czechoslovakia's forced withdrawal from the Marshall Plan, there was concern in the West lest a similar fate befall Czechoslovakia, now the last of the Soviet bloc countries which had not fallen under complete Soviet domination. Both the Department of State and its listening posts abroad observed events carefully and weighed the possibilities of America's future policies towards Czechoslovakia. Already in late July of 1947, H. Freeman Matthews, the Director of the Department's Office of European Affairs, addressed a secret communication to the Under Secretary of State, Dean Acheson, in which he attempted to chart "the probable course of developments in Czechoslovakia and possible action by the United States in regard thereto." Briefly surveying some of the recent events, such as the journey of the Czechoslovak ministers to Moscow, the Communist dominance in the government and the overall political climate and state of personal freedom, Matthews turned to foreign affairs. In an attempt to explain "Czechoslovak subservience to Soviet wishes," he suggested that it was due to the Czechs' conviction of an "ever present recurrent German threat, the memory of Munich, and the confidence in the alliance with the Soviet Union as the most certain security against a resurgent Germany," but also to the realization, on the part of the moderates, that their chances of resisting events were none too good, in view of the "slightest prospect of effective assistance from any source." Expanded Czechoslovak trade and cultural relations with the U.S.S.R. and Eastern Europe only further tended "to bring about the integration of Czechoslovakia with the other countries in the Soviet orbit."

Speculating about future Soviet interference in Czechoslovak domestic affairs, Matthews considered it a distinct possibility, pointing to Communist attempts to "disentegrate [sic] the Slovak Democrats, with the Czech parties standing aside," the purge of "saboteurs" in the "Catholic or National Socialist parties," and the split within the ranks of the Social Democrats "into a 'Unity' party and an unrecognized rump." These were all good prognostications, as the future would show.

He subsequently recommended the following course of action for the United States government in its future relations with Prague: The withholding of "consideration of any grant of credit," since such action would only aid the present Communist leadership in strengthening and consolidating its hold. Such, after all, had been the case with "our generous UNRRA aid," which provided the Communists with an opportunity to prove that governments led by them could obtain Western aid. "If reconstruction loans and large commercial loans were made available at this time to the nationalized Czech industry they would only provide much needed capital to finance the Two-Year Plan, to the success of which Communist prestige is committed." Similarly, reconstruction loans by the International Bank should be suspended until future trends in Czechoslovak politics could be seen more clearly.

In contrast to these stern economic measures, the Czechoslovak people should be dealt with courteously, and cultural relations as well as private trade should be supported. Issues stemming from Lend-Lease, debts of the U.S. Army, etc., should be handled in "an amicable spirit of concession and cooperation," since "none of these sources of difference is worth incurring Czech ill-will."

Czechoslovak parties which manifested their anti-Communism too belligerently should be discouraged from doing so, and the dangers of such action should be pointed out to them. "A strictly hands-off attitude should be maintained." In case of a Communist coup or terror against opposition groups, the United States should "establish as a matter of public record the character and extent of Soviet responsibility." The case should be brought before the United Nations, and asylum should be granted to Czechoslovak refugees in the United States zones of occupation in Germany and Austria.

So much, then, for the punitive action and the steps to be taken in case Czechoslovakia succumbed to Soviet domination. If, however, the Czechs were to continue their previous independence in domestic matters, "every attempt should be made to promote cultural interchange . . . to carry on an active information program in Czechoslovakia, to develop and strengthen contacts with leaders among the non-Communist groups. . . ." Also, in case of such a development, the "United States should encourage in every feasible way the growth of trade between Czechoslovakia and Western European countries even though this may prove of some temporary advantage to the Communist Party by assisting the implementation of the Two-Year Plan." Long-range benefits would clearly outweigh such temporary advantages to the Communists. Even though things did not look too bright at the present, "in view of the many evidences that the eventual objective of the Soviet Government is complete control of all countries within the Soviet orbit," the United States, while cautious, should be ready.[1]

Such were the proposed policies of Washington. Although it was not very likely that the moderates would be able to hold their positions, the United States should have contingency plans. But, as the news about Czechoslovakia kept arriving in the American capital, the need for such plans seemed ever more remote. Typical of some of the pessimistic signals was a dispatch of the United States Embassy in London. In it, Washington was apprised of the attitude of the British Foreign Office towards events in Czechoslovakia: the Foreign Office "is definitely worried about recent political developments in Czechoslovakia. It is felt in London that Communists are making progress there and in elections next spring will make real gains." According to the dispatch, "the Communists were exploiting [the] situation created by Czechoslovakia's withdrawal from participation in [the] Marshall proposals and endeavoring to influence [the] Czech masses to vote for closer cooperation with the U.S.S.R. and [the] East European zone." Thus, in spite of President Beneš' predictions to the contrary, the British Foreign Office felt that the strength of the Czechoslovak Communist Party was increasing.[2]

From closer quarters, the American Embassy in Prague, came a report emanating from sources close to the Slovak Democratic Party which pointed to the uncertainty of Czechoslovakia's immediate political future. Communist strategy, it was argued, "was still fluid and precise application in coming months will depend on the world situation." Much also depended on the general climate of East-West political relations. If antagonism between the two "became deeper, Communist efforts [in Czechoslovakia] will become greater." Ambassador Steinhardt, who talked at length with some of the leaders of the Slovak Democrats, concurred in their views. He further reported that "Democratic leaders believe, from a document they obtained secretly that the Communists plan no violent action for the time being." This same document, referring to a clandestine Communist attempt to arm the masses of Slovak partisans, also mentioned the failure of this endeavor and indicated that other means to overcome democratic opposition would have to be found. Thus, while definitely less pessi-

mistic than London, there clearly was concern in the American
diplomatic community in Prague about Czechoslovakia's future political course.[3]
   The two reports are in marked contrast to a dispatch from Prague of
only a week before. In it, the Embassy had appraised the country's
future in somewhat brighter and more optimistic terms:

> The Communists have undoubtedly lost some ground with the
> electorate since May 1946 and would probably not venture on new
> elections without a firm alliance with a tame Social Democracy. At all
> events, whatever their object and their time table may be, there can be
> little question that both the over-all Moscow party line and the
> struggle for position within the Czech party itself will result in a
> continued tactic of provoking recurring political crisis [sic] which
> create the atmosphere of tension and disorder on which the Russians
> thrive.[4]

The increased apprehension which now characterized the analyses of
the Czechoslovak situation by U.S. diplomats was in itself sufficient
indication of the steadily worsening political climate in the country.
Already on October 21st, a bare three weeks after his cautiously
optimistic prognosis, Steinhardt called the internal and the international situation as relating to Czechoslovakia "more bitter and
tense."[5] Again pointing to the overall international situation as a
determining factor for Czechoslovakia's internal conditions, he
singled out the recent "Cominform manifesto"[6] and the frequent
heated exchanges between East and West in the United Nations as
ominous factors. The increasing references to the U.S.S.R. were in
themselves a good indication of the gravity of the situation.
   Some non-Communist politicians who confided in the American
Ambassador were asking him and his staff their opinion "as to whether
the Soviet Army would move in in the last analysis, if a completely
subservient Czechoslovak government could not otherwise be established." Others, seemingly less pessimistic, "reassure themselves in
their soul-searching by reasoning that the Kremlin must realize that
military occupation of Czechoslovakia must surely lead to war, probably not at once, but within a period of a year or two (as in 1938–39),
and that the Soviet Union is not prepared to undertake now a severe
risk of war."[7]
   In an interesting distinction between Hungarian and Czechoslovak
conditions, Steinhardt pointed out that Soviet intervention directly

into Czechoslovakia would necessitate an invasion of Soviet troops into the country, whereas in Hungary no such drastic step was required, given the fact that Soviet troops had already been stationed there. Finally, the Ambassador referred to the hopes of those Czechs who equated Washington policymakers with Bismarck, in the sense that, like the German Chancellor, they were well aware that "the master of Bohemia was the master of Europe" and that the United Nations was not likely to permit such a prestigious position to fall into Soviet hands.[8] One can only charitably conclude that Laurence Steinhardt was wrong on both counts, in his prognosis of Bohemia's future as well as in his estimate of Washington's political acumen.

Late in October, Steinhardt submitted a long report dealing once again with the "increase in political tension" in Czechoslovakia. This time, the Ambassador felt compelled to explain at some length the "character and history" of the Czechoslovaks, which he thought important for a proper understanding of the whole Czech situation. Referring to the Czechs as "industrious, individualistic, complaining and stubborn," he also called them "highly literate" and showered much praise on their desire for modernity and their democratic instincts. In this respect, as indeed in many others, they differed from the rest of Slavdom. Only in one respect did they exhibit typically Slav characteristics — in "their hatred of the Germans." So much for the virtues of the Czechs. As for their vices, Steinhardt cited "nobility and courage as usually inconspicuous in the Czech character. For centuries they have survived by bowing their heads to the waves of conquest which have rolled over Europe."[9] These remarks added little, if anything, to a true understanding of the situation. As on occasion he had done before, Steinhardt had pontificated about things of which he had only routine knowledge. As was the case with his disastrous prognostications of the 1946 election results, he once again confounded his sincere liking of the Czechs and their democratic cause with a thorough knowledge of things Czech which he simply did not possess.

After this attempt to explain the historical and psychological elements in the whole Czechoslovak situation, Steinhardt returned to safer ground and briefly summarized Czechoslovak events since 1945. As he saw it, things had gone relatively well until the summer of 1947 when "another picture began to unfold." A variety of factors ranging from crop shortages to mismanagement of some of the nationalized industries contributed to the present unsatisfactory state of affairs. Failure by the Soviet Union to deliver much needed wheat and raw materials, and the political tension among the Great Powers further aggravated the Czechoslovak political situation. This in turn led to a reaction of fear among the democratic-minded part of the population; they began to fear "(1) a Soviet coup such as occurred in Hungary, (2) economic privation, and (3) isolation from the West." [10] However, and in spite of the indications by a few highly placed anti-Communists that they might leave the country if the situation got worse, "there [was] no general hysteria in this direction." Furthermore, most Czechoslovaks felt that continuous cooperation with the U.S.S.R. gave them some degree of protection against a direct Soviet invasion and, consequently, "that [this] policy must be maintained if the country is to retain its present limited degree of autonomy." [11]

In view of all this, Steinhardt felt that "the tension described appears to be playing into our hands and to call for no immediate change in our policy of (1) no loans, (2) continued business relations where possible, and (3) keeping the hopes alive of loans at some time in the undefined future." [12] At the very time when the Ambassador from the United States advised his government to continue its policy of economic restraint, and contrary to what he had just reported to Washington, the U.S.S.R. was delivering large shipments of wheat to Czechoslovakia. No doubt, given their own precarious economic state, the Russians could ill afford to export valuable foodstuffs, but, unlike their American counterparts in Washington and Prague, Soviet diplomats correctly assessed the political advantages to be gained from such a gesture. While Laurence Steinhardt was philosophizing about Czech history and mentality, hoping that things would somehow work themselves out in favor of the democratic cause, large signs all over the country reminded the Czechoslovak population of its "friend in need," as the Communists, sponsoring this propaganda, would affectionately refer to the "Big Soviet brother."

A much more realistic approach to the whole problem emerges from the Ambassador's next communication. In it, he correctly recognized the principal strength of the Communists among the Czechoslovak electorate: the successful exploitation of the people's fears of German strength and potential revenge. Whatever else Czechs and Slovaks might have thought about Communism and Soviet Russia, even many a non-Communist viewed that party and its Russian sponsors as the main bulwark against a resurgent Germany. Whatever other pro-Western trends and likings much of the population might exhibit, and in spite of a dislike for Marxism by a majority of the people, the fear of Germany "continues to supresss their more normal reactions and to prevent many voters from voting their convictions." This, in turn, was instantly recognized by the Communists, who were "exploiting to the fullest the insidious fear-complex engendered by the German war-time regime." Thus, the U.S. policy recently proclaimed by Secretary Byrnes of rehabilitating devastated Germany could not have come at a more opportune time for the Prague Communists. In addition, so Steinhardt concluded, the "[Communist] party continues to be aggressive and vocal . . . it now seem[ed] improbable that there would be any important diminution in the number of Communist votes in the next election unless the non-Communist parties [were] able effectively to seize and hold the offensive, of which at present there [were] no real indications."[13]

The Ambassador's comments on the lack of initiative on the part of the non-Communist parties were well taken. Only infrequently, when Communist demands would go too far, would their opponents make common cause and resort to joint action. For example, during a government meeting in early November, they rejected a Communist request for participation in the meetings by partisans and representatives of industrial and agricultural workers' organizations, all Communist controlled. This rare display of harmony and common purpose among the non-Communists encouraged Steinhardt and prompted him to remark that ". . . barring any unforeseen developments and on the assumption that the anti-Communist leaders maintain their cooperation of the past three or four days and do not succumb to fear, it is quite possible that the present crisis will be surmounted without any fundamental change in [the] character of the government."[14] That such a show of strength did not miss its intended effect is best illustrated by the fact that in spite of protests by the excluded trade unions and workers' organizations, the non-Communists weathered the storm. Already on the following day, Steinhardt reported that "meanwhile [the] atmosphere in Praha [was] calm and the Communist press [was] somewhat less violent than on similar previous occasions."[15]

Such intervals of relative peace and calm were brief and not necessarily indicative of the overall picture. While the Communist Minister of Information, Václav Kopecký, continued his tirade against the West,[16] Prime Minister Gottwald, in a meeting with Beneš, told the President "that it was becoming increasingly difficult for him, as Prime Minister and leader of the Communist Party, to function and that in order to obtain desired 'cooperation' from [the] non-Communist leaders, it might become necessary to purge [the] non-Communist parties." To this open threat of unilateral action, Beneš is reported to have responded equally bluntly by telling Gottwald that such a purge would "have to begin with [him]."[17] Such brutal frankness in a formal exchange of views between President and Prime Minister is in itself indicative of the seriousness of the crisis.

The possibility of a Communist coup was being seriously considered for the first time in late November. It had been mentioned before in some of the Embassy's dispatches, but so far largely in a purely hypothetical context. This time, the threat of a coup was being presented as a real possibility. "I believe it may be possible," the Ambassador wrote, "that the Communists, thwarted in their attempt to gain control within the parliamentary framework, may decide to stay without it and use force. However, that will be for Praha, if not Moscow to decide. And time will tell the result. At the same time, no matter what, I imagine they will step up their anti-American attack."[18] This distinction between Czechoslovak Communists and the Soviet Union is critical. Rarely, if ever before, did Steinhardt emphasize the difference between them. In retrospect, one can only speculate whether recognition, by American policymakers, of this important fact might not have decisively influenced United States policy towards Czechoslovakia. As it turned out, this belated recognition on the Ambassador's part that Czechoslovak Communism might indeed have some identity of its own was only to come in his last report prior to the coup. Steinhardt, who had been in ill health for some time, returned to the United States to seek medical treatment and did not return to Prague until February 21, 1948. By that time, he was little more than a silent spectator to the Communist coup.

Thus, as had been the case on previous occasions of the Ambassador's absence, Counselor John Bruins assumed charge of the Prague Embassy. While some of his earlier reports reveal a guarded optimism, Bruins, like his chief of mission, harbored no illusions about the gravity of the overall situation. He might well have reported with some satisfaction that in the recently held student elections at Charles University the Communist candidates were soundly trounced, defeated in some of their traditional strongholds,[19] but, important as such a specific success of their opponents was, it could only briefly divert attention from the overall picture. By mid-December, Bruins wrote that the "Embassy's contacts agreed that [the] present comparative political calm [was] unlikely to last beyond mid-January when Communists [were] expected to begin [their] pressure campaign." Once again, both prognosis and timing were "based on the expected termination of the London Foreign Ministers Conference." But, like

Steinhardt in his prior communications, Bruins regretted the fact that the "Czechoslovak moderates seem unable to shake their defensive psychosis and seize [the] present opportunity to take [the] initiative."[20] Bruins returned to the prospect of a possible coup a few days later. He reported on his latest contacts with Czechoslovak politicians and men in public life. While Prime Minister Gottwald, in a recent interview with an American correspondent, saw no need to use force in the Communists' attempt to gain 51% of the vote in the forthcoming elections and was "serenely confident" that such a result could be achieved by legal means, there were other indications which at least pointed to the contrary.[21] Purges of ranking non-Communist officials in the police, particularly in the special security forces, as well as similar cleansing operations in the Army, were in themselves indications of the Communists' unwillingness to achieve their aims by democratic methods. Finally, a report from Vice Consul Claiborne Pell in the Slovak capital of Bratislava, where he obtained an interview with the Secretary-General of the Slovak Communist Party, Štefan Baštovanský, produced no clear-cut response. In a discussion pertaining to the aims of the Communists in Czechoslovakia, Baštovanský assured his questioner that these were "limited" and "specific" in scope. When pressed by Pell "as to whether the Slovak Communists would depart from Parliamentary methods to attain their objectives, if thwarted within the Parliamentary framework, *he likewise would not categorically reply, but said he didn't think force would be necessary.*" To Pell's remark that Moscow, in both theory and practice, had never ruled out violence as a means of achieving desired aims and that his evasiveness on this point differed markedly from the capital of world Communism, Baštovanský "wriggled" and insisted "that Czechoslovak Communism and Russian Communism were horses of two different colors." From all this, Pell concluded that the Slovak Communists who "were certain they could not gain even a sizable minority of the Slovak vote" by legal means, simply "had not yet made a fixed decision whether or not to take extra-legal measures to win."[22]

President Beneš' Christmas message sought to calm passions and to a degree even chided the political left when he accused it of "professing socialism" as a "morally superior way of life." The President's praise for the university students, who had, in the recent university elections, purged their own governing bodies of Communist influence, was another tactic on Beneš' part to show where his own sympathies lay.[23] But, noble as such attempts were, they were also futile because they simply did not constitute effective counterpressure to the current fullfledged Communist offensive.

Bruins sent Steinhardt an extensive report early in the new year in order to apprise him of the rapidly changing events. Yet, in spite of the rather tense situation in Prague, the chargé dealt largely with internal embassy matters and only briefly alluded to Czechoslovak politics. "There are the usual number of rumors and alarms. Some of the alarmists place us definitely behind the Iron Curtain by the 15th of January including M. Bidault according to an info telegram from Caffrey today. I believe that the election campaign will soon be stepped up but do not thus far have the feeling of any dire impending events hanging over our heads."[24]

As the moderates were slowly losing ground, Bruins decided that the time had come to bolster their morale and to strengthen their political position by support from the West. Well aware "of very friendly pro-Western sentiment in this country," he suggested that the United States "make some gesture before the elections." The chargé was also mindful that outright financial help "would immediately be open to the charge of trying to buy the souls of Central Europeans"; he therefore proposed "a quick Commercial Treaty or Cultural Treaty or both." Such action, he thought, "would show that [the United States] does not intend to 'desert' this country." In turn, from a purely propagandistic viewpoint, a cultural treaty would be a minor coup, since such a treaty would be the first of its kind concluded with any country in Europe. Provided that the ambassador would approve such a course of action, he beseeched Steinhardt to get "something done promptly," being all too familiar, from his own long diplomatic experience, with the "tempo of our [United States'] usual treaty correspondence." It was not too late and, according to Bruins, the Communists were now somewhat more vulnerable in view of the fact that the U.S.S.R. was now reliably reported as being opposed to the transfer of other minorities (especially Hungarians) from Czecho-slovakia, a point that could be ably exploited by the fiercely nationalist Communist opposition.[25]

On February 5th, a report by the U.S. Military attaché in Prague, Lt. Col. Foote, mentioned "vicious criticism of the U.S." in the Czech press as a violation of an agreement concluded in the fall of 1947 between Steinhardt and Gottwald.[26] The focus of the Communist attacks against the United States centered once again on the whole question of the liberation of Prague, an issue which by now had become a favorite anti-American theme in the Communist press. This time, though, the story was further embellished by additional informa-tion furnished by Soviet officers "who allegedly took part in the liberation by the RED ARMY." The United States was further being accused of restoring the "old NAZI intelligence net" in conjunction with the British in their respective zones of occupied Germany.[27] Colonel Foote gauged Czech reactions correctly when he stated that "such articles, if repeated often enough, are bound to sow some seeds of belief in the Czech mind and will certainly be used to their best propaganda advantage against democratic leaders in the election."[28] Like other foreign observers, he rightly pointed to the continuous Czechoslovak fear of a resurgent Germany and that country's dependence on the U.S.S.R. for the prevention of just such an occurrence.

As late as January 28th, less than a month before the Prague coup, Bruins expressed the opinion that "80 per cent of [the] Czech people favor Western style democracy over Communism but timidity and expedience render most of them inarticulate." In an eleventh-hour attempt to make up for lost time and anxious to "materially consolidate this pro-Western sentiment," Bruins strongly urged the State Department to conclude "without delay" both a commercial and a cultural treaty with Czechoslovakia.[29] He had done so before, but this time he took the proposed American offensive one step further by suggesting the publication of the "American documents in Czechoslovakia on [the] true story of [the] liberation of Praha."[30]

In Steinhardt's absence, Bruins proceeded with laying the groundwork for the commercial treaty. In consultation with Acting Foreign Minister Clementis and Minister of Foreign Trade Ripka, he seemed to have satisfied himself that the Communists would not obstruct conclusion of such an agreement; on the contrary, "they [were] well aware [that] Czechoslovakia needs increased trade with [the] U.S." The chargé hoped to conclude the preparatory stages "so that when [the Ambassador] returns there [would] be concrete basis for negotiations." In view of the overall uncertain conditions in Eastern Europe, he advocated a short-term commercial treaty in preference to some long-term arrangement.[31]

A similarly expedient and unceremonious approach was to be taken in the proposed cultural agreement. Here, Bruins referred to a cultural treaty concluded only recently (June, 1947) between Czechoslovakia and the United Kingdom by the simple diplomatic device of an exchange of notes. In both instances, however, it was the propaganda value rather than the intrinsic benefits of commercial or cultural arrangements between the two countries which Bruins intended to exploit: "What they [Czechoslovaks] need most is moral support.

They do not want to feel deserted."[32] In respect to the documents relating to the liberation of Prague, Bruins' contemplated exploitation for propaganda purposes would obviously have been even more of a trump card. He therefore took the necessary steps to obtain their declassification and release by the Department of the Army at the earliest possible date.

It would seem obvious from all the above that John Bruins entertained earnest hopes that the hour was not too late and that the situation in Czechoslovakia could be redressed in favor of the moderate parties. His contacts in President Beneš' entourage led him to believe so, since he claimed to have reliable information emanating from "trusted sources close to the President" that Beneš would "insist" on a non-Communist Prime Minister after the 1948 elections, "if the Communists did not gain materially in them."[33] In other words, it was not necessary for any one non-Communist party to emerge as the strongest as long as the moderates as a group did not lose ground to the Communists. Bruins' report constitutes one of the strongest, if not the strongest, appeals made by American diplomacy on behalf of Czechoslovakia. It also represents one of the few attempts to deal with Czechoslovakia methodically and with a clearly defined goal, something conspicuously absent in the preceding post-war period.

Steinhardt, still in the United States, obviously approved of Bruins' initiative; in a letter addressed to Harold C. Vedeler of the State Department's Central European Division, he supported both the commercial and cultural treaties. Like Bruins, he too had propaganda and moral support for the moderates as his main objective when he told Vedeler that "even if it [the commercial treaty] is of no consequence and has to be revised in the near future," it was of signal importance nonetheless.[34] He referred to the proposed cultural treaty in similarly nonchalant terms, expressing the view that "just a few pious words that commit no one to anything . . . [were] better than nothing." In an almost underhanded manner, Steinhardt added that even a simple "declaration of intent" which gullible Czechoslovak newspaper readers would hardly distinguish from a formal treaty might serve the purpose: "I think we could get away with this."[35] Both remarks are an expressive commentary on the sad state of affairs into which Washington's relations with Prague had now fallen.

With unprecedented speed, Washington agreed in principle to the opening of negotiations on both commercial and cultural fronts. First Vedeler[36] and then Secretary of State Marshall[37] himself gave the necessary preliminary authorizations. As things turned out, the effectiveness of the proposed measures never came to a test.

While Washington, at last, began to take concrete steps to shore up its position in Czechoslovakia, events in Prague, as seen from an American point of view, took a decisive turn for the worse. On January 29th, Bruins reported that the "main Communist thrust [was] now directed against Czechoslovak 'reactionaries' in general and National Socialists [now accused of close collaboration with the Slovak Democrats] in particular and [the] United States' 'imperialist' foreign policy." The specific charge against the United States consisted in its "motivating [an] anti-Soviet campaign (publication of German F.O. documents) to conceal United States plans in Germany." Bruins considered such "mobilization of Communist heavy artillery" against National Socialists and the two other outspokenly anti-Communist parties, the Populists and the Slovak Democrats, "logical in view of . . . the unimaginative and ineffective Catholic Populist Party campaign and [the] weakening of [the] Slovak Democratic Party" under Communist pressure.[38]

Three days later, the Prague Embassy, for the first time, dealt with the issue which eventually proved to be the crux of the governmental crisis preceding the coup. A report centered on the question of the Communist Minister of the Interior's high-handed and illegal conduct. In particular, Minister Nosek was accused of "terroristic methods used by the police" and of "discrimination against non-Communists in [the] Czechoslovak police."[39] For this, Nosek had been under attack for the past two months, first by the National Assembly's Security Committee (chaired by the National Socialist deputy Ota Hora) and, more recently, by the non-Communist ministers in the regular meetings of the government. After some detailed discussions of what exactly had happened, Bruins commented that such Communist tactics (replacement of non-Communists by Communists in the various security organs) had successfully been used in other East European countries and were now "being implemented here apparently in preparation for eventualities." Not even Bruins' final sentence, in which he characterized the new "common stand taken by National Socialists and Social Democrats" as one useful in "bringing the issue before [the] public," could conceal the chargé's grave concern with the steadily worsening political situation.[40]

XII

The Final Days

The gravity of the situation notwithstanding, the parliamentary session of February 5th, devoted primarily to fixing an exact date for the elections due to be held in the spring of 1948, gave no overt indication that the division among the parties was more than usual. While each of them tried to have elections at a date which they considered most suitable for their own cause, the overall tone of the discussions did not appear out of the ordinary.[1] In his comments on the session, Bruins wrote that the Communists preferred May 2 to any other date, "presumably to obtain benefit of May Day publicity"; he added, however, that "there [was] no indication that [the] Communists [were] trying to avoid any election at all." In conclusion, he expressed the view that "it appears [that] the election date [would] be settled by compromise."[2]

The atmosphere was entirely different in both sessions of the government on February 17th and the gathering of the National Front on the following day. On both occasions, the National Socialists attempted to force the Communists to instruct Interior Minister Nosek to rescind his discriminatory orders dealing with the removal of ranking, non-Communist police officers. Prime Minister Gottwald, who up until then had temporized on the whole matter by arguing that Nosek's illness made it impossible for him to defend himself in person, obviously had run out of excuses and now attempted to defer the matter on technical grounds. Gottwald was particularly hard pressed on the police issue in view of the fact that this time even the Social Democrats had joined ranks with the other non-Communist parties in their insistence on an adequate explanation by the Minister of the Interior. Since the Prime Minister, in the government's meeting of February 13th, had explicitly promised that such an explanation would indeed be forthcoming, his situation had become increasingly embarrassing. To extricate himself from this delicate position, Gottwald, in the session of the National Front of February 18th, now argued that he was adjourning the meeting on procedural grounds since it had originally been called to deal with the issue of a new constitution and those present lacked the authorization to discuss other matters.[3]

The most important factor in this particular crisis, as far as the American Embassy was concerned, was the defection of the Social Democrats, who until then had usually cast their votes with the Communists on all major issues. Bruins seems to have detected a new line in the Social Democratic political orientation, inasmuch as they had begun to differentiate between constitutional matters and issues pertaining to the basic workings of the democratic process as opposed to general economic and socio-political matters. While in the latter they continued to support Communist objectives, though adhering to their own socialist tradition, they opposed the Communists on the former, reminding the electorate that they were as much a democratic as a socialist party. The chargé, however, was undecided as to whether the National Socialists' "bring[ing] to a head at this time" of the whole police issue was good strategy and ultimately "beneficial to their long-term objectives."[4]

On February 20th, Ambassador Steinhardt returned to his post in Prague. A personal note from Jan Masaryk awaited him; it welcomed him and made brief mention of the overall state of affairs: "the situation is messed up and not clear — vederemo" were the words in which the Czechoslovak Foreign Minister characterized things.[5] Steinhardt himself sent two dispatches to Washington on the very day of his arrival. In the first of these he repeated some of the matters reported by Bruins on the previous day, while adding some important new information to the effect that Gottwald had complained to Beneš that "the other parties were 'ganging up' on the Communist Party and asked what [the] President would do if Gov [sic] resigned." To this, Beneš was said to have replied that he would appoint the "leader of the strongest party [Gottwald] to form a new cabinet — but on condition [that] the new Cabinet was agreeable to all Nat Front parties. This would imply only a Cabinet reshuffle." Just as important as this additional item of news was Steinhardt's other piece of new informa-tion in which he referred to a Communist communiqué demanding, for the first time, the setting up of a "real National Front representing all classes [of] working people of cities and villages under [the] leader-ship [of] Klement Gottwald . . . to defend [the] people's democratic régime."[6] This call for a governing body including organizations other than political parties, together with a meeting of the state-wide Congress of Workers' Councils for February 22, alarmed Steinhardt, who considered all these recent developments extremely serious. The

enormous amount of pressure by the Communists and the simultaneous full-scale mobilization of all workers' organizations and trade
unions, traditionally loyal to them, boded ill for the future. Just as
threatening, however, was the firm stand by the non-Communist
parties, particularly on the police issue. In view of all this, the
Ambassador concluded that "any prediction as to future developments would be hazardous."[7]

Steinhardt's second message of the same day was mildly optimistic.
In this report, he stated that the "National Socialists have seized the
offensive and recognize that [the] police issue is Communist's *[sic]*
weakest point and the one on which Social Democrats will abandon
Communists." But he also reported that the former Soviet Ambassador to Czechoslovakia, Valerian Zorin, had "unexpectedly" arrived
in Prague the afternoon of the previous day; Steinhardt was somewhat
skeptical about the official version of this given in the Czechoslovak
press, according to which Zorin simply wished to attend a pro-Soviet
rally. It was more likely, Steinhardt opined, "that Moscow [was]
suddenly taking [a] more active interest in [the] local political situation
and [the] plight of the Czechoslovak CP." Still, he felt that all non-
Communist parties were looking forward "with restrained optimism
and [the] intention of exercising firmness" to the crucial cabinet
meeting to be held that same afternoon.[8]

Since the session of the Czechoslovak cabinet on February 20th had
failed to resolve the issue of the Communist police appointments in a
way acceptable to their adversaries, and since Gottwald gave no
indication that the appointments would be cancelled, the twelve
cabinet members representing the National Socialists, Catholic
People's Party and Slovak Democrats tendered their resignations that
same evening. It was now President Beneš' move; he could accept or
refuse them. In taking the latter course of action, he could demon-
strate his solidarity with the resigning ministers. Beneš, already seriously ill and under great pressure, at first temporized. He spent the
better part of the night conferring with various cabinet members, both
Communist and non-Communist.

So much for some of the facts on which both Communist and non-
Communist sources seem to be in a reasonable state of agreement. But
there remains much dispute about just what happened during the
fateful days of February 22–24th; it is here that the two disputants
quite obviously differ in their respective interpretations.

Karel Kaplan, writing in *Historica* and focusing his narrative on
Beneš, claims that "Dr. Beneš, in accepting the resignations of the

bourgeois ministers did, after all, play a positive role" in the February coup. Since this particular sentence in Kaplan's article is documented by material from the Archives of the Central Committee of the Communist Party of Czechoslovakia, it seems reasonable to assume that Kaplan's work constitutes more or less official party line on this matter.[9] Still, "Beneš' desire to save the bourgeoisie" and "his positive role in February show a considerable divergence between the aim and its realization." Kaplan then goes on to explain that Beneš' change of mind was occasioned primarily by his realization that the bourgeoisie could not be saved, that the "strength of the people's movement" could not be broken, and that any attempt to try to save the resigning ministers would "only mean that he would end like them — with a complete loss of prestige."[10]

Thus, it was the "People's Movement" which "inadvertently enabled Dr. Edvard Beneš to play what, after all, was a positive role in the decisive conflict between the proletariat and the bourgeoisie, and that in contravention of his subjective desires."[11]

Another group of Prague historians, writing in the ominous year of 1968, when it was possible for them to appraise events somewhat more critically, come to different conclusions. They tend to support the view that Beneš, by and large, was in agreement with the politics of abstention of the moderate parties, but they claim that his knowledge of the proposed resignations of their ministers was sketchy at best. When informed by the National Socialist Ministers Zenkl and Ripka that the resignation of the non-Communist members of the cabinet was a distinct possibility, he supported such a course of action on the assumption that the Social Democrats would do likewise. This, in turn, would accelerate the holding of new elections, after which the political parties might cooperate once again. Rather than put the blame squarely on Beneš who, they claim, had really only two chances of active interference in the crisis — acceptance of the resignations or his own abdication and subsequent announcement of all that had happened publicly — they tend to examine the roles of the National Assembly and the Army, two potential pillars of support for the moderates, as well as those of the police and the numerous mass organizations. They blame the non-Communist deputies for their failure to call an extraordinary session of Parliament, in which the government crisis could be discussed, and for their continuous reliance on Beneš, from whom they expected the ultimate decision.[12] The Army, in turn, was intimidated by the spectacular show of strength of the various pro-Communist mass organizations, who took to the streets to make known their point of view. On February 23rd, when the crisis was at its height, General Svoboda, the officially non-partisan but pro-Communist army commander, addressed a meeting of the Central Action Committee of the National Front and, on behalf of the army, made clear that it would remain faithful to the people and not become the instrument of any individual or group of people. This non-participation of the armed forces contrasted sharply with the openly pro-Communist role played by the police: "In February, 1948 it was possible to exclude the army from direct participation in the events and, in so doing, to realize the aims of the Communist Party."[13]

On the side of the Czechoslovak exiles, Jaromír Smutný, chief of President Beneš' chancellery and obviously a first-hand participant in the drama, gives a somewhat different version. In referring to the resigning ministers' meeting with Beneš, he quotes the President as accepting their resignations, but clearly gives the impression that Beneš did so as a gesture of support for their point of view. He encouraged them to stand firm and promised to do likewise. Similarly, the President is reported to have been in favor of forcing a government crisis at the earliest possible occasion, since he considered it of importance in view of the forthcoming elections.[14]

Not everyone among the participants of that meeting seemed equally convinced that Beneš would indeed back the resigning ministers. Vice-Premier Šrámek, leader of the Catholic People's Party, expressed open doubts about it.[15] Nonetheless, the anti-Communist ministers now tried to enlist the support of the last major non-Communist party, the Social Democrats. As will be recalled, the Congress of that party in November of 1947 had unseated the pro-Communist Fierlinger from the party's chairmanship, but in so doing had by no means brought about a complete volte-face in the party's political orientation. There had, however, been an important shift in attitude regarding matters constitutional and pertinent to democratic rights and freedom. Here, the new trend towards a traditional concept of democracy as opposed to the Communist version of people's democracy was most noticeable; this now encouraged the resigning ministers in their quest for support from the Social Democrats. After all, it was precisely this kind of an issue that provoked the government crisis and the ministers' resignations. It seems surprising, then, that the Social Democratic cabinet members did not make common cause with their non-Communist colleagues in view of the strong support which they had given them previously in various speeches on this very issue. In retrospect, the Social Democrats' stand has been variously interpreted as cowardice, indecisiveness and even as an act of patriotism and high statesmanship: cowardice for fear of being upbraided by their Communist mentors, indecisiveness because of the new alignment of forces within the party which split the old unity, and finally, patriotic and statesman-like due to their unwillingness to split the nation in two at this crucial moment in its history. Be this as it may, the fact remains that they did not tender their resignations. The complete isolation of the Communists which their opponents had hoped to effect did not thus come about.

Instead, it was the Communists who almost immediately went over to the offensive. Able organizers and excellent strategists that they were, they mobilized trade unions, farm workers and, above all, the by now well-armed workers' militia units in calling for a mass meeting of these organizations for February twenty-second. Such public displays of force had stood them in good stead before, and they were determined to take full advantage of the precedent. It was precisely the inability of the moderate parties to counter these visual and highly effective displays of party loyalty in similar ways which had always hampered them in their showdowns with the Communists. The fact that the opposition was heterogeneous, composed of segments from various political parties which, only recently, had found a major joint platform, did not help matters either. The Communists had ridden out the storm.

Judging from its numerous dispatches during the days of the government crisis, the American Embassy in Prague seemed to be fairly accurately informed about all these happenings. On February 21st, Steinhardt reported that "the basic Communist strategy at present [was an] attempt to 'Discredit and Isolate Resigning Ministers' from their own supporters and to constitute a *new* so-called 'National Front' with Communist stooges by presenting trade unions, group organizations, partisans and other Communist dominated groups including left-wing Socialists." As to the alternatives still open, the Ambassador spoke of a Communist plan for an outright takeover of the government as opposed to "Beneš' exercise [of] his constitutional authority in the hope of forcing Communists to modify their program." Just how far the Communists would go in such a modification "to give their conduct a semblance of legality would appear to depend on the nature of instructions they have received from Moscow and their appraisal of the reaction of the Czechoslovak public who are by nature phlegmatic and not given to violent reactions."[16] While Steinhardt's comments about the nature of the moderates' political reactions is accurate enough, it does not appear that the Czechoslovak Communists were anxiously waiting for instructions from Moscow in the execution of their plans; they carried them out on their own. This is best borne out by the various specific moves in which they were now engaged and which, once again, bespoke their superior organization. On February 23rd, the embassy dispatch mentioned: the issuance of rifles to the Communist-controlled Prague police; the order, by the Minister of the Interior, declaring current Czechoslovak passports invalid; the arrest of various prominent non-Communist officials; the taking over of the Bratislava radio station, so far controlled by the Slovak Democrats, by the Ministry of the Interior; and the indefinite furloughing of all non-Communist employees at the Prague radio station. Lieutenant Rychly, the Embassy's attaché for naval questions, is reported to "have recognized several individuals as having been among those who incited disorder in Spain, Yugoslavia and Poland" now doing the same thing in Prague.[17] Whether the agitators spotted by Rychly were Russians or Czechoslovaks is not made clear, though presumably the former in view of the places mentioned. The following day, Steinhardt painted an even gloomier picture. The typesetters of some prominent non-Communist dailies and weeklies had refused to go to work and the Communists had also succeeded in cutting off the necessary supplies of paper to some of the opposition press. Action committees were being formed all over the country, in factories, mines, public offices, and non-Communist employees were discharged. A rumor, according to which the Fierlinger-dominated left-wing faction of the Social Democratic Party had forcibly taken over the party's headquarters, is also contained in the report. A whole galaxy of actions made it painfully clear to the Ambassador that the Communists had taken the offensive. As for their opponents, he could only report that "according to reliable reports Communist leaders are not encountering too much difficulty in finding fairly representative National Socialists and members of [the] People's Party prepared to enter a new government."[18]

It was becoming increasingly obvious that the non-Communist parties had not only lost the initiative but, even worse, that their resistance to the attacking Communists was rapidly faltering. Their last hope now rested with President Beneš. The beleaguered head of state announced, late on February 23rd, that he would address the population by radio within the next few days to explain the situation and to calm spirits. His speech was never to be made. Instead, he now tried desperately to stave off mounting Communist pressure to dismiss the resigning ministers. To a letter from Prime Minister Gottwald, of February 21st, Beneš replied on the 24th that he "fully felt the great responsibility in this fateful hour of [Czechoslovakia's] national life." He expressed an awareness that the overwhelming majority of the country's population desired socialism as a way of life, but he also insisted that such a goal had to be achieved by democratic means: "You know my sincerely democratic creed. I cannot but stay faithful to that creed even at this moment because democracy according to my belief is the only reliable and durable basis of decent and dignified human life." He appealed to Gottwald for support in a solution of the government crisis by parliamentary and constitutional means.[19]

The President's appeal to Gottwald fell on deaf ears. Already the following day, Beneš received an official reply from the Communist Party of Czechoslovakia, signed on its behalf by Party Chairman Gottwald and Secretary-General Rudolf Slánský. It was no longer possible for the Communists to negotiate with the resigning representatives of the other parties since they ceased to be representative of the true feelings of their constituents. On the contrary, rank-and-file members of these parties now themselves desired "a rebirth of their own parties and the National Front." In other words, only "progressive elements" were to be included in the new government, as previously proposed to Beneš by Gottwald. The reply urged Beneš "to recognize the correctness of the [Communist Party's] conclusion" and to "agree with its proposals."[30]

By the evening of February 25th, it was all over. Beneš capitulated, formally accepted the tendered resignations of the National Socialist, Populist and Slovak Democratic ministers, and appointed a new government in accordance with Gottwald's wishes. The Communist triumph was complete.

Whatever doubts Washington might still have had about the ultimate outcome of the events in Prague were quickly dispelled by a cable from the office of the U.S. Military Government in Bavaria to its head office in Frankfurt. It was therein reported that the Czech-Bavarian border had been sealed off as of the previous night, that border guards had been replaced by troops, and that "there [were] indications of a revolution [in Czechoslovakia]."[21]

All Washington could do was to sift through the pieces. In this connection, it is of interest to retrace the steps envisaged by some of the State Department's European and Central European desk officers. In a "Memorandum of Conversation" dealing with "the current crisis in Czechoslovakia," Llewellyn Thompson, Jacob Beam and Harold

Vedeler discussed the situation with Armand Bérard and Arnauld Wapler, Minister and Counselor, respectively, of the French Embassy in Washington. In the talks held on February 24th, the Americans made clear to their French colleagues that the crisis "had come as a surprise." In spite of some indications, in the fall of 1947, "that the Communists had begun a campaign to win complete power through extra-legal means . . ." there was nonetheless "a wide-spread feeling in Czechoslovakia that if the projected [forthcoming] elections were free the Communists could expect some loss in public support." It was precisely to avoid such a result, or so at least some of the State Department's Central and East European hands seemed to speculate, "that impelled the Communists to take provocative steps ending in an attempt to seize power." Then, trying to justify their own conduct in the whole matter, the State Department representatives referred to "various suggestions" entertained by them "for official action," although they did not yet think that the time was ripe to use any of them, at least not "until the outcome [in Prague] was reasonably certain." It was felt in Washington "that with respect to [America's] friends in Czechoslovakia two considerations should be borne in mind: (1) to keep from arousing false hopes among the non-Communists and (2) to avoid the suggestion that the situation seemed hopeless." Well-intentioned and fatuous as such thoughts might have been, they also represented the thinking of traditionalist diplomacy. The Czechoslovak situation, quite obviously, could not readily be integrated into such a conventional perspective. Stronger medicine was needed and Americans were either unwilling or unable to dispense it.

Bérard then expressed the view that since the Communists "had already seized power" and "since he saw no means by which the non-Communists could recover their position," some form of protest was about all that could be effected. In this connection, he asked if the recall of Ambassador Steinhardt was being contemplated. To this, Thompson replied that "the Department saw certain advantages in keeping diplomatic representation in the satellite countries and would probably treat the new government of Czechoslovakia in the same way as other Communist-dominated governments of Eastern Europe." Some form of American protest would be forthcoming "but not before Beneš had an opportunity to act."

In an interesting analogy between Munich, in 1938, and the current Czechoslovak crisis, Bérard compared the impact of the surrender to Hitler to the present capitulation to the Russians: "As Munich left the French disturbed because it meant the surrender of Czechoslovakia to the Germans so this Communist seizure of power aroused French anxieties with respect to the Soviets." Bérard felt that "what could happen in Czechoslovakia could also happen in Italy and France," where the unsatisfactory economic situation was fertile ground for the Communists. Thompson simply turned the argument around when he attempted to calm Bérard's fears with the observation that what the Communists had done in Czechoslovakia might serve as a warning to Italian non-Communists and encourage them to unite and "consolidate their strength against the Communists for the coming elections."[22]

In a parallel move, the American chargé d'affaires in Paris, trying to coordinate American, British and French efforts in a contemplated joint action of protest, met with Foreign Minister Bidault who, in the presence of the British Ambassador, expressed his views on the Czechoslovak crisis. While he "accepted in principle [a] joint Franco-British-American action," he nonetheless "opposed a démarche in Prague on the grounds that if Beneš holds," such an intervention would do more harm than good, inasmuch as it would "counterbalance such benefits as we now enjoy from the presence and intervention of [Soviet Ambassador] Zorine [sic]." Contrariwise, should Beneš yield, a likely possibility according to Bidault, "such a démarche would be pointless and [would] constitute a rebuff to [the] U.S."[23] Secretary of State Marshall in turn considered the "issuing of [a] strong statement on Czechoslovak developments but before doing so" requested Steinhardt's "appraisal of the situation."[24]

Steinhardt obviously thought in these very same terms; in his response, he suggested such a "strong statement by the Secretary" which, he thought, "would have a sobering effect on the Czechoslovak Communists who are at present flushed with victory." After this rather routine suggestion, the Ambassador resorted to the oft-invoked "democratic traditions" and institutions of the country, a remark frequently made by him and other Western observers, and believed to be some special coat of protection which the Czechs possessed against any form of totalitarian evil. He suggested to Secretary Marshall that in view of the fact that Czechoslovakia had a democratic past, while most of the other East European countries taken over by the Soviets had not, Stalin would listen particularly carefully to an American protest over Czechoslovakia. Such a protest might also "influence [Beneš'] course of action," since the President "had not yet clarified his position." What there remained to be clarified in it, a day after his surrender, Steinhardt did not say. The American protest was to be tendered by Marshall himself, "because of his great personal prestige in Czechoslovakia" and was to be strongly worded, in order to achieve the desired effect.[25]

Since the United States, Great Britain and France had made known their views in a joint declaration of the previous day, Marshall replied that "for the moment" this tripartite declaration "replaces [Steinhardt's] suggested statement." He promised "to review the matter . . . in [the] light [of] continuing developments." Subsequently, perhaps in the expectation that propaganda broadcasts would undo, or at least offset, some of the harm brought about by an inept diplomacy, Marshall let Steinhardt know that he "urgently require[d] current guidance for [the] Voice of America . . . in order to combat falsification now being propagated in Zecho [Czechoslovakia]."[26]

To add even further to his disappointment, Marshall, on March 1st, received word from Steinhardt that the "effect in Czechoslovakia [of the] tripartite declaration has been to give little comfort to remaining dispersed moderate elements." Quite to the contrary, the rather meekly worded declaration "embolden[ed] the Communists because of their belief that [this] statement indicates that western powers intend to do little about [the] present situation other than issue condemnatory statements."[27] Steinhardt now suggested to the Secretary of State that he imitate Bidault's example with a definite threat of economic sanctions, since the words of the French Foreign Minister "had come as a real shock to [the] Communists and appear to be causing them some hesitancy lest they be the forerunner of effective economic sanctions. Even many [were] aware of [the] strangulation that would result to [the] country's economy from economic sanctions."[28]

Now that the political battle was over, there was an attempt to recover at least some of the lost ground by economic measures. Thus, for example, it was suggested to the State Department by its Prague Embassy that "a mild form of economic sanctions" could come in the form of a stern warning by "some fairly high officials in the Department" that Americans who intended to visit Prague in the summer of 1948 for the Sokol festival[29] ought to abstain from proposed visits, in light of the fact that their contact with Czechoslovak citizens might endanger the latter's safety. The Czechoslovak press, in the past few days, had stepped up its accusations against "American . . . imperialists" and contact with them would constitute a definite risk for their Czech relatives and acquaintances. Furthermore, since the Prague government "is looking forward to dollars brought in by [the] tourist trade next summer," this would be a good way to cross such calculations.[30] A mild form of economic sanctions, indeed; it was certainly not likely to assure the dispersed Czechoslovak opposition about America's intention to restore democracy to their country.

XIII

After the Coup

Unable to prevent what had happened, Americans and Czech moderates alike now tried to explain why and how it had come about.[1] Among the few remaining contacts which the American Embassy managed to maintain with some of its Czech sources, the persons of Jan Masaryk and Jaromír Smutný were easily the most important and most knowledgeable.

Two days after the swearing in of the new government in Prague, Jan Masaryk, in conversation with Steinhardt, gave the Ambassador a fairly detailed account of the events of the past few days. According to the Czechoslovak Foreign Minister, Beneš had no previous knowledge of the intention of the twelve ministers to resign, for "their action had come as a complete surprise to him." The President at first had no intention of accepting the resignations; on the contrary, he was contemplating his own resignation without accepting theirs and without approving a new government, as desired by Gottwald. The fact that Beneš did eventually accept and give in to Communist pressure is ascribed by Masaryk to his extremely poor health and overall physical condition and his "confused state of mind." Beneš' lifelong devotion to politics and his love of office may have been instrumental in delaying his resignation. Similarly, a keen apprehension that either Fierlinger or Zdeněk Nejedlý, the one-time Communist Minister of Education, both individuals openly disliked by Beneš, would succeed him, may well have influenced the President's decision to remain in office, at least for the time being.

As to Beneš' announced radio address to the Czech people, a speech that was never given, Masaryk claimed that the President's physical condition, "particularly his difficulty in articulating," had made it impossible for him to speak. There was "no evidence that Beneš would have been denied the use of [the] radio." Finally, as to the President's future, Masaryk was rather pessimistic. The ailing head of state was leaving Prague that very day and was expected to resign shortly thereafter. Nor was Masaryk's prognosis for Edvard Beneš' health any more reassuring. "He would not live long," he said to Steinhardt, for the President "was a broken man."[2] Both of Masaryk's predictions were essentially correct: Beneš resigned the presidency in June and died in September of the same year.

Smutný, the head of the presidential chancellery and a long-time collaborator of Beneš', talked to Steinhardt a few days later; he concurred with Masaryk in his account of the initial stages of the coup. He, too, claimed that "the President was not prepared for the twelve resignations" and that "for several days Beneš contemplated refusing to accept [the] resignations or to approve the new government and contemplated resigning." From then on, however, Smutný's account of the fateful days was radically different from Masaryk's. According to him, "[Beneš] decided to accept the new govt [sic] when he was informed that Communists not being certain their putsch would succeed relied upon a considerable armed force on Czechoslovak eastern frontier." While Smutný was unable to identify the "exact location of this force, he said that the President had taken at face value the information that the force existed."[3] The reference to such a Soviet force, stationed on the country's eastern frontier and ready to intervene on the Communists' behalf, should such intervention become necessary, was the first of its kind. While the U.S.S.R. no doubt had troop formations both on its own territory bordering Czechoslovakia as well as in Poland, Rumania and Hungary, it does not appear from available evidence that an invasion of Czechoslovakia, such as occurred in 1968, had been contemplated at the time. There can be no doubt that the Czechoslovak Communists must have derived strength and comfort from the fact that Soviet troops were stationed around most of Czechoslovakia's frontiers, while American military formations, numerically vastly inferior, were positioned along a relatively short stretch (some 250 miles) of Czechoslovakia's western frontier.

As for Beneš' future plans, Smutný told Steinhardt that, for the present at least, the President would remain in Czechoslovakia. "If he [Beneš] leaves the country — for the second time — he is convinced all semblance to resistance ot [sic] putsch among the people to Communist domination will collapse as they will feel deserted." Furthermore, the President reasoned that he could be of no value to Czechoslovakia and its people from abroad. If, "on the other hand, he resigns and remains in [the] country he will be the focal point of resistance by [sic] Communist domination." Beneš' present intentions to remain were being reinforced by requests from all sides "that he should not leave yet." Eventually, the President would "decide whether he will be more of a nuisance to the Communist Govt [sic] in or out of office and will make his decision accordingly." In order to facilitate his future role as an obstacle to the Communists, he hoped that, for the time being at least, he would be spared criticism by the Western press. Finally, Smutný mentioned Beneš's awareness of the danger to which he exposed himself by remaining. He was conscious of the fact that the Communists would eventually "throw him out of office," but he also doubted that they would permit him to leave the country legally. The President also expressed fears that he would be put on "trial as a traitor" and that plans to indict him "had . . . been carefully formulated by the Communists."[4]

While Smutný's reference to the readiness of Soviet troops is, of course, a weighty argument, it remains largely unsubstantiated in other accounts. Similarly, and in spite of the President's physical and mental condition, it is surprising, to say the least, that a statesman of Beneš' experience would undertake political action of momentous importance without first ascertaining some of the basic factors in the situation. General Hasal, the chief of the President's military chancellery, certainly would have had some knowledge of major Soviet troop movements and of their positioning on the country's borders. He was a man loyal to Beneš and would not have failed to bring such information to the President's immediate attention. In view of this, Smutný's statement that the Soviet forces were a major factor in Beneš' decision to accept the new government is open to serious question.

The one other significant comment on Russian participation in the Czechoslovak coup can be traced to a conversation between Jozef Lettrich, prominent member of the Slovak Democratic Party, and Charles W. Yost, one-time First Secretary of the U.S. Embassy in Prague and subsequently chargé d'affaires of the American legation in Vienna. On March 26th, in the Austrian capital, Lettrich, who by then had escaped from Czechoslovakia, sought out Yost and told him that "there is no doubt . . . that the Communist moves which followed were directly coordinated, if not planned in detail, by Moscow and the Cominform in Belgrade. There was a clear threat of intervention by Soviet armies." He further claimed that "the arrival of ZORIN [sic], the Soviet Vice Commisar [sic] of Foreign Affairs, at the time of the crisis was no coincidence. He was obviously despatched by Moscow in order to make sure that the Czech Communists did not miss what might be their last opportunity to definitely fasten Communism on their country." But, having told Yost all this, Lettrich refrained from establishing a direct link between Moscow and Prague. "There is no direct evidence of coordination between Zorin and Gottwald . . ."

although "Zorin had not come to Czechoslovakia to deal with wheat shipments." Finally, and obviously in an effort to absolve himself and other non-Communist politicians of any possible blame for the outcome of events, Lettrich told Yost that "the key to the situation lay with President Beneš rather than with Gottwald. Thus, while Beneš hesitated to accept the resignations of the non-Communist ministers, the Communists stepped up their activities through the resistance organizations and the trade unions, and also through pressure on the Social Democrats."[5]

Be this as it may, the Prague government, for rather obvious reasons, treated the coup as a purely internal matter and, on March 4th, Steinhardt reported the Czechoslovak Ministry of Information had made every effort in its radio and press releases to portray it in just such a light. According to the Prague news media, "foreign imperialistic plots were threatening [the] republic which barely escaped from this menace by a change in government and [the] elimination of cabinet members who were associated with foreign imperialists." In this and similar statements, Steinhardt saw both an excuse for and a first step towards "totalitarian Communist control of all branches of government and industry."[6]

All this notwithstanding, the Ambassador, in a brief review of the causes of the February crisis, reported on the following day that "two facts" stood out among the various causes which brought it about: "[the] (1) immediate formation [of] action committees all over [the] country, which purged all types of economic, political, sporting and beneficial organizations. This could not have occurred spontaneously and without previous preparation; (2) the parade and discipline of [the] factory militia on the old town [sic] square in Praha which included about six thousand civilians . . . armed with new rifles indicated a degree of precision in the manual of arms which must have called for considerable preparation and training." Steinhardt suggested that these two factors should be given special prominence in the appropriate Voice of America broadcasts.[7]

While thus giving much credit to the Czechoslovak Communists, Steinhardt's preliminary analysis[8] of the Prague coup makes no mention of any kind of Soviet participation or preparedness. He was not alone in crediting superior Communist discipline, planning and overall organization for much of the success of the coup. An intelligence report of the Department of the Navy illustrates, in some detail, the actual take-over by Communists of an important government office. A United States citizen of Czech descent, a former "classmate of

Jan Masaryk's in 1896 and 1900" and "an associate of Edvard Beneš'"
with whom he served in the Czechoslovak government in 1918, had the
following to say about the take-over, by Communist officials, of the
Czechoslovak Ministry of Foreign Affairs. The source, referred to as
"believed to be reliable," had lunch there on February 24th when,
suddenly, "an attendant instructed everyone to attend a meeting in a
special hall upstairs." The source did not know the persons who
conducted the meeting, but reported that it was called for the purpose
of an appeal to Beneš in an attempt to put pressure on the President to
accept Gottwald's new cabinet, since only a Communist government
could obtain badly needed food supplies from the Soviet Union.
Subsequently, the speaker, who declared himself a member of the
"Communist Committee of Action," made a motion to the effect that
the Ministry should be immediately taken over by the Action Committee. The next passage of the report is particularly revealing since,
"according to the source, the vote in favor of the motion was that of the
decidedly minority pro-Communists present; however, there was no
opposing vote."[9] In many ways, this show of hands at the Foreign
Ministry on that fateful February 24th characterizes the attitude of the
nation at large — anti-Communist, but both unwilling and unable to
say so at the crucial moment. The next sentence in the report only
tends to confirm such a view. It stated that "there was a dumbfounded
acceptance through lack of any leadership in opposition." Once again,
a symptom all too typical for Czechoslovak politics after 1945. Not
even Jan Masaryk, who was present at the meeting, provided any
guiding hand or direction, as might have been expected from a
prominent member of the government who, after all, was in charge of
the very ministry about to be taken over by the Action Committee.
Obviously as equally stunned as all the others, he is reported to have
left the room immediately after the vote with a rather ironic one-
sentence remark: "'Gentlemen, I wish you luck, I am going now in [sic]
bed.'" To this remark, the American source added that "a more
accurate translation in quoting Masaryk [was] difficult."[10] Perhaps
the Foreign Minister, for one last time, tried to charm his audience
with a sample of his wry wit, or even a slightly off-color remark. These
may have stood him in good stead on previous occasions, but they
proved of little avail this time. It was a sad and pathetic exit for the
Foreign Minister, the enigmatic son of a famous father.

    After reporting that similar take-overs by Action Committees had
been staged in many government offices and industrial plants, "no
business or governmental agency being too insignificant," the source

then reported on his attempt to see President Beneš, his one-time "school-friend and classmate." After repeated attempts to do so, he finally got his audience with Beneš "on or about 1 March 1948" in the President's country seat of Sezimovo Ústí, where Beneš had just taken up residence. While the military guard permitted the visitor to enter the grounds, he never actually got to see the President, merely being "met by the President's niece, JIRINKA *[sic]*, and advised by the lady that BENEŠ *[sic]* was prohibited from seeing anyone."[11]

After some of the dust had settled, Steinhardt dispatched a long and detailed communication to Washington in which he wished "to supplement the Embassy's coverage of the Czechoslovak Government crisis of February 1948 by certain descriptive and analytical comments." The unusually long resumé started out with the statement that the February crisis "was probably inherent in the situation ever since the consummation of the Czechoslovak-Soviet Treaty" of December, 1943. A thousand years of Czech history, as well as Czechoslovakia's geographical position in the very center of Europe, helped to explain why the Czechs gave in. They had never been fighters, and had reached moments of glory only when there was a "power vacuum" in the region; the most recent example of this was in 1918, under the leadership of Czechoslovakia's first President, T. G. Masaryk. This, and the frequent waves of emigration which "repeatedly drained off the cream of the population, leaving a residue of small farmers and artisans, who have never seemed able to exercise firmness, courage and noble traits in time of crisis, but rather have chosen to bow to political storms..." account for the Czechs' instinctive desire for survival and their preference to submit rather than fight.

Another Czech trait was their inability to play off mighty neighbors against each other "and to indulge in double-talk." This they had done fairly successfully since 1945 ("for example the statements of Jan Masaryk during the past two years") and, as long as such a pose suited the Soviets, all was well. However, "[the Czechoslovak] alliance with Russia combined with the present aggressive Soviet political policy in Europe has prevented the Czechs for the present from 'having it both ways,' as the recent crisis demonstrated."

So much then for the Czech part of the blame. It was now the turn of Czechoslovakia's allies to come under Steinhardt's scrutiny. His resumé of the Czechoslovak alliance system began with a simple but ominous sentence: "The Czechs have had bad experience with their allies." The first had been at Munich, where France and England deserted them, and more recently, with the Western powers in general.

The greatest American mistake, according to Steinhardt, was the conduct of U.S. policy during World War II. Whereas the Russians were already concerned with the forthcoming new order in Europe, the U.S. was primarily interested in winning the war. This Soviet emphasis on matters political rather than purely military "contributed to [America's] loss of influence in Central and Eastern Europe." The Czechs were convinced that "'we wrote them off' or, in other words, consigned them to the Soviet sphere of influence." Subsequent American actions only strengthened their belief that such was indeed the case: "Our attitude at Yalta and Potsdam on boundaries and reparations and especially the halting of our army in May 1945, thus permitting Soviet forces to liberate Praha confirmed our stand in the minds of the Czechs. Hindsight now indicates that further attention by us to the political aspects of the war might have given us control of Central Europe at a nominal cost."[12]

As for the U.S.S.R. and Czechoslovakia's alliance with the Soviets, "it offered the Czechoslovaks tangible benefits only as long as the Soviet Union chose to abstain from an aggressive European policy." Since, however, "the Soviets continued to be aggressive, it was only a matter of time before a crisis would be precipitated in Czechoslovakia." The exact moment was not really important; what did count was partly the right opportunity, but more particularly, the will of Russia. It was "fundamentally a Moscow decision," Steinhardt claimed.

The Ambassador was just as convinced that "it [was] now clear that the decision of the twelve ministers . . . to resign was taken with the direct encouragement and consent of President Beneš." During the crucial five-day period, when Beneš pondered his course of action, he received strong support from the ministers or their representatives, encouraging him to refuse the resignations. It was Beneš' "weakness . . . which is hardly excusable on the grounds of his sub-normal physical health," which brought about the "debacle." The President "was greatly frightened by the Soviet specter" and reported that threats by Gottwald and the Trade Union Movement made him fear the outbreak of "internal strife and the consequent necessity by Soviet troops in surrounding countries to come in to 'restore order.'" Steinhardt, however, disclaimed "evidence of any troop concentration on the borders of Czechoslovakia." On the contrary, he believed that "on similar recent occasions" Finland and Iran were exposed to even greater Soviet pressure which they resisted successfully. The failure to resist, on the part of the Czechs, was ascribed by Steinhardt to the "lack of unity . . . indecision and lack of positive action on the part of the moderate forces." The Communists, quite naturally, "took full advantage" of it. Direct Soviet interference was being disclaimed by the Ambassador. Zorin's arrival in Prague, on February 19th, "cannot be placed under the heading of direct interference." From Zorin's conversations, of which the U.S. Embassy managed to get "creditable reports," it simply could not be deduced that Zorin came either to foment or to supervise the Communist coup. The Soviet role in the Prague events of February, 1948 could not be compared with Russian interference into Rumanian affairs in 1945: "Zorin is not a forceful, door-slamming type and his activities are not comparable to those of Vishinsky [sic] in Bucharest during the crisis there." Only the swift formation and the high state of preparedness of the various "Action committees" constituted "definite indication of preparedness and may have had Soviet aid . . . They may have been directly encouraged by Soviet support."[13]

After some discussion surrounding the mysterious death of Foreign Minister Jan Masaryk, during which Steinhardt concluded that "from a political viewpoint, it made very little difference whether it was suicide or murder," the Ambassador addressed himself to the simple question of why the Communists won. His answer to it was equally simple: "The Communists were aggressive and bold, and were sufficiently organized to take advantage of the situation. The non-Communists had no adhesion as a group, did not recognize the issue as one of Communism against non-Communism, and continued to place their individual party loyalties and personal ambitions ahead of their opposition to Communism. This, combined with the weak leadership at the top, particularly on the part of the President, caused the debacle." It was as simple as that.

There followed remarks on the present [April, 1948] state of the country and a rather interesting observation to the effect that "there are many people who believe that their only salvation will be in a war between the United States and the Soviet Union." Steinhardt thought that this indicated the same type of mentality as during World War II, when the Czechs entertained similar hopes of being liberated by action from abroad.

Some general observations on future U.S. diplomatic conduct vis-à-vis Czechoslovakia were followed by four specific suggestions of what America might and should have done to have kept Czechoslovakia in the democratic fold. Of the four — "1) radio and other propaganda . . . 2) negotiations of treaties (small countries are flattered by such attentions) . . . 3) assistance (sale, not gifts) of much needed commodities . . . 4) direct internal interferences . . ." — only the first of the above measures would any longer be of utility in Czechoslovakia." The Soviets had used radio and other means of propaganda with enormous effect, while American "fair play" had led nowhere. "Greater use by us of Soviet methods might result in both positive and preventative benefits."[14]

The report is at once a strong indictment of the Czechoslovak moderates and, to a lesser extent, of American policy towards Czechoslovakia. It does, however, stop short of claiming that, had the moderates been made of sturdier stuff and had the Americans been better and tougher diplomats, events in Prague would have been different. There is the straightforward recognition of Communist strength, superior organization and preparedness. It is difficult to disagree with some of Steinhardt's observations, although it is doubtful that the Ambassador was anywhere nearly as knowledgeable of the Czechs' past, their traits and habits, as his report seems to indicate. Although there can be no question about Steinhardt's genuine sympathy for the people of the country to which he was accredited, there is no substantial evidence of any kind which would make it possible for him to pose as an expert of things Czech as, on occasion, he was wont to do. His sweeping generalizations during the 1946 election campaign and his utterly wrong predictions about their outcome[15] indicate this curious blend in the man who had Czechoslovakia's cause at heart, but who was given to an overestimation of his own capabilties in correctly judging the country's pulse.

Only weeks after the coup it became patently evident that, for the immediate future at least, the American role in Prague would be a nominal one. While the Embassy would continue to function, it would do so more or less pro forma and to the extent that American missions carried on their business in other East European countries. The special role Steinhardt and his Embassy had once thought to play, in view of Czechoslovakia's then still unusual position in the Russian political orbit, had come to an end. So had Steinhardt's usefulness as head of the American mission in Prague. As he himself described to Marcia Davenport[16] only days after his reassignment to Ottawa: "I was not sorry to leave Prague, partly because all our friends have 'departed,' for one reason or another, partly because conditions are deteriorating so rapidly, and partly because I felt that there was very little more that I could do under existing conditions."[17] In another communication, this one to his friend Miloš Hanák, the one-time Czechoslovak envoy to Turkey whom Steinhardt had known ever since his own tenure of office in the Turkish capital, the Ambassador sounded equally dispirited: "Prague is not and can never be the same for us since our friends have been driven out of their own Country." Although he reassured Hanák, who by that time had taken up residence in the United States, "that some day we shall all have a 'Reunion in Prague'"[18] he was obviously relieved to have been given an assignment where the pace and overall conditions of his work would be more routine. He expressed his feelings to Sumner Welles, when he told him "what a relief it will be to live once again under normal conditions . . . after all these years in Peru, the Soviet Union, Turkey and the past six months in Prague."[19]

In turn, his friends, both fellow diplomats and others, seemed to appreciate Steinhardt's craving and need for an assignment to a more conventional diplomatic post. Stan Griffis, the U.S. Ambassador in Poland and obviously one who could speak from first-hand experience, sent him a brief note of encouragement in mid-March: "I know what a murderous time you must have been through and my instinct and knowledge of you tells me how well you must have handled an almost impossible situation. Accordingly, this note is merely a note of high regard, sympathy and good wishes to you as you sit on top of your volcano. Mine at this moment is fortunately not in the state of eruption."[20] Dorothy Thackrey, editor and publisher of the *New York Post* and a long-time friend of Steinhardt's, in congratulating him on the appointment to Canada, added rather caustically: "I know how happy you will be to get back into civilization."[21]

While the new Czechoslovak Foreign Minister, Vlado Clementis, assured Steinhardt that he had "no intention to change anything in our relations whether personal or intergovernmental,"[22] both Washington and Ambassador Steinhardt saw quite clearly that an era had come to an end and that there was no longer any need to maintain a fairly large Embassy in the Czechoslovak capital. Christian Ravndal, the Director General of the United States Foreign Service and the man in charge of appointments, wrote to Steinhardt in late May and suggested that "in view of the changed situation in Czechoslovakia," he had been "wondering whether a reduction of staff of the U.S. mission would not be justified." To soften the impact of the blow, Ravndal assured Steinhardt that his "work is important, we know this, but there will be less and less to do."[23]

While Steinhardt saw the wisdom of Ravndal's proposal and told him so in his reply,[24] he also wrote to Emil Kekich, his former political officer at the Prague Embassy, telling him that it was "useless to seek to persuade the Department to assign a staff to Prague any larger than the policy calls for." He could not "conscientiously recommend to the Department continuance of a staff in Prague as large as that in 1947 — having regard to the Communist seizure of control, and the inevitable reduction in the activities of the Embassy. . . ." It would seem "more important . . . under the circumstances . . . to emphasize to the Department that the staff be of high calibre and that as many Americans as possible be substituted for alien employees."[25]

By October, both Steinhardt and John Bruins, who had been second in rank at the Prague Embassy and had repeatedly substituted for an absent ambassador, were at their new posts: the former in Ottawa and the latter at the National War College in Washington. From there, Bruins wrote his former chief: "I trust you are now pleasantly ensconced in Ottawa and that, like we, you are enjoying the pleasant glow of having left our Czechoslovak problems behind us."[26]

No fair-minded person ought to begrudge Steinhardt his new post. It was, after all, routine State Department practice to re-assign a man who had served in what by then was classified as a "hardship post" to a more regular station. He more than deserved the much milder diplomatic climate of the Canadian capital. It is, however, much more difficult to express similarly charitable views about America's Czechoslovak policy and the role played in it by Laurence Steinhardt. Looking back on the last three years, it is next to impossible to discern any systematic or long-range approach to or any basic understanding of the problems of Czechoslovakia by the U.S. Department of State. To what extent such a course was mandated by Teheran and Yalta is just as unfathomable, but this, here at least, is not really the point at issue. What does matter is that once in his post in Prague, Steinhardt carried on in a manner which might well have served its purpose in a conventional station, but which was hardly sufficient counterweight to the well-coordinated diplomatic efforts of the Soviet Union. It may be argued that American acknowledgement of Soviet influence in Eastern Europe prevented the same type of aggressive propaganda as was used by the U.S.S.R. The fact remains that nothing definite had been decided about the ultimate fate of the country, that Czechoslovakia did have free elections in 1946 and that there was a marked difference between the overall political climate of the country as compared with the rest of Eastern Europe. Thus, the United States may well be charged with not having even attempted to play an important part in Czechoslovakia's affairs. With constant apprehension that the Soviets might be offended if the United States overstepped the boundaries of fair play in a part of the world assigned to its opponent, Washington never bothered to bring the issue to a test.

Similar charges must be raised when it comes to matters economic. Here, different considerations accounted for American half-heartedness, or outright inactivity. The United States was to trade with Czechoslovakia in a manner customary in the free world — one granted favors to friends and kindred spirits and then one expected reciprocal treatment in return. Such an attitude may well constitute sound enough traditional economic practice, but it did not lend itself to a situation where innovative and unorthodox thinking was the order of the day. Although in a far worse economic situation than the United States, the U.S.S.R. delivered the much needed foodstuffs to the Czechs at the very moment when such deliveries created a maximum political and propagandistic impact. Subsequent American trade practices with Yugoslavia and other countries who were not on particularly friendly terms with the United States confirm their political soundness.

Steinhardt's inability to change such traditional thinking among American policymakers casts him in the role of a conventional rather than innovative or outstanding diplomat. It is understood that Washington and not its embassies all over the world make United States foreign policy, but this established practice in any country's policy does not absolve the respective head of mission, the man who is on the spot and supposedly an expert on the affairs of the country to which he is accredited, from attempting to influence policy if he feels that it is ineffective or outrightly wrong. It is precisely in this respect that Steinhardt did not act to best advantage. In spite of an occasional suggestion that Czechoslovakia, on account of its peculiar situation between East and West, needed special attention, the Ambassador did not seem to have any kind of well thought-out plan for the unusual treatment which the unusual circumstances in the country called for.

Admittedly, such instances when ambassadors show the way rather than merely take and execute directions from home are infrequent. Nor do the enormous growth and complexity, to say nothing of the radically changed nature of present-day international relations, lend themselves to the kind of personal diplomacy of olden days. Yet, even when all this is taken into consideration, it simply does not appear that Steinhardt, or anyone else at the Prague Embassy, was willing to take the risk of a major difference of opinion with Washington. Even John Bruins' last minute suggestion for a trade treaty and a commercial agreement — things which, after all, had been pondered over for more than two years — were stop-gap measures rather than any kind of radical, substantive changes of approach.

It is similarly unclear and incomprehensible why the one readily available propaganda trump card — the true story of the liberation of Prague and the documentation supporting it — was not utilized with maximum efficiency. The Embassy, all too familiar with the bureaucratic procedures and eternal procrastination on the part of Washington, ought to have suggested its use long before it actually did, having witnessed the effective use of aggressive propaganda on the part of the Russians. As was the case with the contemplated proposal for a trade agreement, which came after the Russians had actually made delivery of sorely needed grain, the United States only then began to think about propaganda as a means of salvaging Czechoslovakia, after the Russians had done so effectively for years.

Finally, the question of whether Czechoslovakia had indeed been abandoned and conceded to the Russians at Yalta must be examined. There are references to such an assumption in some of Steinhardt's messages to Washington. They do, however, convey the feelings and thoughts of some Czechs, as reported by Steinhardt, rather than his own or the American official point of view. The conduct of American diplomacy towards Czechoslovakia was markedly different from the line Washington took towards, say, Bucharest or Budapest. The size of the Embassy's staff and the nature of its activities also differed vastly from those of an American mission "behind the Iron Curtain." The very fact that there was an embassy in Prague while, with the exceptions of Poland and Yugoslavia, the other East European countries had merely U.S. legations or missions, is in itself sufficient indication that the United States did indeed have some special interest in regard to Czechoslovakia. In view of all this, United States policy towards Czechoslovakia during the crucial years 1945–1948 suffered from two rather fundamental weaknesses. The first concerns the Embassy of Laurence A. Steinhardt. With some exceptions, neither the Ambassador nor his staff ever clearly identified or foresaw how some of Czechoslovakia's problems could be pinpointed or solved with United States help. To be sure, specific problems during the post-war years, especially those of an economic nature, were frequently relieved by instant and effective American aid. A long-range policy, however, was lacking.

Secondly, and just as regrettable if not more so, the Embassy's contacts were largely limited to non-Communist politicians. While one might argue that, for rather obvious reasons, American diplomats in Prague could not possibly gain the same access to Communist sources as could their Russian counterparts, there seemed to have been no major attempt to establish some permanent liaison of any sort. Only on rare occasions would Steinhardt confer with Gottwald or other Communist officials, and even then only to deal with specific issues, usually protests against anti-American propaganda spread by radio and press. What good such liaison ultimately might have done is, of course, open to question, but a more evenly oriented network of information would doubtlessly have been to American advantage. The all too visible association of the United States Embassy with the moderates, while conceptually logical, cast the U.S. mission from the very start as an anti-Communist force. Such a pose might have been to some advantage if some of the Czech moderates had been of sturdier stuff than they actually were. This not having been the case, the Americans' reliance on the non-Communists in their gathering of information and appraisals of Czech domestic events proved frequently counter-productive. It gave the Embassy a one-sided view of Czechoslovak events and it exposed it to often needless suspicion on the part of the left.

The Embassy's position was not made any easier by the advice and support it received from Washington. The Department of State and its officials responsible for Czechoslovak affairs unquestionably meant well, but like Steinhardt and his men in Prague, they lacked direction. Caught between the realities of the post-war situation in Eastern Europe and such divergent pressures as American business interests and Western-style democratic freedoms, Washington temporized and muddled, zig-zagging its way through policy decisions. Instead of a long-range policy towards the country, where American hopes for swift restoration of both economic prosperity and a democratic way of life were highest, the United States merely resorted to a series of ad hoc measures. The conditions in Czechoslovakia called for a more dramatic program. Freedom and democracy simply could not be sustained by good wishes and hopes alone. Realities in Czechoslovakia necessitated a bolder defense of mutual hopes and aspirations. Neither the United States nor Czechoslovakia would see another such unique opportunity for more than a generation. Continuous and sustained misunderstandings, arrogance and ignorance on both sides, and lack of will forced the two countries into rival camps against the intentions and best interests of both.

Notes

INTRODUCTION

1. It is perhaps indicative of the extent of United States-Czechoslovak relations in the inter-war years that F. Vondráček, in his book, *The Foreign Policy of Czechoslovakia*, devotes a mere fourteen pages (mostly scant specific references) to Czechoslovakia's relations with the U.S. during those years; see F. Vondráček, *The Foreign Policy of Czechoslovakia* (New York: Columbia University Press, 1937), pp. 451 ff.
2. An invaluable source for the period is George F. Kennan, *From Prague After Munich* (Princeton, N.J.: Princeton University Press, 1968); in it, the author comments on the peculiar status of American diplomatic representation in the so-called Protectorate of Bohemia and Moravia. See especially pp. v and vi.
3. Steinhardt to Allen, August 26, 1945, Library of Congress, *Steinhardt Papers,* Letterbooks.
4. Steinhardt to Ferris, October 20, 1945, *ibid.*
5. Steinhardt to Francis Williamson, July 28, 1945, *ibid.,* Number 56.
6. *Loc. cit.*
7. *Loc. cit.*
8. Steinhardt to Secretary of State, July 21, 1945, File 860 F.0017, National Archives, *Diplomatic Papers,* Czechoslovakia, Record Group 59.

CHAPTER ONE:
THE LIBERATION OF PRAGUE

1. *Archiv Národního shromáždění — Státní rada, plenum [Archives of the (Czechoslovak) National Assembly — Council of State, Plenum],* February 13, 1945, quoted in Václav Král, *Osvobození Československa* (Prague: Academia, 1975), p. 265.
2. S. M. Shtemenko, *Generalnyj shtab v gody vojny* (Moscow: Kniga vtoraja, 1973), p. 316, quoted in Král, *op. cit.*
3. Bernard Law Montgomery, *The Memoirs of Field-Marshal The Viscount Montgomery of Alamein, K. G.* (London: The World Publishing Company, 1958), pp. 296–97. See also Omar N. Bradley, *A Soldier's Story* (New York: Henry Holt and Company, 1951), p. 549.

4. Intelligence Dissemination Number A-53771, April 11, 1945, National Archives, *Office of Strategic Services,* Record Group 226.

5. Bosý to Portal, April 19, 1945, File 820, National Archives, Czechoslovakia, *Military Affairs,* Record Group 226.

6. Intelligence Dissemination Report, Number A-53420, April 6, 1945, National Archives, *Office of Strategic Services,* Record Group 226.

7. Anthony Biddle (Supreme Headquarters Allied Expeditionary Force) to H. R. Bull, May 4, 1945, File 820, National Archives, Czechoslovakia, *Military Affairs,* Record Group 226.

8. Ripka to Nichols and Ripka to Schoenfeld, April 25, 1945, File 820, *ibid.*

9. Nichols to Foreign Office, April 21, 1945, Public Records Office-FO, File 371-47154.

10. Eduard Taborsky, "The Triumph and Disaster of Eduard Benes,"[sic] *Foreign Affairs,* 36 (1958), pp. 669–84; Táborský was Beneš' secretary at the time of the events described above.

11. Schoenfeld to Department of State, April 21, 1945, *Foreign Relations of the United States,* (1945), IV, 440.

12. Memorandum of Chief of Staff, April 26, 1945, Public Records Office-Cabinet, File 88/36.

13. Churchill to Truman, April 30, 1945, Public Records Office-Premier, File 3/114/3A.

14. Stettinius to Acting Secretary of State, April 28, 1945, File 740.0011 E W/4-2845, National Archives, *Diplomatic Papers,* Record Group 59; see also *Foreign Relations of the United States,* (1945), IV, 444 ff.

15. *Loc. cit.*

16. Král, *op. cit.,* p. 294.

17. See particularly Václav Král, *Pravda o okupaci [The Truth About the Occupation]* (Prague: Naše Vojsko, 1962), pp. 345 ff.

18. Harry S. Truman, *Memoirs: Year of Decisions* (Garden City, New York: Doubleday and Co., Inc., 1955), pp. 216–17; Alfred H. Chandler *et al.,* eds., *The Papers of Dwight David Eisenhower: The War Years* (Baltimore: Johns Hopkins Press, 1970), IV, 2662 ff.; Omar N. Bradley, *op. cit.,* p. 549; Forrest C. Pogue, "The Decision to Halt at the Elbe," in *Command Decisions,* ed. K. R. Greenfield (Washington, D.C.: Department of the Army, 1954), pp. 479–92. For a German version concerning events in Prague during those days, see Walter Gorlitz, ed., *The Memoirs of Field Marshal Keitel* (London: Kimber, 1965).

19. Grew to Caffery (for Murphy), May 6, 1945, File 740.0019/5, National Archives, *Diplomatic Papers,* Control (Germany), Record Group 59.

20. *Loc. cit.*

21. Caffery (transmitting Murphy's message) to Secretary of State, May 11, 1945, File 740.0019/5-1145, *ibid.*

22. Mark S. Steinitz, "Ambassador Laurence A. Steinhardt and United States Relations with Czechoslovakia, 1945–1948," M.A. Thesis, University of Maryland, 1974, p. 23.

23. *Mladá Fronta [The Young Front,* official publication of the Czechoslovak Youth Movement] (Prague), April 29, 1965.

24. J. Smrkovský in *Dějiny a současnost [History and Contemporary Affairs]*, 4 (April 1965), pp. 56ff. This is the same Josef Smrkovský who, as President of the Czechoslovak National Assembly, was Dubček's "number two man" in the ill-fated "Prague Spring," and who, most recently, sharply criticized the Soviet occupation of Czechoslovakia in 1968.

25. Steinhardt to Schoenfeld, May 21, 1945, Library of Congress, *Steinhardt Papers*, Box 83.

26. Memorandum of Conversation between the Czechoslovak Ambassador (Hurban) and some of his staff with Francis Williamson, November 15, 1945, File 860 F.00/11-1545, National Archives, *Diplomatic Papers*, Czechoslovakia, Record Group 59.

27. *Loc. cit.*

28. Steinhardt to Secretary of State, August 12, 1946, File 860 F.00/8-1246, *ibid.*

29. Bruins to Steinhardt, January 23, 1948, Library of Congress, *Steinhardt Papers*, Box 57.

30. Williamson to Steinhardt, January 23, 1948, *ibid.*, Box 83.

CHAPTER TWO:
PROGNOSES, HOPES, AND ASPIRATIONS

1. Winant to Secretary of State, April 5, 1945, File 860 F.00/4-445, National Archives, *Diplomatic Papers*, Great Britain, Record Group 59.

2. Schoenfeld to Secretary of State, April 11, 1945, File 860 F.00/4-1145, National Archives, *Diplomatic Papers*, Czechoslovakia, Record Group 59.

3. Cordell Hull, *Memoirs of Cordell Hull* (New York: The MacMillan Company, 1948), I, 603–04. Most of the factual information about Steinhardt's private and public life can be found in *Who Was Who in America*, II, 1943–1950 (Chicago: The A. N. Marquis Company, 1950), p. 507. It may be of some interest to note that the biographical sketch of the writer Gertrude Stein, on the same page, is shorter than Steinhardt's.

4. Charles E. Bohlen, *Witness to History* (New York: Norton, 1973), pp. 88–89. See also Mark S. Steinitz, "Ambassador Laurence A. Steinhardt and the United States Relations with Czechoslovakia, 1945-1948," Master's thesis, University of Maryland, 1974, p. 34.

5. Steinhardt to Loy W. Henderson, December 19, 1939, Library of Congress, *Steinhardt Papers*, Letterbooks; see Steinitz, *op. cit.*, p. 37 also.

6. Steinitz, *op. cit.*, p. 36.

7. Steinhardt to Francis T. Williamson, July, 1945, Library of Congress, *Steinhardt Papers*, Letterbooks.

8. Steinhardt to Secretary of State, July 24, 1945 (file copy, no file number), National Archives, *Diplomatic Papers*, Czechoslovakia, Record Group 59.

9. Steinhardt to Walton C. Ferris, Assistant Chief, Division of Foreign Service Personnel, October 20, 1945, Library of Congress, *Steinhardt Papers*, Letterbooks.

10. *Loc. cit.*
11. Steinhardt to Francis Williamson, June 22, 1945, *ibid.*
12. Steinhardt to Williamson, September 22, 1945, *ibid.* Steinhardt's ire centered on a foreign service officer previously stationed in Warsaw, about to retire, "whose course and conduct at a post call for a medical examination rather than transfer to [a] potentially equally critical post." Eventually, Claiborne Pell, the present U.S. Senator from Rhode Island, was appointed U.S. Vice-Consul in Bratislava.
13. *Loc. cit.*
14. Steinhardt to Francis Williamson, July 28, 1945, *ibid.*
15. Steinhardt to James Riddleberger, September 1, 1945, *ibid.*
16. Steinhardt to Henry Luce, September 7, 1945, *ibid.*
17. Steinhardt to Williamson, October 1, 1945, *ibid.*
18. Klieforth to Secretary of State, June 15, 1945, File 860 F.00/6-1545, National Archives, *Diplomatic Papers,* Czechoslovakia, Record Group 59; see also *Rudé právo,* July 5, 1945.
19. Steinhardt to Secretary of State, July 21, 1945, *ibid.;* see also *Lidová demokracie,* July 5, 1945.
20. Sawyer to Secretary of State, July 12, 1945, *ibid.*
21. Intelligence Dissemination Number A-21938, early August, 1945, National Archives, *Office of Strategic Services,* Record Group 226.
22. Steinhardt to Williamson, October 1, 1945, Library of Congress, *Steinhardt Papers,* Letterbooks.
23. Steinhardt to Van Slyke, December 17, 1945, *ibid.*
24. Steinhardt to Maurice Hindus, December 18, 1945, *ibid.* Hindus had published an article on Czechoslovakia in *Collier's Magazine* and sent Steinhardt a copy for comment; the two-page comment of Steinhardt's, while generally laudatory, reproaches Hindus for being too pessimistic in his outlook for Czechoslovakia's future.
25. Clipping from *Svobodné noviny* [Czech daily concerned primarily with literary and artistic issues], no date (probably late April, 1946), enclosed in Steinhardt to Secretary of State, May 7, 1946, File 860 F.00/5-746, National Archives, *Diplomatic Papers,* Czechoslovakia, Record Group 59.
26. Steinhardt's correspondence with Smith dates back to July, 1945, and continues, on a fairly regular basis, until the end of the year. Of particular interest are Steinhardt's letters to Smith of August 28, September 1, November 5, November 12, and December 26, 1945. See also Smith to Steinhardt, August 23, 1945; all to be found in Library of Congress, *Steinhardt Papers,* Letterbooks.
27. Steinhardt to Williamson, November 13, 1945, *ibid.*
28. Steinhardt to Williamson, August 28, 1945, *ibid.*
29. Steinhardt to Secretary of State, November 21, 1946, File 860 F.00/11-2146, National Archives, *Diplomatic Papers,* Czechoslovakia, Record Group 59.
30. Steinhardt to Williamson, August 28, 1945, Library of Congress, *Steinhardt Papers,* Letterbooks.
31. The Czechoslovak government and National Assembly, immediately after the war, were of a provisional character. The first post-war elections were held in 1946. See below, Chapter V.

32. Most prominent among them were the claims of the Petschek family, well-known industrialists and coal mine owners in pre-war Czechoslovakia.

33. Steinhardt to John Foster Dulles, October 21, 1947, Library of Congress, *Steinhardt Papers,* Letterbooks.

34. Large iron and steel works, in Moravia, with predominantly foreign ownership.

35. Steinhardt to Dulles, June 26, 1947, Library of Congress, *Steinhardt Papers,* Letterbooks.

36. *Ibid.*

37. *Ibid.*

CHAPTER THREE:
TROOP WITHDRAWAL

1. The first post-war Czechoslovak elections were scheduled for May, 1946.

2. Even General Svoboda, the pro-Communist Minister of Defense and the former commander of the Czechoslovak Brigade in the U.S.S.R., admitted to the American chargé d'affaires that "Red Army behavior [in Czechoslovakia] was bad." Klieforth to Secretary of State, June 17, 1945, File 860 F.00/6-1745, National Archives, *Diplomatic Papers,* Czechoslovakia, Record Group 59.

3. Klieforth to Secretary of State, July 6, 1945, File 860 F.00/7-645, *ibid.*

4. *Loc. cit.*

5. Grew to Klieforth, July 9, 1945, File 860 F.00/7-945, *ibid.*

6. Klieforth to Secretary of State, July 16, 1945, File 860 F.00/7-1645, *ibid.*

7. See in particular Steinhardt to Secretary of State, August 2, 1945, *Foreign Relations of the United States* (1945), IV, 481 ff.; also Steinhardt to Secretary of State, July 23, 1945, *ibid.,* pp. 478-79; Steinhardt to Secretary of State, September 4, 1945, *ibid.,* pp. 488-89.

8. Steinhardt to Secretary of State, September 14, 1945, File 860 F.01/9-1445, National Archives, *Diplomatic Papers,* Czechoslovakia, Record Group 59.

9. Harriman to Secretary of State, July 11, 1945, File 861.46, National Archives, *Diplomatic Papers,* Czechoslovakia, Record Group 59.

10. Record of Meeting of Secretaries of State, War, and Navy, October 16, 1945, *Foreign Relations of the United States* (1945), IV, 496-97.

11. Murphy to Secretary of State, October 17, 1945, *ibid.,* pp. 498 ff.

12. Patterson to Byrnes, October 26, 1945, *ibid.,* pp. 502 ff.

13. Secretary of State to Steinhardt, November 2, 1945, *ibid.,* pp. 506 ff.

14. Steinhardt to Secretary of State, November 8, 1945, *ibid.,* pp. 507-08. For Stalin's reply to Truman, see *loc. cit.*

15. Steinhardt to Secretary of State, November 30, 1945, *ibid.,* p. 509.

16. Hubert Ripka, *Czechoslovakia Enslaved: The Story of the Communist Coup d'Etat* (London: Gollancz, 1951), p. 44.

17. Steinhardt to Secretary of State, July 24, 1945, File 801.46, National Archives, *Diplomatic Papers,* Czechoslovakia, Record Group 59.
18. See below, pp. 50–51.

CHAPTER FOUR:
POST-WAR RECOVERY

1. Masaryk to Steinhardt, October 20, 1945, File 804.4/851, National Archives, *Post Files,* Record Group 319. Svoboda's letter, addressed to Steinhardt and dated October 17, is also enclosed.
2. Steinhardt to Svoboda, October 30, 1945, File number missing, *ibid.;* also see Steinhardt to Byrnes, October 31, 1945, File number missing, *ibid.*
3. Svoboda to Steinhardt, November 8, 1945, File number missing, *ibid.*
4. Byrnes to Steinhardt, December 2, 1945, File number missing, *ibid.*
5. Food items, in particular, were frequently U.S. Army rations (K rations), clearly distinguishable in their khaki-colored containers.
6. Acheson to Steinhardt, September 25, 1945, File 804.4/851, National Archives, *Post Files,* Record Group 319.
7. Byrnes to Steinhardt, October 27, 1945, File number missing, *ibid.*
8. Steinhardt to Secretary of State, September 29, 1945, File number missing, *ibid.*
9. Another equally disturbing incident in the activities of the United States Relief and Rehabilitation Administration occurred in the Moravian capital of Brno. There, according to the reports of non-Communist sources which eventually reached the United States Embassy, the local authorities entrusted with the distribution of supplies channelled major quantities of canned meat into the hands of Soviet occupation troops. Since UNRRA relief was specifically earmarked for the civilian population only, the disclosure of these facts caused a major stir. The Communists acknowledged that the Soviet contingents had indeed been recipients of some of the UNRRA supplies; however, they attempted to cushion the impact of the incident by claiming that, in turn, the Soviet Army had supplied an equal amount of fresh meat to Czechoslovak authorities for use by the civilian population in Brno.
10. Steinhardt to Secretary of State, September 4, 1945, File 611.60 F 31/9-445, National Archives, *Diplomatic Papers,* Czechoslovakia, Record Group 59.
11. For a useful discussion of the subject, see Thomas Paterson, *Soviet-American Confrontation* (Baltimore: Johns Hopkins Press, 1973), chapter 6.
12. Byrnes to Acheson, September 24, 1946, in *Foreign Relations of the United States* (1946), VII, 223.
13. Acheson to Prague Embassy, March 28, 1946, File 860 F.51/3-2846, National Archives, *Diplomatic Papers,* Czechoslovakia, Record Group 59. See also *Foreign Relations of the United States* (1946), VI, 182–83; also Geir Lundestad, *The American Non-Policy Towards Eastern Europe, 1943-1947*

(New York and Oslo: Humanities Press and Universitetsforlaget, 1975), p. 162.

14. *Rudé právo,* August 3, 1945.

15. Steinhardt to Secretary of State, August 25, 1945, File F.00/8-2545, National Archives, *Diplomatic Papers,* Czechoslovakia, Record Group 59.

16. Steinhardt to Secretary of State, August 29, 1945, File 860 F.00/8-2945, *ibid.*

17. Steinhardt to Secretary of State, September 5, 1945, File 860 F.51/9-545, *ibid.*

18. Secretary of State to Steinhardt, September 12, 1945, File 860 F.51/9-1245, *ibid.*

19. Riddleberger to Steinhardt, October 4, 1945, Library of Congress, *Steinhardt Papers,* Letterbooks.

20. Steinhardt to Secretary of State, July 3, 1946, File 860 F.5034/7-346, National Archives, *Diplomatic Papers,* Czechoslovakia, Record Group 59. See also *Foreign Relations of the United States* (1946), VI, 206, fn. 44.

21. Steinhardt to Secretary of State, June 20, 1946, File 860 F.51/6-2046, National Archives, *Diplomatic Papers,* Czechoslovakia, Record Group 59. See also *Foreign Relations of the United States* (1946), IV, 206, fn. 46.

22. Byrnes to Clayton, *Foreign Relations of the United States* (1946), VI, 216–17.

23. *Loc. cit.*

24. Clayton to Byrnes, September 26, 1946, *ibid.,* p. 224.

25. The question of the unused portion of the surplus property credits was further complicated by the Czechoslovak desire to grant Rumania part of its unused portion. Since the Czechs wished to do so at interest rates substantially higher than they themselves paid Washington, the State Department, quite understandably, was unconvinced of the Czechs' "urgent need" of the credits and questioned Prague's ethics in the matter.

26. Riddleberger to Steinhardt, October 3, 1945, Library of Congress, *Steinhardt Papers,* Letterbooks; see also Paterson, *op. cit.,* p. 125.

27. Joseph Kodíček, "The Suspension of the American Loan," *Central European Observer,* 13 (November 8, 1946), 353; also quoted in Paterson, *op. cit.,* p. 125.

28. Here Acheson quotes verbatim the text of Byrnes' telegram to him, sent from Paris on September 24; for complete text see *Foreign Relations of the United States* (1946), VII, 223.

29. Acheson to Steinhardt, October 25, 1946, in *Foreign Relations of the United States* (1946), VI, 235–6.

30. Steinhardt to Secretary of State, October 7, 1946, File 711.60 F/10-746, National Archives, *Diplomatic Papers,* Czechoslovakia, Record Group 59.

31. Gallman [chargé d'affaires] to Secretary of State, November 7, 1946, in *Foreign Relations of the United States* (1946), VI, 234–35.

32. Byrnes to Steinhardt, October 14, 1946, File 711.60 F/10-1446, National Archives, *Diplomatic Papers,* Czechoslovakia, Record Group 59.

33. Steinhardt to Secretary of State, October 11, 1946, File 711.60 F/10-1146, *ibid;* see also *Foreign Relations of the United States* (1946), VI, 230–31.

34. Steinhardt to Riddleberger, June 12, 1946, Library of Congress, *Steinhardt Papers,* Box 54; his emphasis.

35. Steinhardt to Secretary of State, June 19, 1947, File 860 F.00/6-1947, National Archives, *Diplomatic Papers,* Czechoslovakia, Record Group 59.

CHAPTER FIVE:
THE ELECTIONS OF 1946

1. Steinhardt to Secretary of State, September 8, 1945, File 860.00 F/9-845, National Archives, *Diplomatic Papers,* Czechoslovakia, Record Group 59.
2. Steinhardt played a key role in arranging for the joint withdrawal and, in various letters to personal friends, repeatedly pointed this out to them. See above, pp. 33-34.
3. Steinhardt to Dulles, December 26, 1945, Library of Congress, *Steinhardt Papers,* Letterbooks.
4. Although the U.S. Embassy in Prague unquestionably had many contacts among ranking politicians of non-Communist parties, Dr. Petr Zenkl, chairman of the National Socialist Party and one-time Lord Mayor of Prague and Czechoslovak Vice-Premier, was clearly the most important among them. Letter of Julius Firt, one-time political secretary of the Czechoslovak National Socialist Party, to author, June 20, 1976. Firt himself had close contacts with the Americans.
5. Steinhardt to Secretary of State, March 3, 1946, File 860.00 F/3-946, National Archives, *Diplomatic Papers,* Czechoslovakia, Record Group 59.
6. *Loc. cit.* The National Socialists, on the other hand, were the only party which constantly stressed its national and Slavic character. In so doing, it implicitly repudiated the clericalism of the People's Party, which was associated by many Czechs with the former Austro-Hungarian regime. Conversely, it is quite true that although clerics were prominent in the People's Party (Mgr. Šrámek, its chairman, was Vice-Premier and Mgr. Hála was Minister of Posts and Telegraphs), there was an equally strong secular wing in the party, which in many ways was much more straightforward in its struggle against Communist domination than the old Mgr. Šrámek and the rather timid Mgr. Hála. In this connection, see Steinhardt to Secretary of State, February 28, 1946, *ibid.,* in which the Ambassador refers to one of Hála's conciliatory speeches wherein the latter attempts to reassure the Communists of the People's Party's loyalty to the Czechoslovak-Soviet alliance and its repudiation of Franco's régime in Spain.
7. See below, pp. 137, 163.
8. Steinhardt to Secretary of State, May 15, 1946, File 860 F.00/5-1546, National Archives, *Diplomatic Papers,* Czechoslovakia, Record Group 59.
9. *Loc. cit.*
10. Neither Svoboda nor Foreign Minister Masaryk had any official party affiliation. Nonetheless, Svoboda's sympathies were with the left, Masaryk's with the moderates.
11. Steinhardt to Secretary of State, May 23, 1946, File 860 F.00/5-2346, *ibid.*

12. Steinhardt to Secretary of State, May 15, 1946, File 860 F.00/5-1546, *ibid.*

13. Steinhardt to Secretary of State, June 4, 1946, File 860 F.00/6-446, *ibid.*

14. For a useful brief discussion of the election results and for further figures, see Victor S. Mamatey and Radomír Luža, eds., *A History of the Czechoslovak Republic, 1918-1948* (Princeton, N.J.: Princeton University Press, 1973), pp. 403-05.

15. Steinhardt to Secretary of State, May 27, 1946, File 860 F.00/5-2746, National Archives, *Diplomatic Papers,* Czechoslovakia, Record Group 59.

16. For details on this subject, see below, Chapter X.

17. Steinhardt to Secretary of State, May 29, 1946, File 860 F.00/5-2946, National Archives, *Diplomatic Papers,* Czechoslovakia, Record Group 59.

18. Harriman to Secretary of State, May 31, 1946, File 860 F.00/5-3146, *ibid.*

19. Intelligence Report Number 269008, June 1, 1946, National Archives, *Office of Strategic Services,* Record Group 319.

20. Steinhardt to Secretary of State, June 3, 1946, File 860 F.00/6-346, National Archives, *Diplomatic Papers,* Czechoslovakia, Record Group 59.

21. Steinhardt to Secretary of State, May 29, 1946, File 860 F.00/5-2946, *ibid.*

22. Bruins to Secretary of State, June 4, 1946, File 860 F.00/6-446, *ibid.*

23. Bruins to Secretary of State, June 7, 1946, File 860 F.00/6-746, *ibid.*

24. See above, p. 53.

25. To an extent, Gottwald's accusations were correct. Some politicians of the Slovak Democratic Party were indeed implicated in such a liaison, particularly with the now-exiled Foreign Minister of Tiso's former regime, Ferdinand Durčanský.* A subsequent investigation by the government led to the resignation of some leading members of the Democratic Party and a reshuffling among its leadership. There is still much difference of opinion as to whether these connections constituted an actual threat to Czechoslovakia, as claimed by Gottwald and the Communists, or whether they were primarily a political strategem by which the Prime Minister thought to rid himself of some of his political enemies. [*since deceased]

26. Bruins to Secretary of State, June 7, 1946, File 860 F.00/6-745, National Archives, *Diplomatic Papers,* Czechoslovakia, Record Group 59.

27. Bruins to Secretary of State, June 10, 1946, File 860 F.00/6-1046, *ibid.*

28. Steinhardt to Secretary of State, June 9, 1946, File 860 F.00/6-946, *ibid.*

29. Plzeň (better known as Pilsen), capital of Western Bohemia, seat of the important and Communist-dominated Škoda Armament Works, and the world-famous Pilsen Brewery; Olomouc, second-largest Moravian city.

30. The Košice Program, a political platform adopted by the Provisional Czechoslovak Government in April of 1945, in its then capital of Košice, one of the first Czechoslovak cities liberated in World War II. It was agreed upon by all political parties.

31. *Rudé právo,* May 31, 1946.

32. Klement Gottwald, *Spisy [Writings]* (Prague: n.p., 1955), pp. 253-54.

33. Steinhardt to Secretary of State, July 3, 1946, File 860 F.00/7-346, National Archives, *Diplomatic Papers,* Czechoslovakia, Record Group 59; also see *Foreign Relations of the United States* (1946), VI, 205.

CHAPTER SIX:
THE TRANSFER OF THE SUDETEN GERMANS

1. The most reliable and most readily accessible documentation on the thinking of the various members of the London-based Czechoslovak exile government is to be found in L. Otáhalová and M. Červinková, *Dokumenty z historie československé politiky, 1939–1943 [Documents relating to the history of Czechoslovak politics]* (Prague: Academia, 1966), I and II; see particularly documents 61, 71, 105, 115, 149, 153, 173, 209, 210, 211, 222, 164, 199, 325 and 412. It is regrettable that planned subsequent volumes have not as yet been published.

2. Literally translated, the word *odsun* means "the pushing out" of the Sudeten Germans. The word transfer is the one commonly used in English. For a Czech account of the whole operation and its genesis, see Radomír Luža, *The Transfer of the Sudeten Germans* (New York: New York University Press, 1964). The best account from a German point of view is J. W. Brugel, "Die Aussiedlung der Deutschen aus der Tschechoslowakei," *Vierteljahresheftefür Zeitgeschichte* (1960), VIII, 134–64.

3. Speech by Hubert Ripka, quoted in *Czechoslovak News Letter* [official publication of President Beneš' London exile government], February 2, 1945, p. 2.

4. Speeches by Josef Zinner and Gustav Beuer, January 27 and 28, *ibid.*

5. Speech by Hubert Ripka, January 28, 1945, *ibid., p. 3.*

6. Intelligence Report Number 3144.0401, December 9, 1944, National Archives, *Office of Strategic Services,* Record Group 226.

7. "Memorandum by the Committee on Post-War Programs," July 18, 1944, *Foreign Relations of the United States* (1945), IV, 424.

8. Czechoslovak Ministry of Foreign Affairs to Schoenfeld, April 20, 1944, File 711.9, National Archives, *Diplomatic Correspondence,* Czechoslovakia, Record Group 59.

9. *Loc. cit.*

10. Klieforth to Secretary of State, June 28, 1945, File 711.9, *ibid.*

11. See particularly *loc. cit.;* also Grew to U.S. Embassy, Prague, June 15, 1945, *ibid.* and subsequent correspondence between Steinhardt and the Department of State, especially Steinhardt to Secretary of State, August 28, 1945, File 711.9, *ibid.* and Steinhardt to Williamson, October 20, 1945, Library of Congress, *Steinhardt Papers,* Letterbooks.

12. Clementis to Klieforth, July 3, 1945, File 711.9, National Archives, *Diplomatic Papers,* Czechoslovakia, Record Group 59.

13. Grew to American Embassy (Prague), July 15, 1945, File 711.9, *ibid.*

14. Grew to American Embassy (Prague), July 31, 1945, File 711.9, *ibid.*

15. *Loc. cit.*

16. Steinhardt to Jan Masaryk, August 2, 1945, File 711.9, National Archives, *Diplomatic Papers,* Minorities, Record Group 59.

17. Office memorandum, Steinhardt to Klieforth, August 3, 1945, File 711.9, *ibid.*

18. Steinhardt to Secretary of State, August 2, 1945, File 711.9, *ibid.*

19. Office memorandum, Steinhardt to Klieforth, August 3, 1945, File 711.9, *ibid.*

20. Steinhardt to Secretary of State, July 27, 1945, File 840.4016, *ibid.*

21. Steinhardt to Secretary of State, August 11, 1945, File 860 F.00, *ibid.*

22. *Rudé právo [The Red Right],* August 4, 1945.

23. *Práce [Labor],* August 4, 1945.

24. *Svobodné Slovo [The Free Word],* August 4, 1945. For other Czech press excerpts, see also Steinhardt to Secretary of State, August 14, 1945, File 711.9, National Archives, *Diplomatic Papers,* Czechoslovakia, Minorities, Record Group 59.

25. Steinhardt to Secretary of State, August 7, 1945, File 860 F.00/9-745, *ibid.*

26. Clementis to Steinhardt, August 16, 1945, File 711.9/8-1645, *ibid.*

27. Undated, probably early September, 1945.

28. Steinhardt to Secretary of State, October 3, 1945, File 711.9/10-345, *ibid.*

29. *Loc. cit.*

30. *Loc. cit.*

31. Steinhardt to Murphy, December 7, 1945, Library of Congress, *Steinhardt Papers,* Box 83, Number 438.

32. Steinhardt to Williamson, October 20, 1945, *ibid.,* Number 290.

33. Murphy to Secretary of State, September 27, 1946, File 840.4016, National Archives, *Diplomatic Papers,* Germany, Record Group 59.

34. Steinhardt to Secretary of State, October 30, 1945, File 860 F.00/10-3046, National Archives, *Diplomatic Papers,* Czechoslovakia, Record Group 59.

35. *Loc. cit.*

36. See particularly "Agreement concerning the temporary interruption of the transfer of Germans from Czechoslovakia to the U.S. Zone of Germany," November 12, 1946, File AG 383.7/194, National Archives, *Adjutant General Papers,* Record Group 319; also Dastich to Keating, April 23, 1947 and Keating to Dastich, May 3, 1947, *ibid.* Major-General Kenneth Keating handled the transfer at the American end, Brigadier-General František Dastich was his Czechoslovak counterpart in his capacity as Chief of the Czechoslovak military mission.

CHAPTER SEVEN:

CZECHOSLOVAKIA AND THE MARSHALL PLAN

1. *Archiv Předsednictva Vlády* [Archive of the Prime Minister's Office], Protocols of the 95th session of the [Czechoslovak] Government, July 4, 1947, quoted in J. Belda, *et al.,* "K otázce účasti Československa na Marshallově plánu," [Concerning the Question of Czechoslovakia's Participation in the Marshall Plan], *Revue Dějin Socialismu* [Review of the History of Socialism], 8 (1968), 95; for Masaryk's comments in Oslo, see also the report of the U.S.

Ambassador to Norway, Bay, to the Secretary of State: Bay to Secretary of State, June 27, 1947, File 860 F.00/6-2747, National Archives, *Diplomatic Papers,* Czechoslovakia, Record Group 59.

2. *Pravda,* June 22, 1947; see also Belda, *op. cit.,* p. 95.

3. *Archiv Předsednictva Vlády,* Protocols of the 96th session [extraordinary and secret], July 10, 1947, quoted in Belda, *op. cit.,* p. 95; original emphasis.

4. *Archiv Předsednictva Vlády,* Enclosure to the 96th session, July 10, 1947, quoted in Belda, *op. cit.,* p. 96.

5. Telegram by Gottwald, Masaryk and Drtina [Minister of Justice] to Beneš and the Czechoslovak government, July 10, 1947 [enclosure to the 96th session of the government, July 10, 1947], quoted in Belda, *op. cit.,* pp. 96–97.

6. *Loc. cit.*

7. *Loc. cit.*

8. *Loc. cit.*

9. *Loc. cit.*

10. *Loc. cit.*

11. *Loc. cit.* Minister of Information Václav Kopecký and Minister of Transport Jan Kopecký were not related.

12. Steinhardt to Secretary of State, July 15, 1947, File 860 F.00/7-1547, National Archives, *Diplomatic Papers,* Czechoslovakia, Record Group 59.

13. Steinhardt to Riddleberger, July 16, 1947, Library of Congress, *Steinhardt Papers,* Letterbooks.

14. Steinhardt to Secretary of State, July 22, 1947, File 711.60 F/7-2247, National Archives, *Diplomatic Papers,* Czechoslovakia, Record Group 59.

15. Memorandum of Conversation between Hanč and Williamson, Vedeler (and other U.S. officials), July 29, 1947, File 860 F.00/7-2947, *ibid.*

16. *Daily Review* of the Czechoslovak Ministry of Information (Prague), August 2, 1947.

17. Steinhardt to Secretary of State, August 4, 1947, File 860 F.00/8-447, National Archives, *Diplomatic Papers,* Czechoslovakia, Record Group 59.

18. *Loc. cit.*

19. *Loc. cit.*

20. Steinhardt to Secretary of State, July 18, 1947, File 860 F.00/7-1847, *ibid.*

21. Bruins to Steinhardt, August 5, 1947, Library of Congress, *Steinhardt Papers,* Letterbooks.

22. Vedeler to Steinhardt, August 12, 1947, *ibid.*

23. *Loc. cit.*

24. The reference here is to a pool of monetary gold found in Germany and other countries to which the Germans had transferred it. In September of 1946, the United States, the United Kingdom and France established the Tripartite Commission for the Restitution of Monetary Gold to its former owners. Czechoslovakia was one of the claimants.

25. Memorandum of Conversation between Marshall and Masaryk, November 14, 1947, File 860 F.51/11-1447, National Archives, *Diplomatic Papers,* Czechoslovakia, Record Group 59.

CHAPTER EIGHT:
POLITICAL PARTIES

1. The term Populists is used here to denote members of the Catholic People's Party.

2. Literally translated as *Horizons,* it was by far the most outspoken and truly democratic publication during 1945–1948. It is equally important from a literary point of view.

3. For a full text of Šrámek's speech, see *Lidová demokracie [People's Democracy],* the party's daily, of June 10, 1945. See also Klieforth to Secretary of State, June 15, 1945, File 860 F.00/6-1545, National Archives, *Diplomatic Papers,* Czechoslovakia, Record Group 59.

4. *Lidová demokracie,* February 26, 1946.

5. Steinhardt to Secretary of State, February 28, 1946, File 860 F.00/2-2846, National Archives, *Diplomatic Papers,* Czechoslovakia, Record Group 59.

6. In a speech in Vrchlabí (Bohemia), Hála predicted that "new horizons were opening [for Czechoslovakia] in the West and that [Czechoslovak] relations with the West will become more friendly"; quoted in Steinhardt to Secretary of State, April 30, 1947, File 860 F.00/4-3027, *ibid.*

7. Steinhardt to Secretary of State, October 22, 1947, File 860 F.00/10-2247, *ibid.* Procházka was Koželuhová's husband.

8. Parsons to Secretary of State, December 10, 1947, File 860 F.00/12-1047, *ibid.*

9. Jaroslav Pecháček to author, June 6, 1976.

10. Central Intelligence Agency, Information Report Number 11698, February 11, 1948, National Archives, *Records of the Army Chief of Staff,* Record Group 62.

11. Packages, containing explosives, were mailed to some of the most prominent anti-Communist politicians in 1947, and Krajina, one of the addressees, later uncovered and publicized their Communist origin. This incident, as well as the above-mentioned knowledge of Communist activities in Gestapo jails, made him particularly hated by his Communist foes.

12. Bruins to Secretary of State, March 13, 1947, File 860 F.00/3-1347, National Archives, *Diplomatic Papers,* Czechoslovakia, Record Group 59.

13. *Loc. cit.*

14. Julius Firt to author, June 20, 1976.

15. Steinhardt to Secretary of State, June 10, 1947, File 860 F.00/6-1047, National Archives, *Diplomatic Papers,* Czechoslovakia, Record Group 59.

16. Unsigned Embassy dispatch to Secretary of State, July 1, 1947, File 860 F.00/7-147, *ibid;* see also *Svobodné slovo,* June 22, 1947.

17. Unsigned Embassy dispatch to Secretary of State, August 19, 1947, File 860 F.00/8-1947, *ibid.*

18. Yost to Secretary of State, August 28, 1947, File 860 F.00/8-2847, *ibid.*

19. Yost to Secretary of State, September 9, 1947, File 860 F.00/9-947, *ibid.*

20. *Svobodné slovo,* September 1, 1947. Excerpts of Stránsky's speech and comments on it can be found in Yost to Secretary of State, September 4, 1947,

File 860 F.00/9-447, National Archives, *Diplomatic Papers,* Czechoslovakia, Record Group 59.

21. Yost to Secretary of State, September 4, 1947, File 860 F.00/9-447, *ibid.*
22. A secret report from the U.S. military attaché in Prague, Colonel J. A. Michela, dated April 14, 1948, deals at length with some of these allegations. Michela's source was a "judge of the People's Court in PANCRAC *[sic]* in PRAHA," a member of the Czechoslovak court which passed judgment on Karl Hermann Frank, the German State Secretary in the so-called Protectorate of Bohemia and Moravia. Included in Michela's report is "a copy of the signed confession of Hermann ZANDER, Secretary of the Gestapo in PRAHA," in which Zander accuses such well-known pre-war Czech Communists as the brothers Synek and Edvard Urks of having betrayed the whole Czechoslovak Communist underground organization to the Gestapo. See Report Number R-141-48 of Col. J. A. Michela, National Archives, *Post Files,* Praha, Box 2953, Record Group 319.
23. See above, Chapter VIII, fn. 10. It may be remembered in this context that Krajina incurred similar Communist disfavor for being the prime mover in the attempt to ferret out and to prosecute the instigator(s) of the bomb plot against the three democratic Ministers. See also Steinhardt to Secretary of State, September 20, 1946, File 860 F.00/9-2046, National Archives, *Diplomatic Papers,* Czechoslovakia, Record Group 59.
24. *Svobodné slovo,* December 18, 1947.
25. See below, p. 126.
26. *Svobodný zítřek [A Free Tomorrow],* December 4, 1947; see also Bruins to Secretary of State, December 12, 1947, File 860 F.00/12-1247, National Archives, *Diplomatic Papers,* Czechoslovakia, Record Group 59.
27. Julius Firt to author, June 20, 1976.
28. *Intelligence File,* SO 11579, January 10, 1948, Records of the Army Staff, Office of the Assistant Chief of Staff, G-2, Record Group 319.
29. See p. 98.
30. A useful summary of the origins of Czechoslovak communism is to be found in H. Gordon Skilling, "The Formation of a Communist Party in Czechoslovakia," *The American Slavic and East European Review,* 14, No. 3 (October 1955), 346–58. More exhaustive is P. Reimann, *Geschichte der Kommunistischen Partei der Tschechoslowakei* (Berlin: Hoym, 1929).
31. Klieforth to Secretary of State, June 4, 1945, File 860 F.00/6-445, National Archives, *Diplomatic Papers,* Czechoslovakia, Record Group 59.
32. Steinhardt to Secretary of State, July 27, 1945, File 860 F.00/7-2745, *ibid.*
33. See in particular Steinhardt to Francis Williamson, July 28, 1945, Library of Congress, *Steinhardt Papers,* Box 83; also Steinhardt to George Van Allen, December 18, 1945, *ibid.*
34. Bruins to Secretary of State, June 7, 1946, File 860 F.00/6-746, National Archives, *Diplomatic Papers,* Czechoslovakia, Record Group 59.
35. *Loc. cit.*
36. In spite of some charges to the contrary, the elections of 1946 were relatively free. See Steinhardt to Secretary of State, May 29, 1946, File 860 F.00/5-2946, *ibid.* and above, see pp. 54 ff.
37. Steinhardt to Secretary of State, January 7, 1947, File 860 F.00/1-747, National Archives, *Diplomatic Papers,* Czechoslovakia, Record Group 59.

38. Bruins to Secretary of State, January 24, 1947, File 860 F.00/1-2447, *ibid.*

39. Steinhardt to Bruins, February 13, 1947, Library of Congress, *Steinhardt Papers,* Letterbooks.

40. Steinhardt to Secretary of State, June 11, 1947, File 860 F.00/6-1147, National Archives, *Diplomatic Papers,* Czechoslovakia, Record Group 59.

41. See above, Chapter VII.

42. Yost to Secretary of State, August 13, 1947, File 860 F.00/8-1347, *ibid.*

43. *Loc. cit.*

44. *Rudé právo,* August 17, 1947.

45. Yost to Secretary of State, September 9, 1947, File 860 F.00/9-947, National Archives, *Diplomatic Papers,* Czechoslovakia, Record Group 59.

46. The ratio of the Czechoslovak crown to the dollar was 50:1. In other words, even at this official exchange rate, one million Czech crowns represented $20,000.

47. Yost to Secretary of State, September 5, 1947, File 860 F.00/9-547, *ibid.*

48. *Loc. cit.*

49. *New York Herald-Tribune* [European edition], September 28, 1947.

50. Steinhardt to Secretary of State, October 23, 1947, File 860 F.00/10-2347, National Archives, *Diplomatic Papers,* Czechoslovakia, Record Group 59.

51. Steinhardt to Secretary of State, October 30, 1947, File 860 F.00/10-3047, *ibid.*

52. Steinhardt to Secretary of State, November 20, 1947, File 860 F.00/11-2047, *ibid.*

53. See below, pp. 128, 130.

54. Steinhardt to Secretary of State, November 24, 1947, File 860 F.00/11-2447, National Archives, *Diplomatic Papers,* Czechoslovakia, Record Group 59.

55. Steinhardt to Secretary of State, November 5, 1947, File 860 F.00/11-547, *ibid.*

56. The Ambassador underwent an operation in December and did not return to his post until February 21, 1948.

57. Bruins to Secretary of State, November 28, 1947, File 860 F.00/11-2847, *ibid.*

58. Bruins to Secretary of State, December 10, 1947, File 860 F.00/12-1047, *ibid.*

59. Bruins to Secretary of State, December 12, 1947, File 860 F.00/12-1247, *ibid.*

60. Bruins to Secretary of State, December 22, 1947, File 860 F.00/12-2247, *ibid.*

61. Steinhardt to Secretary of State, November 24, 1947, File 860 F.00/11-2447, *ibid.;* also Claiborne Pell to author, June 29, 1976; also interview with Senator Claiborne Pell, Syracuse, New York, May 8, 1976.

CHAPTER NINE:
THE SLOVAK CRISIS OF 1947

1. Originally, there were only two political parties in Slovakia, Democrats and Communists; subsequently, the Social Democratic and Freedom Parties, both of minor political consequence, joined their ranks.

2. On March 30, 1946, leaders of the Slovak Democratic Party, mostly Protestants, concluded an agreement with the ranking Catholic deputies of the party, according to which Catholics were to receive their fair share of appointments to state and party offices. The agreement, referred to as the "April agreement," in spite of its actual date of March 30, established a ratio of 7:3 in favor of the Catholics in the division of offices. For details, see J. Belda *et al.*, *Na rozhraní dvou epoch [Between Two Epochs]* (Prague: n.p., 1968), pp. 69–70, also fn. p. 70; M. Vartíková, *Roky rozhodnutia [Years of Decision]* (Bratislava: n.p., 1964), pp. 99–110. It is interesting to note that Jozef Lettrich, chairman of the Slovak Democratic Party, makes only brief mention of this understanding, referring to it simply as "an intra-party agreement concerning Catholic matters." He gives its date as March 31, 1946. See J. Lettrich, *History of Modern Slovakia* (New York: Praeger, 1955), p. 239. Similarly, Josef Kirschbaum, former official of Tiso's regime, merely refers to "an agreement of the Protestant leaders of the Democratic Party with the representatives of the Slovak Catholics, signed on March 30, 1946." See Joseph Kirschbaum, *Slovakia: Nation at the Crossroads of Central Europe* (New York: Speller, 1960), p. 198. However, both Lettrich and Kirschbaum, the exiles, as well as Belda and Vartíková, concur in stressing the importance of the agreement in respect to the Democrats' victory in the 1946 elections.

3. The final vote against the granting of a pardon was 17–6; only the three ministers of the Slovak Democrats and their three colleagues from the Catholic People's Party supported the request for clemency. See Belda, *op. cit.*, p. 173.

4. *Čas [Time]*, September 15, 1947.

5. Yost to Secretary of State, September 16, 1947, File 860 F.00/9-1647, National Archives, *Diplomatic Papers, Czechoslovakia*, Record Group 59.

6. *Loc. cit.* Claiborne Pell is the present Senator from Rhode Island.

7. Slovak Action Committee (signed and enclosed by Ďurčanský and Polakovič) to Marshall, September 23, 1947, File 860 F.00/9-2347, *ibid.*

8. Slovak Action Committee to Ross, April 30, 1947, File 860 F.00/4-3047, *ibid.*

9. Slovak Action Committee to Matthews, April 30, 1947, File 860 F.00/4-3047, *ibid.*

10. Secretary of State to Tittman, April 23, 1947, File 860 F.00/4-2347, *ibid.*

11. Tittman to Secretary of State, December 10, 1947, File 860 F.00/12-1047, *ibid.*

12. The first letters go back to late 1945 and the drive continued until late 1947. Eventually, the State Department, declaring that Ďurčanský was a war criminal, no longer acknowledged letters from the Slovak Action Committee,

although letters from individual American organizations and private persons would receive an occasional non-committal response.

13. *Čas,* September 27, 1947.

14. Steinhardt to Secretary of State, October 17, 1947, File 860 F.00/10-1747, National Archives, *Diplomatic Papers,* Czechoslovakia, Record Group 59.

15. Steinhardt to Secretary of State, October 31, 1947, File 860 F.00/10-3147, *ibid.*

16. During the inter-war years, many members of the Czechoslovak Communist Party were either of German or Hungarian origin; while Czechoslovak citizens, their background, education, and the milieu of their daily lives was often neither Czech nor Slovak.

17. *Čas,* October 5, 1947. A complete translation of the editorial can be found in an appendix to Steinhardt's report to Washington: see Steinhardt to Secretary of State, October 8, 1947, File 860 F.00/10-847, National Archives, *Diplomatic Papers,* Czechoslovakia, Record Group 59.

18. Steinhardt to Secretary of State, November 20, 1947, File 860 F.00/11-2047, *ibid.*

19. This was doubly important, since the three expelled Slovak Democratic deputies were to be tried in Slovak courts.

20. Steinhardt to Secretary of State, November 13, 1947, File 860 F.00/11-1347, *ibid.*

21. Steinhardt to Secretary of State, November 20, 1947, File 860 F.00/11-2047, *ibid.*

22. Steinhardt to Williamson (Acting Assistant Chief, Division of Central European Affairs, Department of State), October 1, 1947, Library of Congress, *Steinhardt Papers,* Letterbooks.

23. Victor S. Mamatey and Radomír Luža, *A History of the Czechoslovak Republic* (Princeton, N.J.: Princeton University Press, 1973), p. 411.

24. For an official Prague version of the Slovak crisis, see V. Jarošová and O. Jaroš, *Slovenské robotnictvo b boji o moc, 1944-1948 [The Slovak Working Class in its Struggle for Power]*(Bratislava: n.p., 1965), pp. 221-52.

CHAPTER TEN:
THE CONGRESS OF THE SOCIAL DEMOCRATIC PARTY

1. The first post-war Czechoslovak government was based in the Slovak city of Košice. Only in May of 1945 did the government move to Prague. For a detailed account of the party's activities during the war years, see Jiří Horák, "The Czechoslovak Social Democratic Party, 1938-1945," Diss. Columbia University, 1960.

2. See above, pp. 52-3.

3. Steinhardt to Secretary of State, October 24, 1946, File 860 F.00/10-2446, National Archives, *Diplomatic Papers,* Czechoslovakia, Record Group 59.

4. Bruins to Secretary of State, February 5, 1947, File 860 F.00/2-547, *ibid.*

5. Steinhardt to Secretary of State, May 27, 1947, File 860 F.00/5-2747, *ibid.*

6. The full text of the speech can be found in *Právo lidu,* May 27, 1947.

7. Steinhardt to Secretary of State, June 2, 1947, File 860 F.00/6-247, National Archives, *Diplomatic Papers,* Czechoslovakia, Record Group 59.

8. Bruins to Secretary of State, June 9, 1947, File 860 F.00/6-947, *ibid.*

9. Steinhardt to Secretary of State, June 19, 1947, File 860 F.00/6-1947, *ibid.*

10. *Rudé právo,* September 12, 1947; *Právo lidu,* September 12, 1947; see also Yost to Secretary of State, File 860 F.00/9-1247, National Archives, *Diplomatic Papers,* Czechoslovakia, Record Group 59.

11. Yost to Secretary of State, September 15, 1947, File 860 F.00/9-1547, *ibid.*

12. *Loc. cit.*

13. *Loc. cit.*

14. Beneš's relationship with Fierlinger had undergone a significant change over the years. Fierlinger was at first the President's confidant and trusted envoy; this is substantiated by the fact that Beneš, still in London as head of the Czechoslovak government in exile, refused to listen to reports that Fierlinger, who remained at his post as Czechoslovak Minister to the U.S.S.R. during the war, was more in the service of Moscow than Prague. The appointment of Fierlinger as the first Czechoslovak post-war Prime Minister, while no doubt equally motivated by other considerations, expressed anew the President's confidence in Fierlinger. Only afterwards did Beneš begin to distrust him and, by all available evidence, to despise him. Fierlinger, an ambitious and vain man, resented Beneš' popularity and came to think of himself as some sort of left-wing dictator of the country after the war. See, among others, Klieforth to Secretary of State, July 12, 1945, File 860 F.00/7-1245, *ibid.*

15. Yost to Secretary of State, September 15, 1947, File 860 F.00/9-1547, *ibid.*

16. See in particular Yost to Secretary of State, September 15, 1947, File 860 F.00/9-1547, *ibid.* and Steinhardt to Secretary of State, October 12, 1947, File 860 F.00/10-1247, *ibid.*

17. See in particular Steinhardt to Secretary of State, October 10, 1947, File 860 F.00/10-1047, *ibid.;* Steinhardt to Secretary of State, October 2, 1947, File 860 F.00/10-247, *ibid.;* Steinhardt to Secretary of State, October 12, 1947, File 860 F.00/10-1247, *ibid.*

18. Steinhardt to Secretary of State, October 17, 1947, File 860 F.00/10-2747, *ibid.*

19. Steinhardt to Secretary of State, October 27, 1947, File 860 F.00/10-2747, *ibid.*

20. Steinhardt to Secretary of State, September 23, 1947, File 860 F.00/9-2347, *ibid.*

21. Steinhardt to Secretary of State, October 2, 1947, File 860 F.00/10-247, *ibid.*

22. *Loc. cit.*

23. *Loc. cit.*

24. See above, pp. 124–25.

25. Steinhardt to Secretary of State, October 31, 1947, File 860 F.00/10-3147, National Archives, *Diplomatic Papers,* Czechoslovakia, Record Group 59.

26. *Právo lidu,* October 19, 1947.

27. Steinhardt to Secretary of State, November 17, 1947, File 860 F.00/11-1747, National Archives, *Diplomatic Papers,* Czechoslovakia, Record Group 59.

28. *Rudé právo,* November 17, 1947; it is interesting to note that Fierlinger published his remarks in the Communist daily rather than the organ of his own party, *Právo lidu.*

29. *Loc. cit.*

30. *New York Times,* December 4, 1947; see also Bruins to Secretary of State, December 10, 1947, File 860 F.00/12-1047, National Archives, *Diplomatic Papers,* Czechoslovakia, Record Group 59.

31. *Loc. cit.*

32. Steinhardt to Secretary of State, November 24, 1947, File 860 F.00/11-2447, *ibid.*

33. General Čeněk Kudláček to the author. General Kudláček, a ranking officer in Beneš' London exile government and a close associate of the then Czechoslovak Defense Minister. General Sergěj Ingr, related some of Beneš' difficulties with Fierlinger, who was then the Czechoslovak Ambassador to the Soviet Union. In brief, and according to Kudláček, Beneš and Ingr became convinced that Fierlinger not only regularly informed the Soviet leadership of Beneš' intentions, but also sabotaged all such directives and instructions of his government which did not seem in the interest of Moscow. It took Beneš considerable time to attach credence to the numerous reports which he had received about the activities of his Ambassador in Moscow, his old-time associate from pre-Munich days. An intimate friendship between Madame Beneš and Madame Fierlinger further complicated Beneš' position, and, according to some sources, on occasion forced the President's hand.

34. *Právo lidu,* December 7, 1947; see also Bruins to Secretary of State, December 8, 1947, File 860 F.00/12-847, National Archives, *Diplomatic Papers,* Czechoslovakia, Record Group 59.

35. Bruins to Secretary of State, November 28, 1947, File 860 F.00/11-2847, *ibid.*

36. *Svět práce [The World of Labor],* November 20, 1947, quoted in Belda, *op. cit.,* pp. 202–03.

37. Belda, *op. cit.,* pp. 203–04.

38. Laušman received 283 votes against 182 for Fierlinger.

CHAPTER ELEVEN:

THE FINAL MONTHS

1. Director, Office of European Affairs [H. Freeman Matthews] to Under Secretary of State [Dean Acheson], July 22, 1947, National Archives, *Records of the Central European Division,* General Records, Folder: Under Secretary, Record Group 59. I am indebted for this document to Mr. Mark S. Steinitz.

2. Hawkins to Secretary of State, October 1, 1947, File 860 F.00/10-147, National Archives, *Diplomatic Papers,* Great Britain, Record Group 59.

3. Steinhardt to Secretary of State, September 29, 1947, File 860 F.00/9-2947, National Archives, *Diplomatic Papers,* Czechoslovakia, Record Group 59.

4. Steinhardt to Secretary of State, September 23, 1947, File 860 F.00/9-2347, *ibid.*

5. Steinhardt to Secretary of State, October 21, 1947, File 860 F.00/10-2147, *ibid.*

6. The reference here is to a major policy statement by Andrei Zhdanov, Politburo member and leading ideologist of the Soviet party, in September, 1947. In it, Zhdanov divided the world into two camps, the peace-loving U.S.S.R. and its allies versus a capitalist and aggressive West.

7. Steinhardt to Secretary of State, October 21, 1947, File 860 F.00/10-2147, National Archives, *Diplomatic Papers,* Czechoslovakia, Record Group 59.

8. *Loc. cit.*

9. Steinhardt to Secretary of State, October 29, 1947, File 860 F.00/10-2947, *ibid.*

10. *Loc. cit.*

11. *Loc. cit.*

12. *Loc. cit.*

13. Steinhardt to Secretary of State, November 3, 1947, File 860 F.00/11-347, *ibid.*

14. Steinhardt to Secretary of State, November 6, 1947, File 860 F.00/11-647, *ibid.*

15. Steinhardt to Secretary of State, November 6, 1947, File 860 F.00/11-747, *ibid.*

16. In a speech before the Socialist Academy, Kopecký stated that Czechoslovakia was fortunate to have been liberated by the Soviet Army rather than the Western forces since, otherwise, the country would have gone the way of France or even Greece. He made it clear that, in the future, Czechoslovakia must continue to stand on the side of the anti-imperialist forces. See *Rudé právo,* November 10, 1947.

17. Steinhardt to Secretary of State, November 20, 1947, File 860 F.00/11-2047, National Archives, *Diplomatic Papers,* Czechoslovakia, Record Group 59.

18. Steinhardt to Secretary of State, November 24, 1947, File 860 F.00/11-2447, *ibid.*

19. Bruins to Secretary of State, December 12, 1947, File 860 F.00/12-1247, *ibid.*

20. *Loc. cit.*

21. Bruins to Secretary of State, December 16, 1947, File 860 F.00/12-1647, *ibid.*

22. *Loc. cit.*

23. *Svobodné slovo,* December 24, 1947; see also Bruins to Secretary of State, December 29, 1947, File 860 F.00/12-2947, National Archives, *Diplomatic Papers,* Czechoslovakia, Record Group 59.

24. Bruins to Steinhardt, January 6, 1948, Library of Congress, *Steinhardt*

Papers, Letterbooks; the reference is to Jefferson Caffrey, United States Ambassador to France.

25. Bruins to Steinhardt, January 20, 1948, *ibid.*

26. Intelligence Report Number R-59-48, February 5, 1948, National Archives, *Post Reports*, Prague, Record Group 319.

27. *Loc. cit.*

28. *Loc. cit.*

29. Bruins to Secretary of State, January 28, 1948, File 860 F.00/1-2848, National Archives, *Diplomatic Papers*, Czechoslovakia, Record Group 59.

30. *Loc. cit.*

31. *Loc. cit.*

32. *Loc. cit.*

33. *Loc. cit.*

34. Steinhardt to Vedeler, January 23, 1948, Library of Congress, *Steinhardt Papers*, Letterbooks, Personal Letters.

35. Steinhardt to Vedeler, February 3, 1948, *ibid.*

36. Vedeler to Steinhardt, January 30, 1948, Library of Congress, *Steinhardt Papers*, General Correspondence.

37. Marshall to Embassy in Czechoslovakia, February 4, 1948, *Foreign Relations of the United States* (1948), IV, 735.

38. Bruins to Secretary of State, January 29, 1948, File 860 F.00/1-2948, National Archives, *Diplomatic Papers*, Czechoslovakia, Record Group 59.

39. Bruins to Secretary of State, February 2, 1948, File 860 F.00/2-248, *ibid.*

40. *Loc. cit.*

CHAPTER TWELVE:

THE FINAL DAYS

1. *Svobodné slovo*, February 6, 1948.

2. Bruins to Secretary of State, February 11, 1948, File 860 F.00/2-1148, National Archives, *Diplomatic Papers*, Czechoslovakia, Record Group 59.

3. *Rudé právo*, February 18, 1948; *Svobodné slovo*, February 19, 1948.

4. Bruins to Secretary of State, February 19, 1948 (Telegram Number 160), File 860 F.00/2-1948, National Archives, *Diplomatic Papers*, Czechoslovakia, Record Group 59; see also Bruins to Secretary of State, February 19, 1948 (Airgram A-177), File 860 F.00/2-1948, *ibid.*

5. Jan Masaryk to Steinhardt, February 20, 1948, Library of Congress, *Steinhardt Papers*, Letterbooks.

6. Steinhardt to Secretary of State, February 20, 1948 (Airgram A-178), File 860 F.00/2-2048, National Archives, *Diplomatic Papers*, Czechoslovakia, Record Group 59.

7. *Loc. cit.*

8. *Loc. cit.*

9. Karel Kaplan, "On the Role of Dr. Edvard Beneš in February 1948," *Historica*, 5 (1963), 240, fn. 1.

10. *Ibid.,* p. 265.
11. *Loc. cit.*
12. Josef Belda *et al., Na rozhraní dvou epoch* (Prague: n.p., 1968), pp. 252–62.
13. *Ibid.,* pp. 247 ff.
14. Jaromír Smutný, *Únorový převrat I [The February Revolution I]* (London: n.p., 1958), p. 14.
15. *Ibid.,* p. 16.
16. Steinhardt to Secretary of State, February 21, 1948, File 860 F.00/2-2148, National Archives, *Diplomatic Papers,* Czechoslovakia, Record Group 59.
17. Steinhardt to Secretary of State, February 23, 1948, File 860 F.00/2-2348, *ibid.*
18. Steinhardt to Secretary of State, February 24, 1948, File 860 F.00/2-2448, *ibid.*
19. Beneš' letter was made public by an announcement of the Czechoslovak News Bureau (ČTK) and was subsequently printed in the press.
20. Press release by the Czechoslovak News Agency, subsequently reprinted in *Rudé právo,* February 25, 1948.
21. Intelligence Division to OMGUS, February 25, 1948, National Archives, *Adjutant General Papers,* 383.7, OMG, Bavaria, Record Group 319.
22. Memorandum of Conversation between Armand Bérard and Arnauld Wapler with Llewellyn Thompson, Jacob Bean and Harold Vedeler, February 24, 1948, File 860 F.00/2-2448, National Archives, *Diplomatic Papers,* Czechoslovakia, Record Group 59.
23. Bonbright to Secretary of State, February 25, 1948, File 860 F.00/2-2548, *ibid.*
24. Marshall to Steinhardt, February 25, 1948, File 860 F.00/2-2548, *ibid.*
25. Steinhardt to Secretary of State, February 26, 1948, File 860 F.00/2-2648, *ibid.*
26. Marshall to Steinhardt, February 26, 1948, File 860 F.00/2-2648, *ibid.*
27. Steinhardt to Marshall, March 1, 1948, File 860 F.00/3-148, *ibid.*
28. *Loc. cit.*
29. This is a Czech gymnastic festival held every four years. A sort of national Olympics that goes back to pre-World War I days, it has traditionally served as a major national manifestation. The Sokol organization has many branches in the United States and large contingents of American Sokols would regularly attend the Prague rallies.
30. Steinhardt to Secretary of State, March 2, 1948, File 860 F.00/3-248, National Archives, *Diplomatic Papers,* Czechoslovakia, Record Group 59.

CHAPTER THIRTEEN:
AFTER THE COUP

1. It is obviously not the purpose here to discuss the various already-published accounts of the Prague coup of 1948. Some of the more reliable ones

are to be found in the bibliography. Rather, it is intended to supplement the extant knowledge by the addition of newly-released materials.

2. Steinhardt to Secretary of State, February 27, 1948, File 860 F.00/2-2748, National Archives, *Diplomatic Papers,* Czechoslovakia, Record Group 59; it is erroneously dated as February 7, 1948 and listed as 2-748. The context of the letter makes such a date utterly impossible.

3. Steinhardt to Secretary of State, March 3, 1948, File 860 F.00/3-348, *ibid.*

4. *Loc. cit.* For a more detailed account of the chancellor's recollections of the February days, see Jaromír Smutný, *Únorový převrat* (London: n.p., 1958).

5. Yost to Secretary of State, March 26, 1948, Number 0456541, National Archives, *Records of the Chief of Staff of the Army,* Record Group 319.

6. Steinhardt to Secretary of State, March 4, 1948, File 860 F.00/3-448, National Archives, *Diplomatic Papers,* Czechoslovakia, Record Group 59. See also *Rudé právo,* March 1, 1948.

7. Steinhardt to Secretary of State, March 5, 1948, File 860 F.00/3-548, National Archives, *Diplomatic Papers,* Czechoslovakia, Record Group 59.

8. For a fuller account of Steinhardt's, see pp. 151–52.

9. Intelligence Report Number 472811, May 26, 1948, National Archives, Box 3060, Record Group 319.

10. *Loc. cit.*

11. *Loc. cit.* It is interesting to note that at the beginning of the Intelligence Report, the source is identified as having been a schoolmate of Masaryk's and an associate of Beneš' in the Czechoslovak government of 1918. Later, in the text of the report, Beneš is given as the schoolmate and Masaryk as the government associate. It would seem, however, from the overall context of his testimony, that this is a genuine error, most likely committed by the report's compiler.

12. Steinhardt to Secretary of State, April 30, 1948, File 860 F.00/4-3048, *Foreign Relations of the United States* (1948), IV, 747 ff.

13. *Loc. cit.*

14. *Loc. cit.*

15. See above, pp. 51–52.

16. An American writer and close personal friend of Jan Masaryk, the Steinhardt family kept up a regular correspondence with Miss Davenport after Masaryk's death.

17. Steinhardt to Marcia Davenport, October 8, 1948, Library of Congress, *Steinhardt Papers,* Letterbooks.

18. Steinhardt to Miloš Hanák, August 20, 1948, *ibid.*

19. Steinhardt to Sumner Welles, August 20, 1948, *ibid.*

20. Stan Griffis to Steinhardt, March 18, 1948, *ibid.*

21. Dorothy Thackrey to Steinhardt, August 20, 1948, *ibid.*

22. Vlado Clementis to Steinhardt, March 26, 1948, *ibid.*

23. Christian Ravndal to Steinhardt, May 26, 1948, *ibid.*

24. Steinhardt to Christian Ravndal, July 19, 1948, *ibid.*

25. Steinhardt to Emil Kekich, August 18, 1948, *ibid.*

26. Bruins to Steinhardt, October 24, 1948, *ibid.*

Bibliography

PRIMARY SOURCES (Manuscripts)

General Records of the Department of State, Record Group 59, National Archives, Main Building, Washington, D.C.; contains *Diplomatic Papers of the Department of State relating to Czechoslovakia*.

General Records, Post Files, Record Group 84, National Archives, Federal Records Center Building, Suitland, Maryland.

General Records, Office of Strategic Services, Record Group 226, National Archives, Main Building, Washington, D.C.

General Records, Army Chief of Staff, Record Group 319, National Archives, Federal Records Center Building, Suitland, Maryland.

General Records, Army Assistant Chief of Staff, Record Group 319, National Archives, Federal Records Center Building, Suitland, Maryland.

PRIMARY SOURCES (Printed)

Foreign Relations of the United States, 1945, vol. IV, Washington, D.C.: Government Printing Office, 1968.

———, 1946, vol. VI, Washington, D.C.: Government Printing Office, 1969.

———, 1947, vol. IV, Washington, D.C.: Government Printing Office, 1972.

———, 1948, vol. IV, Washington, D.C.: Government Printing Office, 1974.

Otáhalová, L. and Červinková, M. *Dokumenty z historie československé politiky, 1939-1943 [Documents Relating to the History of Czechoslovak Politics]*. Prague, 1966.

BOOKS

Ambrose, Stephen E. *Rise to Globalism: American Foreign Policy, 1938-1970*. Baltimore, 1972.

Bartošek, Karel. *Pražské povstání 1945 [The Prague Uprising of 1945]*. Prague, 1965.

Belda, Josef, *et al. Na rozhraní dvou epoch [Between Two Epochs]*. Prague, 1968.

Beneš, Edvard. *Memoirs of Dr. Edvard Beneš, From Munich to New War and New Victory*. Boston, 1954.

Bohlen, Charles E. *Witness to History*. New York, 1973.

Bouček, Miroslav. *Praha v únoru 1948. O práci pražské stranické organizace v únorových dnech 1948 [Prague in February, 1948. Concerning the*

Activities of the Prague Party Organization during February of 1948]. Prague, 1963.

Bradley, Omar N. *A Soldier's Story.* New York, 1951.

Československá revoluce v letech 1944–1948. Sborník příspěvků z konference historiků k 20. výročí osvobození ČSSR [The Czechoslovak Revolution during the Years 1944–1948. Collection of Contributions by the Conference of Historians on the Occasion of the Twentieth Anniversary of the Liberation of the Czechoslovak Socialist Republic]. Prague, 1966.

Chandler, Alfred *et al.*, eds. *The Papers of Dwight David Eisenhower: The War Years,* Vol. IV. Baltimore, 1970.

Diamond, William. *Czechoslovakia Between East and West.* London, 1947.

Ducháček, Ivan. *The Strategy of Communist Infiltration: The Case of Czechoslovakia.* New Haven, 1949.

Gaddis, John L. *The United States and the Origins of the Cold War, 1941–1947.* New York, 1972.

Görlitz, Walter, ed. *The Memoirs of Field Marshal Keitel.* London, 1965.

Gottwald, Klement. *Spisy [Writings].* Prague, 1955.

Hoensch, Jörgen K. *Geschichte der Tschechoslowakischen Republik 1918 bis 1965.* Stuttgart, 1966.

Horecký, Paul L., ed. *East Central Europe: A Guide to Basic Publications.* Chicago, 1969.

Hull, Cordell. *Memoirs of Cordell Hull.* New York, 1948.

Kennan, George F. *From Prague to Munich.* Princeton, N.J., 1968.

Kertesz, Stephen D., ed. *The Fate of East Central Europe, Hopes and Failures of American Foreign Policy.* South Bend, Ind., 1956.

Kirschbaum, Joseph M. *Slovakia: Nation at the Crossroads of Central Europe.* New York, 1960.

Korbel, Josef. *The Communist Subversion of Czechoslovakia, 1938–1948, The Failure of Coexistence.* Princeton, N.J., 1959.

Král, Václav. *Cestou k únoru [Towards February].* Prague, 1963.

_____. *Osvobození Československa [The Liberation of Czechoslovakia].* Prague, 1975.

Kuhn, Heinrich. *Der Kommunismus in der Tschechoslowakei.* Cologne, 1965.

Künstlinger, Rudolf. *Parteidiktatur oder demokratischer Sozialismus: Der tschechoslowakische Weg nach 1945.* Starnberg, 1972.

La Feber, Walter. *America, Russia, and the Cold War, 1945–1971.* New York, 1972.

Lettrich, Jozef. *History of Modern Slovakia.* New York, 1955.

Lundestad, Geir. *The American Non-Policy towards Eastern Europe.* New York and Oslo, 1975.

Luža, Radomír. *The Transfer of the Sudeten Germans, A Study of Czech-German Relations, 1933–1962.* New York, 1964.

Machotka, Otokar, ed. *Pražské povstání 1945 [The Prague Uprising, 1945].* Washington, 1965.

Mamatey, Victor S. and Luža, Radomír, eds. *A History of the Czechoslovak Republic, 1918–1948.* Princeton, N.J., 1973.

Montgomery, Bernard Law. *The Memoirs of Field-Marshal The Viscount Montgomery of Alamein, K.G.* New York, 1958.

Opat, Jaroslav O. *O novou demokracii, 1945-1948. Příspěvek k dějinám národně demokratické revoluce v Československu v letech 1945-1948 [For a New Democracy, 1945-1948. A Contribution to the History of the National Democratic Revolution in Czechoslovakia in 1945-1948].* Prague, 1966.

Osvobození 1945 [Liberation 1945]. Washington, D.C., n.d. (probably 1975).

Paterson, Thomas. *The Origins of the Cold War.* Lexington, Mass., 1970.

_____. *Soviet-American Confrontation.* Baltimore, 1973.

Pogue, Forest C. *The Supreme Command: The European Theatre of Operations.* Washington, 1954.

Prečan, Vilém. *Slovenský katolicizmus pred februárom [Slovak Catholicism before February].* Bratislava, 1961.

Rechcígl, Miloslav, Jr., ed. *The Czechoslovak Contribution to World Culture.* The Hague, 1964.

Reimann, Paul. *Geschichte der Kommunistischen Partei der Tschechoslowakei.* Hamburg, 1931.

Říha, Oldřich, and Mésaroš, Július, eds. *Přehled československých dějin [Survey of Czechoslovak History].* 3 vols. Prague, 1958-1960.

Ripka, Hubert. *Czechoslovakia Enslaved: The Story of the Communist Coup d'État.* London, 1950.

Smutný, Jaromír. *Únorový převrat 1948 [The February Upheaval of 1948].* 5 vols. London, 1953-1957. Mimeographed.

Szulc, Tad. *Czechoslovakia Since World War II.* New York, 1970.

Taborsky, Edward. *Communism in Czechoslovakia, 1948-1960.* Princeton, N.J., 1960.

Truman, Harry S. *Memoirs: Year of Decisions.* New York, 1955.

United Nations Relief and Rehabilitation Administration, European Regional Office. *Agriculture and Food in Czechoslovakia.* London, 1946.

_____. *Industrial Rehabilitation in Czechoslovakia.* London, 1947.

_____. *Foreign Trade in Czechoslovakia.* London, 1947.

_____. *Transport Rehabilitation in Czechoslovakia.* London, 1947.

Vartíková, M. *Roky rozhodnutia [Years of Decision].* Bratislava, 1964.

Vondracek, Felix. *The Foreign Policy of Czechoslovakia.* New York, 1937.

Who Was Who in America. Vol. II, 1943-1950. Chicago, 1950.

Zinner, Paul E. *Communist Strategy and Tactics in Czechoslovakia, 1918-1948.* New York, 1963.

UNPUBLISHED MANUSCRIPTS

Horák, Jiří. "The Czechoslovak Social Democratic Party, 1938-1945." Doctoral dissertation, Columbia University, 1960.

Steinitz, Mark S. "Ambassador Laurence A. Steinhardt and United States Relations with Czechoslovakia, 1945-1948." Master's thesis, University of Maryland, 1974.

198   THE UNITED STATES IN PRAGUE

ARTICLES

J. Belda, M. Bouček, M. Deyl, Zd. Deyl and M. Klimeš. "K otázce účasti Československa na Marshallově plánu" ["Concerning Czechoslovakia's Participation in the Marshall Plan"], *Revue dejin socialismu* (1968), 81–100.

Beneš, Edvard. "Czechoslovakia's Plans for Peace," *Foreign Affairs,* 23 (October, 1944), 26–37.

———. "Postwar Czechoslovakia," *Foreign Affairs,* 24 (April, 1946), 26–37.

Brügel, J. W. "Die Aussiedlung der Deutschen aus der Tschechoslowakei," *Vierteljahrshefte fuer Zeitgeschichte,* 8 (April, 1960), 134–64.

———. "Die sudetendeutsche Frage auf der Potsdam Konferenze," *Vierteljahrshefte fuer Zeitgeschichte,* 10 (January, 1962), 56–61.

Kodíček, Joseph. "The Suspension of the American Loan," *Central European Observer,* 13 (November 8, 1946).

Kořalková, Květa. "K československo-polským vztahům létech 1945–1948" ["Concerning Czechoslovak-Polish Relations During the Years 1945–1948"], *Slovanské historické studie,* No. 5, 309–336.

Lašťovička, Bohuslav. "Vznik a význam košického vládního programu" ["The Origins and Importance of the Košice Government Program"], *Československý časopis historický,* 8 (August, 1960), 449–71.

Opat, Jaroslav. "K metodě studia avýkladu běkterých problémů období 1945–1948" ["Concerning Method and Explanation of Some Problems of the Period 1945–1948"], *Příspévky k dějinám KSČ,* 5 (1965), 65–84.

Pachman, Vladimír. "Boj o odborovou jednotu v letech 1945–1948" ["The Struggle for Unity in the Trade Unions, 1945–1948"], *Československý časopis historický,* 8 (1960), 793–813.

Pogue, Forest C. "The Decision to Halt at the Elbe," in Kent Roberts Greenfield, ed., *Command Decisions,* Washington, D.C., 1959, pp. 479–92.

Skilling, H. Gordon. "The Formation of a Communist Party in Czechoslovakia," *The American Slavic and Eastern European Review,* 14, No. 3 (October, 1955), 346–58.

Sládek, Zdeněk. "Československo-sovětské vztahy v období 1945–1960" ["Czechoslovak-Soviet Relations during the Period 1945–1948"], *Slovenské Studie,* No. 7 (1965).

Taborsky, Edvard. "Benes and the Soviets," *Foreign Affairs,* 27 (January, 1949), 302–14.

———. "Beneš and Stalin: Moscow 1943 and 1945," *Journal of Central European Affairs,* 13 (July, 1953), 165–83.

———. "The Triumph and Disaster of Eduard Benes," *Foreign Affairs,* 36 (July, 1958), 669–84.

Ullmann, Walter. "Czechoslovakia's Crucial Years, 1945–1948: An American View," *East European Quarterly,* 1 (September, 1967), 217–30.

Zámečník, Stanislav. "České květnové povstání," ["The Czech May Rising"], *Historie a vojenství,* No. 2 (1970), 267–301.

Zinner, Paul E. "Marxism in Action: The Seizure of Power in Czechoslovakia," *Foreign Affairs,* 28 (July, 1950), 644–58.

NEWSPAPERS

Čas. Bratislava.
Czechoslovak News Letter. London.
Daily Review of the Czechoslovak Ministry of Information. Prague.
Lidová demokracie. Prague.
Mladá fronta. Prague.
New York Herald Tribune [European Edition]. Paris.
New York Times.
Obzory. Prague.
Práce. Prague.
Právo lidu. Prague.
Rudé Právo. Prague.
Svobodné slovo. Prague.
Svobodný zítřek. Prague.
L'Unità. Rome.

LETTERS

Julius Firt, June 20, 1976.
Vladimír Krajina, August 30, 1976.
Jaroslav Pecháček, June 6, 1976.
Claiborne Pell, June 29, 1976.

INTERVIEWS

Claiborne Pell, May 8, 1976, Syracuse, New York.

Index

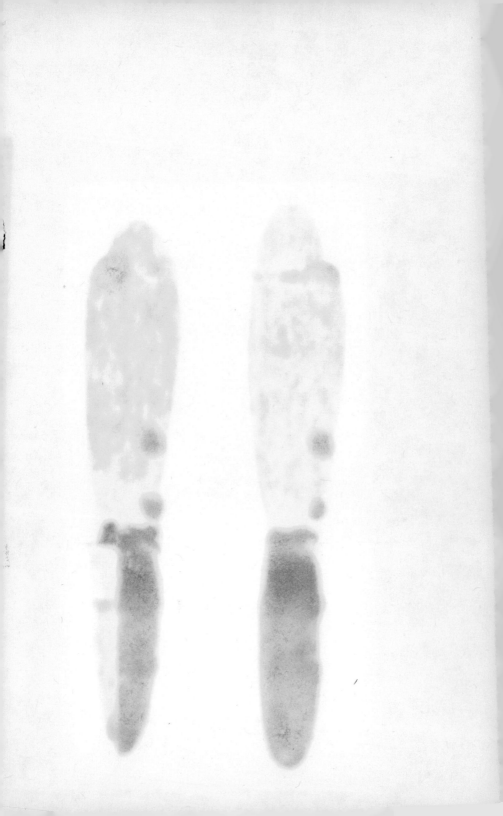